The Council of Europe

The Council of Europe was founded in 1949, in the wake of the second world war, in order to promote European construction through a common democratic and legal area structured around the European Convention on Human Rights.

The Organisation currently comprises 41 member states representing some 800 million Europeans – in other words almost all the countries of the European continent. Since 1989, the Council of Europe has contributed to bringing together the different parts of Europe. The Council develops many forms of co-operation on all the major issues to be addressed by our societies today, including education, social cohesion, protection of national minorities, bioethics, the fight against all forms of intolerance, the prevention of crime and corruption, the consolidation of local democracy and the enhancement of Europe's culture and cultural heritage.

Council of Europe Publishing is the official publisher of the Council of Europe, and reflects the many different aspects of the Council's work, addressing the main challenges facing European society and the world today. Our catalogue of over 1200 titles in French and English includes topics ranging from international law, human rights, ethical and moral issues, society, environment, health, education and culture.

For more information please visit our website: **http://book.coe.int**

Crime and criminal justice in Europe

Council of Europe Publishing

Cover design: Graphic Design Workshop of the Council of Europe
Layout: DTP Unit of the Council of Europe
Edited and published by: Council of Europe Publishing

Council of Europe Publishing
F-67075 Strasbourg Cedex

ISBN 92-871-4378-1

Printed in Germany by Koelblin-Fortuna-Druck

TABLE OF CONTENTS

Preface

Walter Schwimmer
Secretary General of the Council of Europe

When the Berlin Wall fell in 1989, the Council of Europe counted 23 (western) European member states. Since then its membership has increased considerably and now stands at 41. The latest newcomer is Georgia, which became a member in April 1999. This increase in membership implies the need for comprehensive organisational change to deal with new challenges and responsibilities; it also reflects, obviously, profound political and socio-economic changes in central and eastern Europe which affect Europe as a whole.

In the new European landscape the promotion of human rights, the strengthening of pluralist democracy and the improvement of citizens' security are among the key objectives of international co-operation, as highlighted by the heads of state and government on the occasion of the Second Summit of the Council of Europe in October 1997.

Against this background, a fundamental concern must be to promote vigorously a coherent and rational crime policy directed towards the prevention of crime and criminal behaviour, combined with victim support, effective law enforcement, public safety and protection, individualisation of sanctions and measures, and social reintegration of offenders. Such measures must conform to the basic principles of democratic states governed by the rule of law and subject to the paramount aim of guaranteeing human rights, in conformity with the European Convention on Human Rights and the case-law of the organs entrusted with its application. They also need to be based on the comprehensive knowledge acquired by the Council of Europe and reflected in the many specific recommendations and conventions addressing penal, penological and criminological matters.

However, the relevance of empirical facts and the monitoring of new developments in crime and criminal justice for sound decision-making should not be underestimated. It is for this reason that the assessment of trends in crime and criminal justice is a permanent concern of the Council of Europe and its European Committee on Crime Problems. Such an assessment also has a prominent place on the agenda of practically all member states of the Organisation. Periodic events, such as its criminological and penological conferences and colloquia and, in particular, the quinquennial conferences on crime policy have been devised so as to keep these trends under permanent review and to provide those responsible for tackling crime and running criminal-justice institutions with appropriate basic information.

This book is a contribution to that end. It is aimed at providing a succinct overview of European crime problems and crime policies. It is written so as to benefit both the general public interested in these issues as well as practitioners, researchers and academics looking for information on European thinking in this area.

The book covers a vast array of issues, such as the crime picture in Europe, the prevention of criminality, the operation of criminal-justice agencies such as the police and the prosecution, and the complex area of punishment and the treatment of offenders. It also brings attention to trends in criminal legislation and the protection of the legitimate interests of victims.

The preparation of the plan of the book, the selection of its authors and the co-ordination of the individual contributions were carefully monitored by the Criminological Scientific Council. The latter is an advisory body to the European Committee on Crime Problems; it is entrusted with providing guidance, collecting information and making suggestions with a view to preparing and implementing the Council of Europe's work programme in the field of crime problems. Its members are eminent representatives of the criminal sciences. Christopher Nuttall, Chairman of the Criminological Scientific Council from 1996 to 1998, acted as editor and produced both the introduction to the book and its concluding chapter. Several members of the Criminological Scientific Council also contributed as authors, writing on their respective fields of specialisation: Kauko Aromaa (crime trends), Ernesto Savona (legislation), Alenka Šelih (prosecution), Frieder Dünkel and Sonja Snacken (imprisonment). The other contributors are Tony Peters and Ivo Aertsen (victim issues), Hannu Takala (crime prevention), Adelmo Manna and Giacomo Forte – together with Ernesto Savona – (legislation), Amadeu Recasens I Brunet (policing), Andrew Ashworth (sentencing), as well as Anton Van Kalmthout (non-custodial sanctions).

Introduction

Christopher Nuttall

This book addresses a well-defined gap in the literature on crime policy and practice: a comparative study of criminal-justice policy and practice, its approach and philosophy across Europe. This is particularly important because of the rapidly growing exchange of information, from west to east, about crime policy in the member states of the expanded Council of Europe. Countries in both eastern and western Europe are eager to learn from each other's experience and their citizens want to know more about their changing world. This book will interest both the professional trying to solve the problems produced by crime and the interested lay person who wants to understand the new Europe they are living in.

Two areas of vital concern to the justice system – human rights and the treatment of offenders – have been an enormous concern within the Council of Europe over the last fifty years. It would be difficult to overestimate the importance and influence of the European Convention on Human Rights or the European prison rules. Within this context and with a view to the future with the publication of this volume, the Council of Europe seeks to improve the quality of information available and the level of on-going debate on criminal-justice policy.

The authors are all experts in the field of crime policy with a particular interest in comparative studies. A comparison of trends in crime in the first chapter, drawing both on police figures and crime survey data, serves to lay the scene for the rest of this book. Although we are often complacent that we all know what is happening in the crime sector (and how much of it there is), this is a particularly difficult area. In reality, we have only a rough idea of what is happening to crime and little knowledge of its true level. Nevertheless, because crime is such an important social indicator, one of our principal goals must be to understand how it is changing and why.

Victim issues and crime prevention have been both ignored and misunderstood in the past, but a fair and peaceful society requires that fundamentally important areas such as these be addressed and studied. Victims have not only been ignored for far too long but moves over the last two decades towards giving them redress have not gone far enough. It is still not understood that helping victims not only alleviates the misery and suffering of the victim, but it also helps to increase the likelihood that offenders will be convicted. Victims who are treated fairly and with respect by the justice system are better witnesses, thus improving the chances of offenders being caught and punished.

New patterns of legislation, changes in prosecution practice and in sentencing are at the core of the criminal-justice system and make up an important section of this volume. Finally, the book examines sanctions, a central concern for the Council of Europe. The way offenders are treated indicates something fundamental about a country's commitment to democracy, either helping or hindering the reduction of offending. For example, in the United Kingdom a persistent burglar costs society about 1 million pounds over his career. Can we either stop that career starting or cut it off early to avoid such an enormous cost to the public coffers?

The Council of Europe plays a pivotal role in the study of European crime and criminal justice. Its members include the great majority of European states, its influence is broad and it has built up strong relations with the European Union and the United Nations. Within Europe it is more inclusive than the European Union and more specialised than the UN. Because of the very nature of its legal instruments (recommendations and conventions) member states can be more adventurous in the changes and reforms they propose.

The social context of crime policy

Criminal law and procedure are at the very core of society but play different roles depending on the way a community is organised. In authoritarian and elitist states, criminal law is normally designed to enable the rulers to control that part of the population that might not accept their legitimacy. It is part of the power of the state. As a society becomes based on democratic principles, criminal law becomes the vehicle whereby that society deals with its rule-breakers – and protects freedoms, on behalf of all. In such societies the criminal law and its procedure are open to challenge by appeal to a higher body, which interprets these laws and procedures in relation to a broader vision of human rights.

In one set of circumstances, then, laws can drastically reduce the quality of life and in another the same mechanism and procedures can be empowering and form the fundamental building blocks of freedom. A simple example from Britain will illustrate my point.

In the eighteenth century a series of draconian laws was passed in Britain. They dealt with the taking of game and poaching; they were used widely and those who broke them were executed. These laws were not passed for the general good – they were passed to protect the interests of landowners. The 1860s saw a comprehensive review of laws and penalties in Britain. A new law was introduced to stop people putting obstacles on railway lines and hence endangering lives. The maximum penalty was life imprisonment. At the same time the maximum penalty for sending an un-seaworthy ship to sea was fixed at five years. On whose behalf were these laws being framed?

However, by the end of the twentieth century, criminal-justice procedure and its laws had become consistent with the European Convention on Human Rights and with its concern for the rights of the non-powerful and minorities.

The role of public opinion

Criminal-justice policy is vitally important to our quality of life and it tells us a great deal about the kind of society we live in. However, if criminal justice is a basic tool of democracy, what is and what should be the role of the public and what importance should be attached to their opinion?

The views and attitudes of the public (as distinct from criminal justice practitioners) to criminal justice policy affects everyone involved. Crime is important to all societies both because of its actual effects on people and institutions and by its very symbolism as a personification of good and evil.

Modern politicians believe elections can be won or lost on people's perceptions of their ability to handle crime, the police constantly appeal to public opinion to ensure that they get the resources they need, newspapers make a great deal of money out of crime coverage, the judiciary and prosecutors use their interpretation of public opinion to justify their decisions, victims use public pressure to try to improve their own treatment and even offenders appeal to public opinion when they believe they have been treated unjustly. 'Public opinion' can have a major impact on criminal-justice policy.

Should criminal-justice practitioners react to general 'public opinion' or should they react to 'informed' public opinion? These are not necessarily the same. Democracy does not demand that only educated and well-informed people vote or take part in decision-making – so why should we not just test public attitudes and opinion through focus groups and opinion surveys? In the end decision makers will have their own interpretations of public opinion, but we should ensure that the attitudes and opinions they heed are as informed as possible. There is hard evidence that the level of information available to the general public about criminal justice and procedure can influence their attitudes and opinions considerably.

Today in many parts of Europe the majority believes that their criminal-justice systems are not 'tough' enough. Public opinion in certain countries considers that capital punishment should be reintroduced, that a greater proportion of offenders should be sent to prison and that their sentences should be longer. Crime frightens many people. They do not want to be robbed, raped or murdered and they believe the way to reduce their chances of becoming a victim is to treat offenders more severely.

These are very powerful beliefs and many politicians and practitioners react by tightening up their treatment of offenders. They have restricted their policies to those methods that they believe will appease 'public opinion'. Severity is not an effective way of reducing crime but, when it fails, many believe the answer is to be harsher still and penalties are made even more severe. If practitioners and politicians react in such a way, society will suffer all the more by increased criminal activity and greater infringements on its liberty.

In Britain 70% of the population want the return of the death penalty, about 80% say that the courts should be more severe and about 80% say judges are out of touch with ordinary people. But what are these views based on? The evidence from Britain – and throughout much of Europe – is that such views are directly related to the amount of misinformation people receive about crime and criminal justice.

Let us start with capital punishment. Support for the death penalty – at a level of 70% to 80% – is common in the United Kingdom, Canada and the United States. In Canada a study was carried out on what was behind this figure of 80% support. It was found that if people were persuaded that capital punishment was no more a deterrent to murder than life imprisonment, then support for capital punishment fell to just over 40%. Research shows that capital punishment is in fact no more a deterrent than life imprisonment. So how much notice should be taken of the 80% figure of support found in public opinion polls?

A careful study of the relationship between knowledge and attitudes has been carried out in Britain. In the course of two sweeps, the British Crime Survey asked a number of questions of both fact and opinion: Was the level of recorded crime going up or down? How much of total recorded crime is violent? What is the chance that an adult rapist will go to prison if convicted? What is happening to the homicide rate? And so on. The 1996 survey asked about ten such questions.

This survey found that knowledge levels were generally very low. About a quarter of the sample of over 8 000 people did not provide a single correct answer. Just over 200 people provided four out of ten correct answers.

Of the people who knew the least about what was going on in the criminal-justice system (in other words, those who provided no correct answers), nearly 90% stated that sentences were too lenient and 10% said they were about right. Of those who knew a little more and provided four correct answers, around 40% said sentences were about right.

Dependence on public-opinion surveys that suggest the system is too lenient is further challenged by other results from this survey. The sample was asked what would be an appropriate sentence for a 23-year-old, third-time burglar who had taken a television set from a house in the afternoon when no one was at home. Of the sample, 46% said a community penalty would be appropriate. In fact, the court gave this man two years' imprisonment. When faced with an actual case involving a recognisable human being, many people will be much more flexible than simple opinion polls would suggest.

People see crime as a difficult problem with many causes. But many believe that the most effective way to reduce it is through severity. In Britain at least, people believe that the system is much more lenient than it actually is and that there is much more violent crime than there is in reality. It is little wonder that their initial reaction is to demand more severe sentences.

All the evidence points to the fact that providing people with more information renders them more flexible and readier to agree that the criminal-justice system should be pragmatic in its treatment of offenders. The public is not basically retributionist. It is essentially utilitarian and will strongly support actions that they see as reducing crime and victimisation.

CHAPTER 1: TRENDS IN CRIMINALITY

Kauko Aromaa, Research Director,
National Research Institute for Legal Policy, Helsinki

Crime trends until 1990

Trends in West European crime have been analysed since the 1950s,[1] although at the time few European countries were eligible for such analysis, owing to a lack of comparable crime data. The analyses were limited to overall recorded crime, largely equivalent to conventional property crime.

The data situation has since improved, but the difficulties are still considerable. Eastern Europe is a special case, whereas western European countries continue to suffer from their shortcomings despite significant improvements during the 1990s. In particular, the standardised international crime victimisation survey (ICVS) has gained ground and most European countries have now participated in one or several sweeps of the survey. But, as far as trends are concerned, the ICVS is still not sufficiently comprehensive: it focuses on individual citizens, while crimes against corporations make up a significant part of all crime today.

Of authoritative statistics on crime rates and trends,[2] police statistics are generally the most commonly used and provide the broadest coverage. However they are seldom satisfactory[3] and their comparability both over time and across countries remains limited. They also typically reflect what is often called 'conventional' crime and are weak in areas where other crime phenomena – such as corruption, organised crime or economic crime – are concerned. The overall assessment is that "most European nations have experienced sharp rises in registered crime over the past three decades" (that is from 1960 to 1990), that "countries with the lowest rates [of overall victimisation by eleven different types of crime] are characterised by a relatively low level of urbanisation" and that "Crime has gone up from 1955 onwards across western Europe. On average however, the crime problem is still less serious than in the USA."[4]

Project Greater Europe: a situation assessment (1994)

A Council of Europe report assessing the European crime situation in the early 1990s noted important changes from the 1980s onward, when many western European countries experienced an upswing in various types of crime. For one, economic restructuring in all western countries had created turbulence on the crime scene, and secondly, the opening of the borders between East and West quickly began to have multiple effects on many crime-related phenomena, economic and political integration being a multifaceted matter with important consequences on crime as a by-product. The analysis has continued into the late 1980s and the early 1990s.

The Greater Europe project also tried to assess central changes since 1989 in the crime profiles of the member countries, as seen by the country responses to the project questionnaire, which are summarised as follows:

> Some countries, notably geographically peripheral Western European countries, report no significant changes, or at least no changes apparently attributable to [social and political change]. Drug-related crime, especially trafficking, is of particular concern in all countries. New routes via Central and Eastern European countries as well as the abolition of controls at many borders are both seen to be important factors in this respect. The patterns of drug trafficking may have considerably changed as the result of the recent developments in Europe.
>
> In most Western European countries, crime rates in general are reported to have increased. A long, indiscriminate list of offences is mentioned in this respect, including: petty crimes, property crimes, sexual crimes, assaults, shoplifting, burglaries, rape, robbery with violence, armed robbery, thefts, offences against property (armed robbery with violence of banks, security vehicles, supermarkets), violence, particularly domestic, juvenile crime, and gang crime.

The report also shows a list of emerging crime problems that are particularly assumed to be linked to political, economic and social change. In this respect, many countries across the continent were unanimous: organised and/or professional crime and economic crime of various forms, including corruption, were repeatedly and expressly mentioned both in East and West.

The Sourcebook Project and the Fifth United Nations Crime Survey

The Sourcebook Project of the Council of Europe attempted a first comprehensive systematic comparison across all member countries. It did not produce standard, directly comparable indicators of the crime situation but, rather, a compilation of existing statistical information with differences that did not permit comparisons. Also, not all member countries delivered the required data, and the information provided was not always uniform.

A parallel survey was undertaken by the United Nations. Here, too, existing statistics were compiled, with less commentary from all United Nations member countries. In this case as well, the data was incomplete.

The report on the UN survey included a cross-sectional analysis[5] in which European data were commented on.[6] These data dealt primarily with conventional offences: homicides and other violent crime, crimes against motor vehicles, theft, burglary, petty crimes, and violence against women. However, corruption was assessed separately.

Explanations of variations in crime rates apply a theoretical framework where motivational, opportunistic and control factors are related. In the analysis, Europe is dealt with as two blocks: central and eastern Europe as one, and western Europe as the other.

> The motivation to offend would appear to be greater in the countries with economies in transition (the countries in Central and Eastern Europe) than in

Western Europe ... In Central and Eastern Europe ... there is clearly more demand among male adolescents for opportunities to acquire income through criminal activities. In these countries socio-economic deprivation and alcohol abuse appear to help in forming a breeding ground for different forms of crimes of violence. Assaults, homicides and robberies appear to be more prevalent in countries where many young males experience strain. Furthermore, in most Central and Eastern European countries violence against women is relatively high. In addition to strain and alcohol abuse, this specific crime problem is probably related to the low social status of women. For example, the percentage of women with higher education is much lower in most countries in transition than in the European Union member states.

Corruption also appears to be much more common in many Central and Eastern European countries than in North America and Northern Europe. In the short term, the economic crisis in the Russian Federation in particular may exacerbate existing economic and social problems in the region. In the longer term, economic prospects may be better but this will not necessarily reduce crime. Increased affluence in these countries will probably not reduce the prevalence of strain because in the context of a free-market economy the lower social strata will profit less from it than will the higher strata. The rates of unemployment will probably remain high for many years to come.

In most of the countries in transition, people in urban areas typically live in flats, and car ownership is still relatively rare. These factors may have so far inhibited further increases in property crimes. Over the past ten years, in most Central and Eastern European countries the level of affluence has increased. This has been the case in particular in Hungary, Poland, Slovenia and the Baltic states. If the GNP of these countries (which are among the first candidates for entry into the European Union in the twenty-first century) continues to increase, vehicle-related crimes and some forms of petty crime are likely to increase as well. Probably household burglary rates will also increase if households start to possess more expensive commodities, and if investment in anti-burglary devices remains low.

The level of corruption in government circles appears to be lower in the countries where economic restructuring is relatively advanced, for example, in Estonia and Hungary. In fact the level of corruption in these countries is lower than in some Western countries. These are encouraging findings. If the restructuring in other countries in the region continues, the long-term prospects for decreasing levels of corruption seem fairly good.

To sum up, the overall criminological outlook for the countries in transition in our view is relatively bleak. Even if the current economic problems are overcome, rates of crimes of violence will probably remain high, owing to high levels of unemployment among young males and the high consumption of strong alcohol. Also, traditional attitudes towards females are unlikely to change in the short term, and violence against women is likely to remain a serious problem.

In the years to come, the increased affluence of the emerging middle classes, although currently suffering a setback in the Russian Federation, will increase opportunities for crime. More people will be able to afford to live in detached housing and to own cars. With a time lag of a few years, the levels of self-protection will go up and the rate of opportunistic crimes might stop increasing. Some of the crimes prevented, however, are likely to be displaced to become robberies.[7]

Crime rates, profiles and trends in the 1990s

European regions

In this presentation, countries are grouped in a more detailed manner than has been customary.[8] Europe is broken down into nine regions. This is solely for practical purposes, but it is based on the idea that in the open landscape that Europe is beginning to resemble, adjacent countries with intensive interaction are likely to develop roughly similar crime profiles over time. Of course, political, historical and geographical dimensions play a role as well. Countries are only covered insofar as entries on them may be found in the Council of Europe Sourcebook on Crime, the Fifth UN Crime Survey, and the International Crime Victimisation Survey (ICVS).

The subdivision is based on the one suggested by the Council of Europe Committee of Experts in their report on organised crime in Council of Europe member states, although some alterations have been introduced. Thus, Hungary is placed in east central Europe rather than the Balkans as suggested by the Expert Committee. Also, a few extra countries in the European zone were included, even though they were not Council of Europe members.

Crime rates, profiles and trends

European crime rates may, for the first time in the present scope, be compared on the basis of the work reporting the Fifth UN Survey. In this source, most European countries have been indexed according to their crime rates. Sources permit comparisons of only some conventional crime categories, and corruption. The crime indices have been constructed so as to allow the use of police statistics, findings from the ICVS, and additional sources where relevant.

Basic questions we must ask are How much crime?, What kinds of crime? and What trends may be observed? The available data answer this question only to a limited degree. Some categories of traditional crime may be accounted for on the basis of statistics on recorded crime. Additionally, a few types of crimes experienced by individuals as measured in victimisation surveys are compared. Organised crime is presented separately. The presentation is regrettably only for 1990-94, as data for the end-1990s have not yet been made available.

First, the countries in each of the nine European regions are profiled according to the crime ratings they received in the report of the Fifth United Nations Survey on Crime Trends and Operations of Criminal Justice Systems, published in 1998. These ratings refer to the period up to 1995, combining data from police and health statistics, the ICVS, and – for corruption – ICVS data together with two other measures of corruption. Each index is based on the ranking of the countries according to each data source that could be used in the calculation. These rankings were standardised by dividing the rank by the number of countries for which relevant data were available and then multiplying by 100.

The types of crime assessed are listed below, together with an indication of the contents of each crime index used:

- homicide (police-recorded homicides for 1990 and 1994, World Health Organisation causes-of-death data for 1992, Interpol homicide rate 1992, and Centers for Disease Control data for 1994);
- other 'non-fatal' violence (one-year assault, threat, and robbery victimisation according to ICVS data for 1988-95);
- violence against women (five-year rates of female respondents who have been victim of sexual or non-sexual assault, police-recorded rapes 1990 and 1994);
- burglary (police-recorded burglaries 1990 and 1994, one-year rate of burglary victims according to the ICVS 1988-95);
- motor-vehicle crimes (one-year rates of victims of theft from/of car 1988-95, police-recorded rates of stolen vehicles, and of untraced motor vehicles in 1995);
- petty crimes (one-year rates of victims of car vandalism, theft of motorcycle or moped, theft of bicycle, theft of personal belongings, sexual offensive behaviour, threats, all according to the ICVS 1988-95);
- corruption (one-year rate of victims in the ICVS 1988-95, Transparency International corruption index 1995, *World Competitiveness Yearbook* 1997).

All charts and maps providing a visual presentation of the material covered below are available on www.om.fi/optula

The presentation, albeit not complete, covers all police-recorded crime from 1990 to 1997. For most European countries, at least partial information is given. The crime rates per 100000 inhabitants have been indexed in order to arrive at the same baseline: there are great differences between countries regarding the overall volume of recorded crime and trends are more easily grasped if such a standardisation of statistics is adopted. In the index calculations, 1991 was taken as the base year, with a value of 100.

Trends of rates of separate crime categories are also discussed at length. For crime trends in the 1990s, police-recorded crime is used as the main source. These data are from the Council of Europe Sourcebook Project that published its first comprehensive volume in 1999. The trend data cover the period 1990-96. Additionally, national police statistics for a large number of European countries have been consulted. The rates are presented for the following nine crime categories (again, not all crime categories are reported for each country): homicide, assault, robbery, rape, theft, motor vehicle theft, bicycle theft, burglary, domestic burglary, and drug offences.

Major crime trends region by region

Scandinavia (Denmark, Finland, Iceland, Norway, Sweden)

The region

The five Scandinavian countries have a total population of about 24 million. Over the 1990s, each experienced a similar restructuring of the economy following the recession at the beginning of the decade. During the 1990s, Sweden and Finland joined the European Union whereas Norway and Iceland have remained outside this structure. Denmark was already a member. However, Scandinavian passport conventions have made all countries of the region equally accessible for a long time and the position of Norway or Iceland is not significantly different from the other countries as far as free movement is concerned.

Geographically, Scandinavia has been relatively isolated from the rest of Europe, although exchange with eastern neighbours has increased over the 1990s. Finland and Norway share a land border with Russia, Finland has regular sea connections to Estonia, and Sweden has also actively developed routes to the Baltic region. There is a direct land connection to western Europe only from Denmark. During the 1990s, outside crime influences in the region have thus become more prominent than before 1991. Despite this, the region remains relatively isolated.

To understand their crime profiles, a few general characteristics of each country are helpful. Denmark is an affluent country, has a moderate unemployment level and is highly urbanised, with an average level of alcohol consumption. Finland is moderately urbanised, has a relatively high unemployment rate, an above-average level of alcohol consumption and a low number of hard-drug addicts. Iceland is only moderately urbanised. Norway has a relatively low degree of urbanisation, with a relatively high level of social integration. The number of hard-drug addicts is low. Norway is a very affluent country with a low unemployment rate and a moderate level of alcohol consumption. Sweden is affluent, fairly urbanised with an average level of unemployment and a mid-range alcohol consumption level. It has a moderate number of hard-drug addicts.

Crime rates and profiles 1990/1994

Crime profiles for the Scandinavian countries resemble each other rather closely. When comparing average crime scores, the region is at the European average for homicides and motor-vehicle crimes. For non-fatal violence, burglary and petty crime, the average scores are below European averages. For violence against women, the region scores high, and for corruption very low. However, Finland and Sweden score higher on the homicide index than the others. Sweden also receives a high score on petty crime. For crimes against motor vehicles, Sweden and Denmark have above-average scores. Overall, Finland ranks relatively low on property crime and relatively high on violence; Sweden ranks relatively high on both, Denmark ranks high on the property side but low with regard to violence, and Norway ranks low on both. Comparable data were not provided for Iceland.

Crime trends 1990-96/97

The Scandinavian countries display a decrease in police-recorded crime. Norway, however, deviates markedly from this pattern, with a rapid increase after 1995. In fact, it may have lost its previous position as one of the definitive low-crime countries in western Europe. Whether this may be ascribed to the economic development of the country deserves further study. As police-recorded crime is predominantly property-related in this region, this seems to be a plausible explanation. Another explanation may lie in increased immigration from several problem areas to Norway.

Traditional types of property and violent crime at first decreased in this region, and then slowly increased again, corresponding roughly to overall economic development. It is only in the area of narcotics offences that moderate to considerable increases were to be found, Norway having experienced the most marked increase in this respect.

As for motivation, opportunity and control elements, the 1990s were a turbulent period, particularly because of the large increases in unemployment in the early 1990s. Towards the end of the decade, this factor improved systematically, whereas the opportunity dimension gained in strength as the economy again began to grow.

Western Europe (Belgium, Ireland, Luxembourg, the Netherlands, England and Wales, Scotland, Northern Ireland)

The region

For purposes of analysis, this region is broken down into the three Benelux countries and the four British Isles countries. All seven are members of the European Union. Sufficient data exist for all seven. The economic recession of the early 1990s was also experienced in this region, followed by relatively similar restructuring of the economy. The countries of this region together have a population of about 89 million (1997), the Benelux countries have 26 million, and the British Isles countries 62 million inhabitants.

Luxembourg is reported to have a low unemployment rate, but has a high level of alcohol consumption and is very highly urbanised. Belgium is quite similar in these respects and is reported to have less hard-drug addicts than the European Union mean. The Netherlands also shares similar characteristics, although the narcotics market is relatively strong.

England and Wales are highly urbanised, with mid-range unemployment and a high level of alcohol consumption. Narcotics addiction is more widespread than in most other European Union countries. Scotland is less urbanised, with relatively high alcohol consumption and mid-range unemployment. Northern Ireland is relatively affluent and among the less urbanised European countries, a traditional lifestyle still prevailing widely. Its political troubles have probably supported the maintenance of a high level of informal control. Ireland is also a relatively rural traditional country with above-average alcohol consumption. It has a low rate of hard-drug use although this is reported to be on the increase.

Crime rates and profiles 1990/1994

The general crime profiles for these countries are similar. The average regional score for homicides is moderately low, as is the average score on the corruption index. Petty crime is below the European average. For non-lethal violence and violence against women, this region is at the European average. In contrast, relatively high scores are found for burglaries and crimes against motor vehicles. Thus, the region can be characterised as one with moderate or low violence, moderate corruption, rather high serious property crime and moderate petty crime.

In the Benelux countries, deviations from this pattern are provided by Luxembourg with its high motor-vehicle crime rate, the Netherlands with their very low homicide and high petty crime rate and Belgium with its moderately high number of homicides and burglary, a low number of petty crimes and a rather high corruption score. Of the British Isles countries, Ireland, England and Wales have a very low homicide rate. Northern Ireland falls outside the range with a very low score on corruption and a very high homicide rate. Burglary and crimes against motor vehicles in England and Wales together with Scotland are quite high.

Crime trends 1990-96/97

In western Europe, the overall crime trend was a decrease for all countries for which data are reproduced, with Ireland the only minor exception: here, crime rates remained constant, at least up to 1996.

The overall trends of police-recorded crime are relatively uniform across the region. At the beginning of the 1990s an overall growth was clear. After 1992 growth stagnated and rates began to drop. However, Ireland's overall rate of police-recorded crime continued on the same level as in 1991-93.

This impression of overall stagnation shows nuances when the rates are broken down. The same interpretation is confirmed for violent crime, with the exception of rape, which steadily increased at a moderate rate over the 1990s in all countries of the region. A further exception was an increase in robberies in Belgium, England and Wales, and Ireland. Belgium and Luxembourg also experienced a clear increase in narcotics offences.

West central Europe (Austria, Germany, Liechtenstein, Switzerland)

The region

This region has nearly 100 million inhabitants (1997), with 82 million in Germany alone. Switzerland and Liechtenstein have remained outside the European Union, Austria joined the Union only in 1994, whereas Germany has been one of the core countries in European integration. Also, since the fall of the Berlin Wall, Germany shares a long border with Poland, a significant locus for cross-border crime. Germany's many other neighbours (the Benelux countries and France in the west, the Czech Republic in the east, and Denmark in the north, together with long Baltic Sea and Atlantic shorelines) represent ample possibilities for cross-border criminal influences and activities. Austria also shares borders with a number of countries, including Italy, Slovenia, Hungary, Slovakia and the Czech Republic. It is thus on the route from, and represents an entry from, the Balkans into Germany. Together with Switzerland, it is also on the route from Italy to Germany. Switzerland is in a central position to Austria, Italy, France and Germany.

Austria is affluent but not highly urbanised and unemployment has been relatively low. The level of alcohol consumption is above the European average. Germany is highly urbanised and affluent, with a mid-range unemployment rate and considerably high alcohol consumption. Switzerland is the most affluent European country, unemployment is low and alcohol consumption is moderate. Switzerland is not highly urbanised, a relatively small proportion of the population living in large cities. The narcotics situation is more serious in Switzerland than in Germany or Austria. Liechtenstein is urbanised to a low level; other data were not available.

Crime rates and profiles 1990/1994

The region as a whole scores below the European average for homicides, non-lethal violence, burglary and crimes against motor vehicles. Average scores are found for petty crime and corruption, and an above-average score for violence against women. Austria has a homicide rate above both the regional and the European average, Germany is the one of three countries where the score for violence against women is quite high. In Germany, the motor-vehicle crime rate is also above the European average. Switzerland has a much lower score for corruption than the other two. Data on Liechtenstein have not been reported separately from those of Switzerland.

Crime trends 1990-96/97

In west central Europe, the overall trend of all crimes recorded by the police in all three countries remains constant. In Austria, fluctuations were minimal during the 1990s, with a slight tendency to decrease. In Germany, stagnation occurred after a rapid initial increase following the unification of Germany. Switzerland showed a moderate increase in the overall crime rate after 1995. For specific types of crime, the trends are not quite so uniform. The homicide trend was decreasing for Switzerland. In Germany, an initial increase noted up to 1993 was followed by a gradual decline. The Austrian rates fluctuated unsystematically around a low level. Assault rates were quite stable over this period, Germany representing a minor exception with an average annual increase rate of about 7 per cent between 1992 and 1996. Rape was stable in Germany and decreased in Austria. In Switzerland, a decrease in rape between 1990 and 1994 was followed by new increases in 1995 and 1996.

Robbery rates fell in Austria and increased in Germany. In Switzerland growth up to 1993 was followed by a significant decrease in 1994 and 1995 and a small increase in 1996. Thefts decreased in Austria and Switzerland. After an increase up to 1993, a decreasing trend in theft was also observed in Germany. Motor-vehicle thefts decreased in Austria and Switzerland. After a large increase up to 1993, the German rates also began to decline. Bicycle theft rates declined in all three countries. Burglary rates declined in Austria;

in Switzerland figures for 1996 showed an increase after many years of declining rates. In Germany, burglary rates also grew rapidly up to 1993; after this date they began to fall. Domestic burglaries decreased in Austria; in Germany, their rate stabilised after a growth period up to 1993. Switzerland reported no data for this crime category. Drug offence rates grew in all three countries over the whole period from 1990 to 1996, the largest growth being in Switzerland.

South-western Europe (Andorra, France, Italy, Malta, Portugal, San Marino, Spain)

The region

The total population of this region is about 165 million, the three big countries being France, with 59 million, Italy with 57 million and Spain with 39 million. For analytic purposes, a subdivision may be useful. Andorra, Portugal and Spain are one obvious group, Italy and San Marino (and Malta) a second group, and France might best be treated as a third. If taken as a whole, the region shares land borders with the west central Europe region (Austria, Switzerland and Germany) and the Benelux region. Additionally, Italy neighbours on Slovenia in the east. Coastlines, however, make the region open in other directions. Thus, Balkan influences are important to Italy, and African ones are particularly relevant both for Spain and Italy. The Atlantic coast provides an important interface with western influences for Portugal, Spain and France. From the perspective of European influences, its peripheral location means that Portugal is rather isolated. Few data are provided for Andorra.

France has an above-average unemployment rate, is relatively highly urbanised and has a high level of alcohol consumption. Portugal is one of the least affluent and most rural societies in Europe, with relatively strong informal control still prevailing. Alcohol consumption in Portugal is rather high. Spain is relatively urbanised, with a high unemployment rate and an above-average level of alcohol consumption. Its GNP is in the European mid-range. Italy is relatively urbanised, with a high GNP, a relatively high unemployment rate and a high alcohol consumption level. The hard-drug addict rate is very high in Portugal. Spain and Italy also have more hard-drug addicts than the EU countries on average. Malta has a low degree of urbanisation; otherwise few data are available.

Crime rates and profiles 1990/1994

The region averaged a low to moderately low rate for homicides, other violence and petty crime. It was near the European averages for burglary; however, for crimes against motor vehicles and for corruption this region averaged quite high. Notable exceptions to the general pattern were the quite high homicide rates for Portugal and Italy. Also, France had an average score (in European terms) for violence against women, higher than the other countries in this region. For burglaries, Malta scored low, and for crimes against motor vehicles, Portugal took only an average position. The corruption measure gave the highest score for Italy and the lowest one for France, slightly below the European average. No data were provided for Andorra and San Marino.

Crime trends 1990-96/97

In south-western Europe, the 1990s were also a period of small changes. The overall trend in rates of police-recorded crime was a calm one, with moderate fluctuations for this region (for those three countries where data were available). For single crime categories, this impression is nuanced: the Italian homicide rate decreased significantly after 1991. Assault rates in France and Portugal increased moderately over the 1990s; in addition, the rates of rape and narcotics offences increased in France.

The Balkans (Albania, Bosnia, Bulgaria, Croatia, "the former Yugoslav Republic of Macedonia", Romania, Slovenia and Yugoslavia)

The region

The countries in this group have a total population of almost 43 million (1997), Romania being the largest with over 22 million inhabitants. The population of Bulgaria is over 8 million, the remaining four countries having between 2 and 4 million inhabitants each. Romania and Bulgaria have coasts on the Black Sea and borders with the former Yugoslavia/the Balkans, Turkey, Greece and Hungary. Romania shares a northern border with Moldova and Ukraine. The region shares a border only with two European Union countries, Italy (bordering on Slovenia) and Greece (adjoining Bulgaria, "the former Yugoslav Republic of Macedonia" and Albania).

The Balkan wars in the 1990s have greatly influenced, at least for the time being, the role of this region as a narcotics smuggling route towards the west, formerly of considerable importance. Like many other east European countries, Albania is going through a change towards a market-orientated western democracy, with similar problems emerging in the new situation. Bulgaria experienced a similar transition in the early 1990s. After the disintegration of Yugoslavia, Croatia became independent in 1992, at the same time as "the former Yugoslav Republic of Macedonia" and Slovenia. Romania introduced parliamentary democracy in its new constitution of 1991.

Albania was a predominantly rural country with a low GNP and had a very high unemployment rate. Bulgaria had a high unemployment rate, was relatively urbanised and had a low GNP and above-average alcohol consumption. Croatia had a below average GNP, was not very urbanised and had a high unemployment level. "The former Yugoslav Republic of Macedonia" had a very high unemployment rate and low GNP, and was not very urbanised. Romania was also a relatively poor country, not very urbanised, with a very high unemployment rate and a moderate alcohol consumption level. Slovenia had a relatively high unemployment rate. It was affluent by central and eastern European standards and not very urbanised. Yugoslavia was not very urbanised, nor affluent and had a low GNP.

Crime rates and profiles 1990/1994

The countries of this region scored close to the European average in many respects. The homicide rate averages were a little high, and the scores for crimes against motor vehicles and for petty crimes were moderately low. Corruption, in contrast, was high in this region. Deviations from this regional profile were clearest in the case of Bulgaria, which scored high – both in a regional and an all-European comparison – for all crime categories scrutinised. A similar observation may be made of the former Yugoslavia. Albania had a burglary score above both the regional and the European average. "The former Yugoslav Republic of Macedonia" had below-average scores for all types of crime; corruption, however, was at the level for Europe. Croatia was also a relatively low-crime country except for its homicide score, which was quite high. For Romania, the scores for burglary, crimes against motor vehicles and petty crimes were moderately low. Slovenia's crime figures made it an average country for this region.

Crime trends 1990-96/97

In the Balkans, overall data for many countries have not been available. Of the three countries assessed, Bulgaria and Croatia displayed a decrease in recorded crime, after an initial crime increase in the first years of the decade. Romania, in contrast, had been following a very different path, with a rapidly growing crime rate. Data of overall trends in police-recorded crime for this region were available for Bulgaria, Croatia and Romania. The 1990s were a period of rapid growth for Romania, bearing a resemblance to Russian and Baltic developments. In Croatia, an initial crime increase up to 1993 was replaced by a clear decrease that continued up to 1997. Bulgaria showed similar but more moderate fluctuations.

For different crime categories, the changes vary substantially. Homicide trends in this region were generally calm. Even Bulgaria and Albania, which displayed growth trends up to 1993-94, subsequently reported decreases. However, the rates of homicide remained the highest of the region in these two countries. Assault rates were increasing over the entire period in Bulgaria, Romania and "the former Yugoslav Republic of Macedonia". Albania, after an initial increase up to 1993, reported a steady decline. Croatia and Slovenia had stable assault rates. In the early 1990s rapes increased in Bulgaria and in Romania; all other countries of this region shared a decreasing trend. Romanian figures stabilised from 1993 onward, and the Bulgarian ones indicated a slight decrease towards the end of the period.

Robbery rates increased rapidly in Bulgaria up to 1994 but remained constant after that year. The other countries had a rather stable situation in this respect, with Slovenia and "the former Yugoslav Republic of Macedonia" displaying a moderate increase. Bulgaria again reported a large increase in thefts up to 1992, with small decreases in 1995 and 1996. Romania experienced a steady growth of the theft rate, while Croatia and Slovenia reported a decreasing trend. The situation in "the former Yugoslav Republic of Macedonia" remained unchanged over the 1990s. Trends of motor-vehicle thefts were quite similar to other theft trends. After large initial increases,

Bulgaria and Croatia showed a decrease, while Romania, Slovenia, Albania and the Federal Yugoslav Republic of Macedonia showed little change. Bicycle theft showed no systematic change over the 1990s with the exception of Albania, where rates initially increased rapidly, then turned to a decreasing trend that in 1996 reached a lower level than the one for the beginning of the decade. For burglary, after an initial rapid increase up to 1992, Bulgaria again reported declining rates for 1995 and 1996. For Croatia, the rate was decreasing after 1992, for the other countries the rates were rather stable. "The former Yugoslav Republic of Macedonia" also had a clear initial growth up to 1992, after which the rate stabilised. The Bulgarian trend for domestic burglary was one of rapid growth up to 1994. Subsequently, this rate decreased. For the other countries, changes were minimal over the entire period. Drug offences shared a growth trend in all countries of the region, the sharpest increase being reported for Croatia.

East central Europe (the Czech Republic, Hungary, Poland, Slovakia)

The region

These four countries have a total of about 65 million inhabitants (1997). The largest is Poland, with 39 million; the Czech Republic and Hungary both have around 10 million; Slovakia has the smallest population with about 5 million. The region shares a land border with two European Union countries, Germany (Poland, the Czech Republic) and Austria (the Czech Republic and Hungary). In the east, neighbours are the Russian Federation (Kaliningrad region), Lithuania, Belarus and Ukraine; in the south and south-east, Slovenia, Croatia, Yugoslavia and Romania. Poland also has a long Baltic Sea coastline. In the 1990s, all the countries in this region were in transition after a long period of socialist regimes.

The Czech Republic is moderately urbanised, has a low unemployment rate, but also a relatively low GNP and a high level of alcohol consumption. Hungary also is moderately urbanised, with a relatively high unemployment rate and high alcohol consumption. Poland is a moderately urbanised country with a relatively high unemployment rate and low alcohol consumption. Slovakia is moderately urbanised, with a high unemployment rate and moderate alcohol consumption.

Crime rates and profiles 1990/1994

This region had violence scores at the European average; property crime scores were moderately above average. The corruption index had rather high values for this region, with minimal differences between countries. The largest deviations from this regional pattern were the low Hungarian rates for non-lethal violence and petty property crime and the high score regarding violence against women in the Czech Republic.

Crime trends 1990-96/97

Of the countries in east central Europe, Hungary and Poland experienced a very stable situation. The Czech Republic more than doubled its crime rate over the decade, the largest relative increase in a pan-European perspective. The overall rates of police-recorded crime over the 1990s were quite stable in Hungary and Poland, and steadily increasing in the Czech Republic. By crime category, this pattern varied across countries. The crime types that showed recent increases were assault, robbery, theft of motor vehicles and drug offences for Poland, theft, bicycle theft, theft of motor vehicles, burglary, domestic burglary, and drug offences for Hungary, and drug offences for the Czech Republic. For Slovakia, trend data were not available.

South-eastern Europe (Cyprus, Greece, Turkey)

The region

The population of this region amounts to 75 million, Turkey alone having over 63 million inhabitants. The population of Greece is over 10 million, and Cyprus less than one million. These countries share borders with Bulgaria, the former Yugoslavia and Albania; the region also has long Mediterranean and Black Sea coastlines. Turkey also has a land connection to the Near East countries. This region has played a significant role as a route for smuggling narcotics and other merchandise from Asia to Europe. Cyprus is not very urbanised, has a low level of unemployment and is moderately affluent. Greece is moderately urbanised, with affluence in the middle range, moderately high unemployment and moderate alcohol consumption level. Turkey is moderately urbanised, has a relatively high level of unemployment and very low alcohol consumption.

Crime rates and profiles 1990/1994

This region scored very low in a European comparison of homicides and violence against women, and moderately low for burglary and crimes against motor vehicles. Data on non-fatal violence and petty crimes were not available. The average corruption score was the highest among all European regions. Of the three countries in this region, Greece had somewhat higher scores on all the mentioned crime categories, with a score for crimes against motor vehicles equal to the European average.

Crime trends 1990-96/97

For south-east Europe, data were available only for Greece where the overall rate had fallen below the 1991-92 levels. Data on all police-recorded crime were available only for Greece. There, the rate increased up to 1992, then fell rapidly, increasing again in 1995, but still remaining below the 1990 level. For separate crime categories, more trend data are available; in Greece, the crime categories for which clear increasing trends were observed were homicides, thefts, burglaries, motor vehicle thefts and drug offences. In Cyprus, notable increases concerned rapes and drug offences. In Turkey the growth areas were rape, assault, and motor vehicle theft.

The Baltic states (Estonia, Latvia, Lithuania)

The region

After 1991 and the disintegration of the Soviet Union, the three Baltic countries rapidly adopted market economy principles and Western democratic structures; their borders with western Europe have gradually opened and they have expressed an interest in joining the European Union. As in many other eastern European countries, these developments have been paralleled by new crime problems. Bordering Russia, both Estonia and Latvia have been subjected to the considerable influence of Russian crime, in particular since their borders have been relatively open. For Lithuania, neighbouring Belarus and Poland, this influence is smaller but important as well; the route from Russia to Kaliningrad crosses Lithuania. In 1997, the total population of these countries was about 7.5 million (1.4 million in Estonia, 2.4 million in Latvia, and 3.6 million in Lithuania).

In the early 1990s, as totalitarian control structures were replaced by the new regimes, significant changes took place in this region. Income differences grew rapidly and official control mechanisms lost ground, partly as a consequence of corruption. Organised crime structures emerged, developing cross-border co-operation networks. Consequently, motivational, opportunity-related crime increased. After 1991, the social situation of the large Russian minority in each of these countries became weaker; this has sometimes been understood as a further source of criminal motivation.

Estonia has low unemployment, is fairly urbanised, with a relatively low level of affluence. In Latvia unemployment is low and the population is fairly urbanised, with a low level of affluence. Lithuania is fairly urbanised, with a low level of affluence; its unemployment rate is higher than in the two other countries.

Crime rates and profiles 1990/1994

The three Baltic countries averaged high or very high with regard to homicides, non-fatal violence, burglary and petty crimes, as well as corruption. The region was above the European average for crimes against motor vehicles. It is only in regard to violence against women that the region on average was equal to the European score. Differences between the three countries were not great. However, Estonia scored highest in all crime categories except corruption where it approached the European average. Correspondingly, Latvia scored lowest in non-fatal violence and in violence against women.

Crime trends 1990-96/97

Up to 1992, the Baltic states shared the same growth pattern. Later, however, Latvian rates systematically decreased while Estonia and Lithuania both reported overall increases up to 1997. The overall rates of police-recorded crime first showed a uniform increase up to 1992. After this year, however, Latvia began a steady decrease while the other two countries continued a growth trend, albeit one which was not as rapid as in the first years of the decade.

High homicide rates were reached only in the 1990s; falling trends have since been reported for all three countries. Crime statistics for these countries, as to a varying degree in other east European countries formerly under the socialist regime, have surged upwards. Part of the recorded crime increases resulted from statistics reforms that gradually diminished the degree of manipulation of crime statistics that was widespread in earlier years; part of this scenario, however, is generally understood as reflecting real increases, too.

Homicide trends for all three countries were quite similar: in the first years of the decade, rates grew rapidly, with 1994 as the peak year in Estonia and Lithuania, and 1993 in Latvia. Growth was most dramatic in Estonia, but very significant in the two other countries as well. After reaching this peak, homicide rates slowly decreased, the level still being higher than at the beginning of the decade. Assaults displayed a steadier pattern except for Latvia where rates more than doubled in 1992; they subsequently remained on this new level. The Estonian trend was one of a slow increase, and the Lithuanian figures were almost constant throughout the period examined (1990-96). Rape offences increased quickly in Estonia up to 1994, then declined to some extent. In contrast, in Latvia and Lithuania the rates fluctuated around the same level of 5 per 100000 population for the entire period.

Robbery rates also increased steadily in Estonia, growth stopping only in 1996. In Latvia, rates first decreased until 1993, then remaining unchanged. In 1991 and 1992 thefts increased in Estonia and Latvia. Estonian figures fluctuated near the 1992 level, while Latvian rates decreased systematically. In Lithuania, the trend was different, one of slow steady increase over the whole period 1990-96. Motor vehicle thefts increased in all three countries. Most of this growth took place in 1992 for Latvia, in 1993 for Estonia, and in 1994 for Lithuania. Subsequently, a decreasing trend seemed to take over. This may be interpreted as quite significant as the number of motor vehicles in these countries multiplied over the 1990s. Bicycle theft increased steadily in Estonia, but decreased greatly in Latvia. For Lithuania, no data were provided on bicycle theft. Burglary figures were available only from 1992. For Estonia, the subsequent trend was one of growth, possibly stopping in 1996. In Latvia, the trend was slowly decreasing. Lithuania did not report data on burglaries. For domestic burglaries in Estonia, 1991 and 1992 were years of rapid growth; thereafter changes were less significant. In Latvia, rates grew in 1993-94, then declined slightly. In Lithuania, domestic burglaries increased steadily at a moderate pace. Finally, drug offences increased quite rapidly in all three countries year after year. Part of this statistical upswing is understood as being produced by increased control efforts as authorities began to realise that narcotics markets were growing in these countries too.

Eastern Europe (Belarus, Moldova, Russian Federation, Ukraine)

The region

The four countries in this region have a total population of about 183 million, with about 166 million in the European part of Russia, 52 million in Ukraine, 10 million in Belarus, and 4 million in Moldova. After the disintegration of the Soviet Union in 1991, each of these countries experienced major societal changes that still continue. Their economic development has been unstable, with little affluence and rapid growth in income differences. The transition towards democratic market economies has also begun in this region, albeit in a less controlled manner than in many other countries sharing a similar position.

Similarly to events in the Baltic region in the early 1990s, as totalitarian control structures were replaced by the new regimes, significant changes took place. Income differences grew rapidly and official control mechanisms lost ground, in part as a consequence of corruption. Organised crime structures emerged and developed cross-border co-operation networks. Privatisation schemes provided significant opportunities for speculation. Consequently, motivational, opportunity-related and control factors have favoured crime increases.

Moldova has a very low unemployment rate, with a low level of urbanisation and a low level of affluence. Russia has a very high unemployment rate and a high level of alcohol consumption. Poverty is widespread. Ukraine reports a low unemployment level and a below-average GNP; the level of alcohol consumption is average.

Crime rates and profiles 1990/1994

This region displays a twofold profile where regional averages can be particularly misleading. Moldova has a high homicide rate, and also the rate of overall violence is high. The burglary rate is fairly low, as is the rate of motor vehicle crime. Russia has very high rates of lethal and other types of violence. Property crime levels are high. Ukraine also has a high level of violence although the homicide rate is not much above the European average; its property crime rate is high.

Data on corruption are not available for Moldova. Russia holds the top position in the ranking for corruption, whereas Ukraine falls in the mid-range on the corruption index.

Crime trends 1990-96/97

Eastern Europe in this period showed two quite different trends. Moldova reported a systematically declining crime rate, while the trend in the Russian Federation remained constant, at a level about 30% higher than in the early 1990s. No trend data are given for Ukraine.

The homicide trend for Russia displayed a great increase after 1991, remaining on a high level in 1994. No trend data for the two other countries are available. After a peak in 1994, assaults decreased in Russia. Moldova showed practically no change over the 1990s. Rape rates were falling in both Russia and Moldova. Robbery rates were relatively stable after an increase in the early 1990s in both countries. Theft rates were falling in both countries. Motor vehicle theft fell in Russia after 1993; for the other countries, no data are given. After 1992-93, burglary rates fell in both Russia and Moldova. Domestic burglary rates also fell in Russia, after an increase up to 1993. In

Moldova, this rate was rather stable. Drug offences were increasing in both countries. The early 1990s were apparently a growth period in this region for all or most conventional crime categories, homicides most dramatically. Today, the data situation is too unclear to permit more discussion about later years except that, gradually, the overall situation has been improving although not consistently.

Summary

Former Soviet Union member states experienced the most dramatic changes in the 1990s, particularly in violent crime trends. Other former socialist countries showed similar but much less pronounced trends. Western Europe, Scandinavia and several other regions clearly reached a stage of relative consistency; this had already been observed in the late 1980s in many continental western European countries.

Those western European countries with immediate neighbours in eastern or central Europe have experienced more "crime integration" development than others, a simple consequence of their geographical vicinity, allowing more intensive interaction with countries in transition, which have been going through a period of short-term crime growth. Countries on the margins of this east-west interface have remained largely protected from these immediate pressures.

The drug scene seems to have been growing in all European countries, accompanied by organised crime developments that have had a growing influence on other illegal activities, from smuggling of profitable commodities and even people to trade in a variety of other opportunity-dictated commodities. Deregulation policies have resulted in a new situation where operations in the grey economy are also growing, apparently also in countries where this sector has previously not been significant. Black and grey economy operations tend to merge and flow into the legal economy. Money laundering of profits from illegal operations forms part of this development and is reported to be a significant growth industry. In part, this is an obvious reflection of the expansion of the narcotics market on the one hand, and of the grey economy on the other. In part, however, it is also a matter of unstable social circumstances in former Soviet Union member countries that have created pressures to transfer capital away from those economies.

Organised crime

Observations on organised crime

Organised crime has considerable social importance, whether justified or not by facts; because of the elusive nature of the phenomenon, comparable data are scarce. In this dilemma, we have resorted to the most recent data from the Council of Europe project assessing organised crime. However, the interpretability and comparability of data on organised crime and its different aspects are in practice still more of a problem than data on other, traditional crimes. Police registers seldom record it, as most of the observed suspected cases do not come about by individual crime reports – even the count of 'cases' is highly unclear in this realm of the crime problem. Some new data are provided by the EU Multidisciplinary Group report from 1998.

Finnish research has made attempts to understand some of the recent developments in eastern Europe. Several ideas are cited below:

> When discussing the Russian/Eastern European situation, we tend to support (...) a perspective stressing the flexibility, and the opportunistic character of the activities of criminal organisations. Organised crime may be seen as a form of criminal activities that is only poorly and indirectly illuminated by official statistics or by other standard sources. Furthermore, the contents of the phenomenon are difficult to define. It is also an attractive target of myth-making. At present, it is very hard to differentiate between economic crime and other economic activity in Eastern and Central Europe. An established illegal economy has existed for decades in these countries, and patterns of activities that have developed within this economy prevail even today. Various illegal practices (from the viewpoint of the legislation) continue today to be the rule rather than the exception in business activities, and they are usually not considered to be reproachable. Even official estimates of the proportion of the shadow economy out of the total national economy vary between 25% and 50% – the proportion grows as we move from west to east and from north to south – and if compared with the real situation, these estimates across the area are rather too low than too high. In the area, a difference is made between the grey and the black economy; the first includes 'normal' economic crime, the latter covers the 'actual' or 'real' economic crimes. The difference between the two is often difficult to distinguish.
>
> Circumstances favouring large-scale organised economic criminal activities today are good. The privatisation of public properties, the sharply reduced size of the army resulting in a great number of surplus weapons (including nuclear materials) dating from the arms race era, and the new trade channels that have come about after the end of restrictions on travel have created ideal circumstances for operations that produce great profits. The value vacuum in the countries, combined with the large prisoner population and with the large numbers of officials left unemployed since the armed forces and the espionage organisations have been cut down, provide a good background for such operations, and the corruption of the law enforcement authorities provides the peace they need to operate.
>
> Organised crime is not a new phenomenon in the area. However, due to the improved circumstances, and according to estimates by the authorities, the volume of criminal organisations has grown rapidly, and the scale of their activities has grown to larger proportions than before. Criminal groups today control the smuggling/trafficking of stolen goods to and from the area: the primary imports are motor cars, and the primary exports are arms, people, valuable metals and timber. In the widespread smuggling of alcohol, tobacco and consumer electronics, a large number of so-called legal enterprises are involved in addition to professional criminals. In the international narcotics trade, the area has become an important transit route since the wars in former Yugoslavia have cut off the traditional smuggling routes over the Balkans. It is also deemed obvious that the area's own narcotics production is increasing (vacant laboratories and unemployed highly skilled chemists both being easily available).

Another characteristic mode of activity besides smuggling is the 'sale' of security and debt recovery services to business. In part, this is a question of co-operation that benefits both parties, in a part a subordinating of certain branches to the control of criminal groups and channelling the profits for the benefit of these groups (the clearest, albeit not the economically most important, example is the organisation of the kiosk trade in the big cities of Russia). The protection racket has indeed reached unusual proportions specifically in Russia. One background factor in this development is the disorganisation of the law-enforcement structures. Parallel with the privatisation of the economy, also the coercion capacity of the state has been partially privatised – both property and power have been redistributed according to the same general principles and among the same groupings.[9]

The Council of Europe project

No comparable quantitative data on the volume or trends for professional/organised crime are reported, except for the Council of Europe report for the 1996 situation. This analysis assesses characteristics of criminal groups, their criminal activities, places and regions of their criminal activities, their resources, the use of violence, use of influence, money-laundering involvement, and so on. The report makes an overall assessment of "major trends in organised crime in Europe". Here, the extent of organised crime is reported, as well as types of crime, internationalisation, professionalism, linkages between licit and illicit activity and use of violence. The extent of organised crime was reported to be typically low in countries with small populations and a geographically marginal location. Several other countries, in or near the transition countries, report a recent growth of organised crime, while the major western European countries typically report that the situation is more or less the same as in previous years, or stabilised. However, these countries regard organised crime as a serious problem, only Italy indicating a recent decrease in criminal activities of its organised crime groups. Drug trafficking is perceived by most as a primary organised criminal activity that will grow in the near future. Fraud and money laundering are also expected to increase.

Regarding the internationalisation of organised crime, some countries expect domestic groups to continue to hold strong positions. Many, however, see indications of foreign groups becoming increasingly active within their national borders. Most frequently mentioned in this respect are criminal groups of eastern and south-eastern European origins. In the drugs trade, Turkish and Kurdish groups are seen to be important. Also, ethnic Albanian groups are reported to have established networks throughout western Europe, collaborating with Italian, Turkish and other groups. Italian law-enforcement efforts are reported to have forced their criminal organisations to relocate part of their activities outside Italy, namely to neighbouring France, Germany and Spain, but also to eastern Europe. Some countries expect that Russian or equivalent international structures will become integrated with local structures, or that domestic groups will develop closer links with foreign organised groups.

Criminal organisations are reported to have improved their working methods. This increasing professionalism makes it more difficult for law enforcement to observe organised criminal activities. Simultaneously, many countries report that new groups using less sophisticated methods are emerging.

Linkages between licit and illicit activities are also reported to be increasing, in particular in countries in transition where organised criminal groups have become involved in legal companies. Also, social élites and organised crime groups are becoming interconnected. State institutions also risk becoming influenced by organised crime. Besides countries in transition and former members of the Soviet Union, Italy in particular is reported to be undergoing such a development. Many countries express concern over the growing use of violence by organised criminal groups.

An overall assessment concludes that international organised crime in Europe has undergone a significant evolution. In the mid-1980s, organised crime was recognised only by some European states as an important social phenomenon. Now more and more countries have acknowledged that there are criminal organisations active within their borders. Nowadays only a number of relatively small states still maintain that organised crime is not a big issue. Several states, especially some that have dealt with the phenomenon for more than five years (Italy, Germany, and the Netherlands), report that the extent of organised crime seems to be stabilising whereas many of the states where the phenomenon was more recently discovered expect an increase.

The progressive globalisation of national economies and the gradual opening of national borders creates a favourable environment not only for legal but also for illegal organisations operating on an international level.

Assessment

Organised crime has received increasing attention in many different contexts in recent times. Whether this is fully justified in regard to the real changes taking place is hard to tell since there is a continuing lack of reliable and comparable information about the issue. A likely assessment is that the major structural changes in Europe that have taken place over the last decade have indeed made conditions more favourable for organised cross-border criminal activities. However, the newly emerging European prioritisation of 'transnational organised crime' in international fora is a logical consequence of significant expansion in international co-operation. The Council of Europe and the European Union have both grown and have, simultaneously, chosen a path of dynamically increasing co-operative activities (on a global level, the same goes for United Nations activities). If there is to be increased co-operation between nations in crime-related matters, then cross-border and transnational crime phenomena are the obvious targets.

A tentative look at the new European crime scene

The major change in European crime is the massive integration of eastern and western Europe as a consequence of the opening of national borders.

This change has had visible consequences for the entire crime scene. The influence has been not only of 'eastern' pressures moving west but, simultaneously, of 'western' pressures moving east, taking over, infiltrating and making use of eastern structures.[10]

A greying population, with ongoing urbanisation, is becoming increasingly isolated and fearful; populations are becoming increasingly polarised into the 'haves' and the 'have-nots'; the market for private security grows; the crime policy climate grows tougher, enhanced by the growing influx of immigrants from war-ridden countries and elsewhere; advances in control technology support the tendencies of increasing repression, in particular as market-orientated economies hamper the development of integrated crime-control innovations.

In the near future, such developments, taken together, could mean that no dramatic changes in the overall crime situation can be expected, particularly as concerns conventional crime. The major continuing influence on the crime scene is the illegal narcotics business around which important organised crime developments are gaining in importance. The criminal structures that thrive around this central commodity, because of their flexible nature, operate according to opportunity with other commodities, made attractive by changing market situations between regions. Thus, many kinds of other business are implicated as well.

A long period of time will be needed to reverse such tendencies. If – and when – the existing differences in standards of living across Europe are significantly evened out, many of the trends described above will weaken and some may even be reversed. This will only hold provided that circumstances outside Europe do not change so much as to notably influence European conditions. The presently ongoing globalisation tendencies make this unlikely.

Chapter 2: Towards 'restorative justice': victimisation, victim support and trends in criminal justice

Tony Peters and Ivo Aertsen, Catholic University Leuwen

Recent views on victimisation, its consequences and the solutions developed by victim-assistance initiatives and by the criminal-justice system have come a long way. Presented in a European context, they involve complex developments in the criminological sciences and in social and criminal policy over the last three decades.

More than other criminological sciences, victimology has taken an outspoken, applied approach which includes a great diversity of practices and actions orientated towards the protection, support, assistance and strengthening of the legal position of the victims of crime. These practices have been realised within different policy frameworks and legitimise several groups of professionals and citizens to have their say in this field. Victimology and restorative justice are becoming an important field of application in the criminological sciences, a battlefield where many interest groups clash.

Victimology and the victim movement

A short historical and anthropological comment

Over the last two decades victimisation has become a topic of prime criminological interest and is given a top priority on policy agendas; in preceding years the absence of a victim perspective has been the general rule. Of the three protagonists in the committing of a crime, the offender, the victim and the community, criminal justice has always focused on the relationship between the offender and society.[11] Research mainly focuses on the problems of legal protection of the suspect or on the problems of the effectiveness of the system. For a long time the interests of victims of crime have been *"une quantité négligeable"*.[12] Punishment and the social reintegration of the offender polarise the powers of criminal justice.[13] From the moment of reporting the offence the victim experiences "a victimisation by administrative run-around."[14] "Once a case enters the criminal court system, the victim-witness becomes susceptible to a myriad of problems and needs."[15]

However, the history of the administration of criminal justice shows that in non-state societies the victim had a position equal to that of the offender. To avoid revenge and even war, private arrangements to compensate for damage, taking into account the *talio* principle (proportionality) became the usual practice in which mediation was not the exception. "Once the state monopolised the right to criminal prosecution and converted the *wergeld* or the compensation that used to be paid to the victim, into a fine destined to the King's coffers, the victim became the 'forgotten figure', a legal nonentity".[16] "The reduction of the victim to an inconsequential figure coincided with the emergence of the public prosecutor".[17] "The real decline started with the emergence of a criminal law which viewed the criminal act not as an offence against the victim but as an offence against the Sovereign and later the state".[18]

From that moment onward, punishment became the response to crime. With the administration of punishment the offender pays back his or her guilt and debt to the victim and to society. Punishment confirms the authority of the state while obligations towards the victim must be met through civil procedures. The development of the penal approach can be seen as a privileged track for the development of the state.[19] However, historical research shows that until the late eighteenth century, mediation and compensation between offenders and victims played an important role in local justice practices, very often to the displeasure of the king.[20] Within continental European criminal justice the role of the victim has been reduced to the *partie civile* (France, Belgium) or *Nebenklage* (Germany), whereas in the common law countries the role of the victim has remained limited to that of the informant and/or witness.

Different authors of cultural-anthropological studies have stressed the importance of settling conflicts by means of consultation and communication between individuals, groups or families involved in conflict, under the guidance and with the support of their 'elders' or the leaders of the group, as in the case of aboriginal communities.[21] In New Zealand, Australia and Canada recent policies enhancing these traditions now inspire and stimulate new practices of restorative justice outside or inside the criminal-justice procedures (such as family group conferences, healing circles and sentencing circles).

From criminography to victimography

Since the 1960s there has been a clear shift within the criminological sciences from a clinical-psychological to a sociological-interactionist perspective. An important critical reflection concerned the study of the quantity of crime in society.[22] The classical sources of crime statistics have been questioned in a fundamental way by the social-reaction approach of crime (labelling theory), which concentrated on the understanding and analysis of the selectivity of action of the police and the criminal-justice system in dealing with crime. The statistical model, as developed during the nineteenth century by Quetelet and Guerry, portrays the functioning and intervention capacity of "criminal-justice institutions", capacities which have to be distinguished from the reality of the types and quantity of crime.

In order to measure the crime phenomenon researchers embarked on the so-called "dark number of crime", using self-report studies in which a citizen is approached as a suspected offender who is asked to report about possibly committed crimes during the last 6 or 12 months. Discussing the results of these studies, and especially the methodological problems when trying to obtain adequate information from potential offenders, resulted in a further step in the direction of asking citizens to report as potential victims of crime. After a short time a practice of 'victim surveys' developed (see also Chapter 1 on trends in criminality).

This evolution coincided with the growing political interest in the problems of victims of crime, especially in the United States. Since the 1984 presidential election campaign of Barry Goldwater who used street crime and victim problems as one of his campaign topics,[23] the issue has constantly been on the political agenda as the result of the actions of pressure and interest groups. President Johnson's Law Enforcement and the Administration of Justice Commission led to a first National Crime Survey (1966). This same commission was the start of the Law Enforcement Assistance Administration, which generated projects such as rape crisis centres and victim assistance programmes.[24]

These political choices and policy strategies resulted in the frequent use of victim surveys to constantly measure the real dimensions and consequences of crime. Since the 1970s victim surveys, carried out by phone interview, have been organised on a regular basis in the United States, Canada and Europe (in the United Kingdom and Netherlands).

Nevertheless in spite of the fact that victim surveys concentrate primarily on surveying traditional property crime, violent and other street crime and have little or no relevance for measuring sexual aggression and especially intra-family violence,[25] victim surveys have generally been accepted as "the least worst measure of crime". Victim surveys were filled with questions concerning the different experiences of victims, the consequences of this victimisation, the reactions of the police, the prosecutor and the judge, the attitude of potential victims towards crime, insecurity in the neighbourhood and feelings of fear. Victim surveys have become fully-fledged instruments of victimological research and permit extended victimographical analysis, which is much richer than a pure measurement of crime.

However, crime analysis remains an important function of the victim survey. Victim surveys show that, compared to official statistics, crime trends are increasing less rapidly, women commit more crimes and young people commit more – but less serious – crimes, while adults commit more – and more serious – crimes.[26] The British Crime Surveys show that property crimes are reported to the police much less than violent crimes (respectively in 20% and 47% of the cases). Violent crimes are reported even more by women (by 52% of female victims of violent crime.) Men are more at risk of victimisation than women; juveniles and young persons are more at risk than older persons; coloured people are more likely to be victims than other racial groups (especially for violence). Victimisation risks run higher in cities than in the countryside. Household offences (vandalism, burglary and theft) increase faster than personal offences (sexual crime, assaults and other violence). Not reporting crime is in more than half of cases explained by the lack of seriousness of the crime and its consequences; the lack of trust in the police is a second important reason.

Special attention should be given to the International Crime Victims Surveys introduced and co-ordinated by the Dutch Ministry of Justice. Organised in 1989, 1992 and 1996, they have the exceptional advantage that a large number of countries from different continents have participated.

Feminism and victimology

Feminism as a political emancipative movement had a decisive influence on the shift in the content of victimology in the 1970s. Amir, a disciple of Wolfgang, provoked strong negative reactions from feminists with his study on rape (1967). They defined such victimology as "the art of blaming the victim".[27] The shift in victimological thinking can be defined as an explicit orientation of victimology towards actions and interventions in favour of women-victims of sexual aggression, intra-family violence and rape. At the same time there was growing attention for the many forms of neglect, abuse and maltreatment of children. The action-orientated approach to the victim hardly distinguished the ideological moment from the academic one. Victimology was the same as victimagogy.[28] Theorists and empirical researchers have been directly confronted with the social facts that stimulated research concerning the moral, material, physical and psycho-social consequences of victimisation.[29] The thematic development of the cultural legitimisation of the victimisation of women unmasked the socio-cultural justifications of physical violence against women as a part of the socialisation of men, and the prejudices among police and justice personnel as its correlative.[30]

Against such prejudices women's action groups in many European countries have taken the initiative to care about, support and host the victims of rape, abuse and other acts of violence and to accompany them in their contacts with the police and judicial agencies. Women medical doctors, solicitors, nurses and social workers have often spontaneously and voluntarily engaged in actions of solidarity with these groups of victims. Action groups formulated concrete points of view and refused financial support from the authorities in order to maintain their independence. This ideological and social awakening was much more important for the emancipation of women than was the integration of their action as a regular government-supported centre for victim assistance. In the United Kingdom the women's movement preceded by a decade the now-developed network of general victim assistance with rape crisis centres and shelters for abused women. Woman Against Rape, the British collective of prostitutes and Women Against Violence Against Women were initiatives in the war against the sexual and violent oppression of women. The aim was not penal reform but a breakthrough in patriarchal oppression by men.[31]

A decade later (in the early 1980s) government-financed centres for (general) victim assistance mushroomed in the United Kingdom as well as on the continent (The Netherlands, France, Germany and Belgium). They took care of victims of property as well as of violent crimes. In contrast to their feminist precursors, the centres for general victim support not only looked for financial support from government but defined their tasks in close collaboration with policy makers, the police and the judiciary.

In Europe this approach was logical within the framework of the tradition of social welfare. Once a specific need (such as victim assistance) received broad social and political acceptance, there followed a period of institutional development (centres for victim assistance) including the construction of an umbrella structure to co-ordinate local organisations and to represent the interests of the group at governmental level. In Canada and the United States, in opposition to the European approach, the feminist movement has been the starting point and the platform for the fight for the legal position of the victim.[32] The introduction of victim impact statements and victim statements of opinion in court has been the movement's main success symbol.

Victims and the role of international organisations

Victims and the Council of Europe

In Europe as well as in North America the interests and needs of crime victims have been addressed from the early 1970s by local initiatives determined by feminist inspiration and conviction. From the 1980s victim assistance made its way within national umbrella organisations, which acted as partners of government. In Europe different national organisations held international meetings as early as 1986, founding a European umbrella organisation, The European Forum for Victim Services.

The Council of Europe played an early role in supporting the development of victim compensation schemes, of victim assistance and of reorientating police and the judiciary towards the problems of victims of crime. This dialectical process recognised the eminent and pro-active role of the Council of Europe. Taking into account Resolution R (77) 27 of the Committee of Ministers of the Council of Europe on the compensation of victims of crime, the member states were invited to sign the European Convention on the Compensation of Victims of Violent Crime of 24 November 1983. While in some member states, laws on victim compensation already existed (for example in Great Britain, the Netherlands and France) and in other countries such as Belgium the debate continued, the convention functioned as a minimum standard for victim compensation. Countries lacking such a regulation have been strongly stimulated to introduce their own compensation scheme. Belgium accepted a state compensation law for victims of intentional violent acts on 1 August 1985.

Another important initiative of the Council of Europe is the foundation of a group of experts that reported extensively on its investigations and observations concerning the situation of victims of crime in Europe. This state-of-the-art research on the consequences of victimisation has given a strong impulse to communication among scientists and policy makers. The publication offered a substantial basis of knowledge for future scientific research and for the development of a victim policy in Europe. In 1985 the Committee of Ministers of the Council of Europe adopted Recommendation No. R (85) 11 concerning the position of the victim in the framework of criminal law and procedure and in 1987 this same Committee adopted Recommendation No. R (87) 21 concerning assistance to victims and the prevention of victimisation.

The role of the United Nations

The idea of a victims' policy as developed by the Council of Europe since 1977, and translated into a convention and two recommendations, has also inspired the United Nations. Thanks to the preparatory work of the World Society of Victimology in Milan in August 1985, the concerns of crime victims were introduced during the Seventh United Nations Congress on the Prevention of Crime and the Treatment of Offenders. The General Assembly of the United Nations adopted the recommendation of the Congress on 29 November 1985 (General Assembly Resolution 40/34). The recommendation was a plea for better access to the criminal-justice system for victims, as were the convention and recommendations of the Council of Europe. There was also a call for more just treatment, for the use of restitution, compensation and the development of psycho-social assistance. More preventive measures were recommended against crime and the abuse of power. In addition to the European recommendations, the United Nations declaration provides a broader perspective for the protection of victims of ideological, political and cultural abuse of power.

In the United Nations Standard Minimum Rules for Non-custodial Measures (the Tokyo Rules, 1990), there is also an explicit recommendation to care for the victims of crime when alternative (non-custodial) sanctions are imposed. This same concern for victims is included in the Council of Europe Recommendation No. R (92) 16 on community sanctions and measures.

The impact of victimisation and victim assistance

The fear of crime

Fear of crime does not coincide completely with the problems of the consequences of victimisation. Research has clearly demonstrated this as an entirely new area of criminological inquiry[33] so that "Fear of crime is now recognised as a distinct social problem extending well beyond those who have actually been victimised to affect the lives of all those who perceive themselves to be at risk" (Zedner, 1976). Measuring crime by crime surveys, the construction of special prevention projects and neighbourhood watch, all seem to sharpen the sensibility to problems, especially among certain groups of the population, taking into account their age, gender, neighbourhood and ethnic background. In this context Zedner (1997) stresses the so-called "'irrational fear' of women". She refers to Stanko (1988) who says that women are confronted with "hidden violence" from people they know, which is a more acceptable explanation of their fear. This is not always demonstrated in victim surveys.

Consequences of victimisation

The consequences of victimisation are not easy to estimate on the basis of the seriousness of the crime. Victim surveys have widely demonstrated that the majority of people interviewed experience few or no consequences following a victimisation, since the event was not very serious. However qualitative studies demonstrate that in a limited number of cases the consequences may be very serious in the long run as well, and difficult to survive and to cope with.[34]

The characteristics of the victims, their behaviour and coping capacities, their possible experiences with crime, even in the past and the possible influence of other emotional problems are, combined with the social context in which they live, the most important factors which determine the impact of the victimisation. However, the risks of far-reaching consequences are in the first place dependent on types of crimes such as murder, homicide, violence, abuse and rape. These crimes almost always provoke a cumulation of effects ranging from loss of life or serious physical injury to loss of psychological integrity and financial or other material consequences. Often these effects provoke an irreversible loss of quality of life for victims and their milieu.

The results of research[35] show that the impact of burglary is comparable with the effects of crimes of violence (feelings of intrusion and emotional upset) and of rape.[36] The consequences of rape and other sexual crimes have been detected, analysed and described in the context of initiatives by feminist groups in favour of victims. The attitude of distance of these action groups in relation to government and governmental policy has, however, curtailed the development of scientific research in this area.[37] A mainly theoretical study which describes, analyses and discusses in great detail and depth the results of many different publications on victimisation is the standard work published by Ezzat Fattah, *Understanding Criminal Victimisation*[38] in which victimisation has been approached as a dynamic inter-relational phenomenon and human experience.

The organisation of victim assistance

Victim assistance springs from the victim movement of the 1970s. The shift from an offender-orientated (etiological) victimology to a victim-orientated one is largely due to feminism. Women's critical attitude, their orientation towards action, their distrust of the police, the prosecutorial service, the courts and crime policy have resulted in small-scale initiatives such as shelters for (sexually) abused women and children, rape crisis centres and action groups against the abuse of women.

The creation of a general victim assistance structure was started in the early 1980s in most European countries by local grass-roots organisations, where easily accessible assistance and support were offered to victims of all types of crime. Initiatives were soon brought together into national organisations such as NAVSS in Great Britain, INAVEM in France, *Der Weisse Ring* in Germany and the LOS in The Netherlands. Their private character did not obstruct their wish to collaborate with the government and to develop a policy together with social and criminal-justice administrations. After a short time financial and legal support was offered by governments and has grown steadily since the topic of victimisation has received broad social and political attention. Especially during the last decade one can hardly overestimate the role of the media in generalising the interest of the public in problems of victimisation. Television stations particularly have broadcast an endless series of programmes, showing the wider public the many problematic and complex consequences of victimisation by different types of crime.

The authorities were confronted more than ever with the problems of victimisation and were obliged to make clear how they wanted to deal with victims' needs. Social and judicial policy created the need to develop and support new types of organisations for which it was difficult to estimate the necessary investments and budgets. Existing assistance services were not familiar with the special needs of different types of victims, having had limited experience with the majority of crime victims. Since the late 1980s such organised victim assistance has been able to offer a diversified service. This resulted in the creation of 'A European Forum for Victim Services', which functions as a platform for international collaboration in Europe, reaching a number of eastern European countries (Poland, the Czech Republic, Hungary). During yearly meetings information is exchanged and typical models of victim assistance are developed. Recent years have seen the development of a common charter for victim rights.

Victims and the criminal-justice system

The early victim movement in Canada and the United States concentrated on the problems of the legal rights of victims and their position in the administration of criminal justice, and a similar movement could be seen in Europe in the 1990s. However, over the years initiatives were taken which already foreshadowed this interest.

State compensation

Programmes of state compensation were first introduced in Great Britain (1964) and elsewhere (such as the Netherlands and France) in the late 1970s. Today most European countries follow these examples. These practices, introduced by law, aim at financial compensation for victims of (intentional) violent crimes in cases where the offender remains unknown or insolvent. Although remarkable differences exist between the many national systems, especially when defining the group of victims who are eligible to receive compensation and the amount, there are nevertheless clear points of resemblance. Not one of these programmes gives the victim a formal right to financial compensation. State compensation for victims of crime is based on the principle of solidarity. Financial compensation is a discretional decision of a commission which judges each case on the basis of fairness. These principles have also been consolidated when certain countries have changed the law (some several times) in the direction of more flexibility towards compensation (such as by providing an advance loan).

State compensation is a complex, long-lasting procedure leading to success in a rather limited number of cases. The many administrative obligations, the uncertainty about the decision, the long waiting period and the lack of information about the determination of the amount of compensation are frustrating for victims. Added to the frustration which many victims experience in their contacts with the police and the judiciary (court system), the state compensation procedure is often a continuation of 'secondary victimisation'.

The role of the police and the criminal-justice system

Depending on the type of crime, victims report their victimisation (20% for sexual aggression, 88% for burglary and 91.4% for a stolen car).[39] It is thus evident that contacts with the police are of paramount importance. As they are the gate-keepers of the system, access to justice for victims starts with contacting the police. These contacts have therefore been the focus of attention in the development of victim policy since the 1980s. The Council of Europe Recommendation No. R (85) 11, concerning the victim within the framework of criminal law and procedure, explicitly discusses what should be done in member states by the police, the prosecutor when questioning the victim and during court proceedings. The main message is the right to information. At all levels the access to information about the way the case is handled is the basic expectation of every victim. During the last decade considerable progress has been made in the preparation, training and support of the police; more recently prosecutorial services have been concerned about the way victims are received, treated, informed and when necessary referred to more specialised services.

Recommendation No. R (87) 21 concerning assistance to victims and prevention of victimisation stresses the need to co-ordinate the relations between victim assistance and the agencies of the criminal-justice system. More recently Recommendation No. R (98) 13 on intimidation of witnesses and the right of the defence has put the accent on the development of appropriate legislative and practical measures to protect witnesses, often the victims of crime, to enable them to testify freely. Special attention is given to problems experienced in relation to organised crime and in cases of crime within the family.

Training of the police in this area has seen particular progress. It is now widely accepted that all police officers must receive basic training in working with victims of crime. Care for victims thus becomes everyone's concern in the system, not just the exclusive duty of specialists.

Victims and restorative justice

A response to victims' needs

Research on victimisation and victim assistance has revealed specific needs of victims in their relation to the offender.[40] For victims of violence, at least as important as obtaining financial compensation is the need to find answers to questions concerning the offence and the offender. Victims in general express the need for understanding about what happened and in many cases they wish to make clear to the offender the consequences of the crime. These elements are often important issues in coping with the event and its aftermath. When questioned about the desirability and the possible consequences of a meeting with the offender, a significant group of victims confirm that they would welcome the opportunity. Several studies show figures of between 30% and 50% of all victims interviewed: this percentage is even higher when the possibility of indirect (that is, not face-to-face) mediation is offered.[41]

Initiatives regarding mediation between victim and offender have been solicited by the above-mentioned Council of Europe Recommendations No. R (85) 11 and No. R (87) 21. The interest in mediation was in line with the content of the United Nations Declaration of Basic Principles of Justice for Victims of Crime and Abuse of Power (1985). Recommendation No. R (99) 19 by the Council of Europe, concerning mediation in penal matters, recognises, *inter alia,* "the legitimate interest of victims to have a stronger voice in dealing with the consequences of their victimisation, to communicate with the offender and to obtain apology and reparation". One of the benefits of mediation can also be that the victim "may get a more realistic understanding of the offender and his or her behaviour".

Victim-offender mediation is not necessarily limited to a 'diversion practice'. Whereas in victim-assistance programmes the victim remains in an external position *vis-à-vis* the justice system, mediation allows him or her to integrate his/her needs and interests into the criminal-justice process. "Mediation therefore shows that satisfying the interests of the victim, the offender and society at large is not incompatible. (...) The conciliatory nature of mediation can assist the criminal-justice system in fulfilling one of its fundamental objectives, namely contributing to a peaceful and safe society, by restoring balance and social peace after a crime has been committed."[42] Victim-offender mediation should be a service available at all stages of the criminal-justice process. Besides a definition of victim-offender mediation and the mention of some general principles, the recommendation deals with the necessity of a legal basis for mediation, the relation to criminal justice and the operation of mediation services. Much attention is given to the qualifications, selection and training of mediators and the development of standards of practice.

Victim-offender mediation programmes

The recognition of specific victim issues, together with the search for a more meaningful and effective way of working with offenders, has led to the creation of victim-offender mediation or reconciliation programmes in many countries. After the first initiatives in Canada and subsequently in the United States in the 1970s, at the beginning of the 1980s the movement spread to Europe, first in Britain and in several Nordic countries, which simultaneously developed initiatives more or less independently.

Whereas in Norway and Finland mediation has developed apart from probation and victim assistance programmes, in Austria, Germany and the United Kingdom the probation services have taken the lead in organising victim-offender mediation. Austria has played a pioneer role in developing a mediation model for juveniles and has created a well-organised network of services for *Aussergerichtlicher Tatausgleich.* The largest number of mediation services, however, is found in Germany: some 300 services for *Täter-Opfer Ausgleich,* of which here also the large majority (260) are directed at young delinquents.

The fact that in some countries offender-orientated services such as probation have been the driving force behind the early developments has initially placed the victim movement in a somewhat defensive position. Victim support in England and in the United States initially exhibited much resistance to mediation. The fear was that the victim could be "used" in the interests and the treatment of the offender. As mediation methods became more tailored to the needs of the victim, and research results about the positive effects for the victim were made known, this resistance decreased. In France, victim support has played an important stimulating role from the beginning in founding mediation services. In addition, in Belgium a mediation model has been developed for more serious crimes, with the needs of the victim as a point of departure.

The large majority of victim-offender mediation cases in European countries concern relatively minor property offences or less serious violence committed by juveniles who are often first offenders. Violent or more serious crimes by adults or youngsters, however, are not excluded, and some programmes focus especially on such cases.[43] However the quantitative impact of victim-offender mediation programmes in the different European countries remains rather limited.[44]

In a number of European countries victim-offender mediation has received a legal basis, as a part of the Juvenile Justice Act (Austria, Germany, Finland, Poland), the Code of Criminal Procedure (France, Belgium, Finland, Poland), the Criminal Code (Germany, Finland, Poland), or as an autonomous "mediation law" (Norway).

Concerning the process and the effects of victim-offender mediation, a considerable amount of evaluative research data, both of a quantitative and a qualitative nature, has become available.[45] The most important and promising findings concern the degree of satisfaction of the parties, their willingness to participate, the number of agreements reached and the content of the agreements, the compliance rates, the effect on re-offending, the work- and time-consuming process of mediation and its cost-effectiveness.

Restorative justice

The new development of bringing together the victim and the offender has often been identified with 'restorative justice'. But the concept of restorative justice is a broad one[46]: (Anglo-Saxon in origin, the concept is not restricted to a concrete method, a programme or a technique, but goes rather in the direction of a new paradigm or global vision, "changing lenses",[47] the development of another view, not only of the social or criminal-justice reaction that must follow a crime, but also and primarily of the nature of the crime itself. A crime is not seen so much in terms of violating abstract rules of law but rather as a violation of persons and relations. Based upon this vision, the fundamental reaction is aimed at the restoration of damage: damage to the victims, their environment and possibly to society at large, as well as the damage that the offender has provoked in his own social environment. For many, 'restorative justice' is a 'third way' resolutely to be chosen in place of (neo-)retributive criminal law and following the collapse of the rehabilitation model.[48]

A generally accepted definition of restorative justice is given by Tony Marshall in an overview of restorative justice published by the UK Home Office: "Restorative justice is a process whereby parties with a stake in a specific offence resolve collectively how to deal with the aftermath of the offence and its implications for the future". The British Restorative Justice Consortium (1998) sees restorative justice as seeking "to balance the concerns of the victim and the community with the need to reintegrate the offender into society. It seeks to assist the recovery of the victim and enable all parties with a stake in the justice process to participate fruitfully in it".

From these definitions it is clear that 'restorative justice' is not a movement alongside or against the current criminal-justice system. More and more voices are heard calling for maximal integration of this approach within the existing criminal-justice system in order to modify the foundations of the system itself. A second clarification concerns the growing tendency to de-individualise restorative justice. Where in the beginning restorative justice was strongly associated with victim-offender mediation, we now see models that involve not only the two immediate parties to the conflict but also a number of persons or bodies from their surroundings. Nevertheless, within Europe, victim-offender mediation is by far the most important expression of restorative justice. Group-orientated models of restorative justice, initially developed in New Zealand and Australia, are operating only in an experimental way in England.

Restorative justice in Europe at present has at least three important challenges. The first is the need to bring this line of thinking into the dominant conceptions and methods within the administration of criminal justice. A second challenge in the realisation of restorative justice lies in expanding victim-offender mediation to include more categories of (also serious) offences and offenders, and applying a victim-aware approach in the successive stages of the administration of criminal justice, including corrections and after-care. A third task concerns the further establishment of legal frameworks and safeguards and a clarification of the relation of restorative justice programmes to the criminal-justice systems of the different countries.[49]

Chapter 3: Crime prevention in Europe

Hannu Takala, National Council for Crime Prevention, Finland

Old, still new

People have always protected themselves against crime. Owners have tried to see to it that their property is not vulnerable to crimes. The idea of 'defensible space', nowadays central in the strategy called crime prevention through environmental design, can already be found in pre-Industrial Age dwellings. The oldest arguments for punishment are for prevention. Thus, revolutionary social philosophers of the last century wanted to reform living conditions of the urban poor because poverty was seen as the main cause of criminality.

The more recent history of crime prevention began in the 1960s and 1970s. Only then did we have systematic knowledge on the effects of various measures on crime, as well as specific research and planning units for developing methods of crime prevention. The following three decades saw a widening and deepening of the consciousness that combating crime problems effectively requires measures other than punishment. The prevention of crime requires a change in the conditions that facilitate crime. Only recently has crime prevention been developed as a systematic discipline.

Crime prevention can be broadly described as all measures intended to prevent criminal events or an individual's development as a 'criminal' or involvement in a continuation of crimes. This definition also covers the traditional punitive approach where punishment, criminal law and its enforcement are used as a preventive tool.[50]

Not only growth of crime

Increase in crime is the usual reason for an increased interest in crime prevention. However, those countries with the sharpest increase in crime have not necessarily been the first ones to emphasise preventive measures.

A crime prevention agency is established or not when recorded crime has gone up, and establishment of such an agency can be justified on the same grounds several years earlier or later.

A change in the understanding of criminality

In the 1950s and 1960s, important studies on the effects of punishment on crime concluded that severe penalties were shown not to prevent crime[51] or reconvictions.[52] Some interpretations of the results went so far as to say that if crime prevention was the objective, it was preferable to refrain from punishment altogether. At the time, theories of stigmatisation and imprisonment had a strong influence on criminological thinking. Research undermined faith in prison treatment.[53]

This period also gave birth to the criminological idea that the growth of crime, as with geographical or other variations in crime, is generally caused by variations in situational preconditions, or opportunities for crime. Economic and social development, urbanisation, increased traffic and movement in all respects, the growth of commodities on the market and in households and changing ways of life had greatly increased crime opportunities. The importance of opportunity as a major explanation for variations in crime was a new element in criminology.

Therefore it is not surprising that the first countries where crime prevention began to develop were those where opportunities for crime had increased fastest after the second world war.

General policy

At the time when crime prevention agencies were established, new, more goal-orientated and comprehensive planning methods were adopted in several sectors of social policy. Simultaneously, indicators were identified that would help to analyse the problems, alternative measures for tackling them were evaluated and the choice between alternatives was made according to anticipated effects. Especially in the Nordic welfare societies, a strong planning optimism ruled: in the areas of health policy, education, and road traffic safety, as well as in criminal policy, similar planning methods were adopted, regardless of the nature of the specific problems. Early crime prevention vocabulary borrowed terminology from other planning sectors: primary, secondary and tertiary crime prevention, terms usually used as a major classification of crime prevention measures, originated in public health planning.

UK pioneering

The British Standing Committee on Crime Prevention set up in the Home Office in 1966 was the first co-ordinating state agency for crime prevention. The committee brought together representatives of commerce and industry with police and the Home Office to form crime prevention initiatives on a national level. At first its tasks were mainly restricted to developing better protection and to improving security procedures. Britain also started to train police staff specialising in crime prevention and in 1968 the Standing Committee initiated local crime prevention panels to support the police.

Other crime prevention councils were set up in Denmark (1971) and in Sweden (1974). Britain was not a model for the Nordic agencies and Swedish documents seem to be unfamiliar with the fact that a crime prevention agency already existed in Denmark. Sweden quickly marketed the idea of a crime prevention council on the international forum. In the United States, the National Crime Prevention Council was established in 1977.

The Council of Europe

In 1983 the Committee on Crime Problems of the Council of Europe explored the organisation of crime prevention in the member states. The organisational status of crime prevention in Europe in the mid-1980s can be described on the basis of material collected by this committee:

- England and Wales: the Home Office Standing Committee on Crime Prevention (1966), and the Home Office Crime Prevention Unit (1983);
- Denmark: the Council for Crime Prevention (1971);
- Sweden: the National Council for Crime Prevention (1974);
- Scotland: Scotland's Crime Prevention Committee (1975);
- France: the National Council on the Prevention of Violence (1978) followed by the National Council on the Prevention of Crime (1983);
- Netherlands: The National Crime Prevention Co-ordinator and his bureau (1979), and the interdepartmental committee on crime prevention (1983);
- Northern Ireland: The Royal Ulster Constabulary Crime Prevention Branch;
- Norway: the Council for Crime Prevention (1980);
- Belgium: the National Council of Prevention (1984).

In France a network of regional and local crime prevention councils was also developed, and in the Netherlands, Denmark and England, regional and/or local police units specialised in crime prevention. Crime prevention was still considered to be a police task in many European countries. The planning of crime prevention projects or campaigns and advice on protection matters were considered to be responsibilities of the police.

In 1987 the Council of Europe adopted Recommendation No. (87) 19 in which governments of member states are invited to "establish, encourage and support crime prevention agencies at national and/or regional level". The main elements of an organised policy of prevention and the tasks of prevention agencies were to be as follows:

- collecting information on crime and prevention experiments and their results;
- planning, implementing and evaluating prevention programmes;
- co-ordinating preventive activities;
- co-operating with decision makers in developing a rational and effective crime policy; and
- implementing training programmes in the prevention field.

In Finland, the National Council for Crime Prevention was set up in 1989 with explicit reference made to this recommendation. In the year 2000 we can assume that increased international co-operation, rather than the recommendation directly, has influenced the establishment of new crime prevention agencies. Crime prevention councils, planning secretariats and related agencies have become a natural part of state administration. In the Baltic countries the establishment of crime prevention councils is based on the need to construct a modern judicial and administrative machinery. A new crime prevention council was set up in Hungary in 1995 and the National Crime Prevention Council was established in Canada in 1994.

European crime prevention

Crime prevention in European countries is organised in various ways.[54] For example, the secretariat of the Danish crime prevention council is a part of the police administration. Yet, the activities of the council emphasise questions of city planning, grass-roots democracy and citizen participation, and even cultural elements; a particular 'police perspective' on crime prevention is difficult to discern.

There is no common organisational base for European crime prevention. The Council of Europe, with its recommendations and the European Committee on Crime Problems, is the only forum for European crime prevention. The Council has tried to promote crime prevention in its member states. However, the Council has not, perhaps with the exception of co-operation in criminological research, become a forum for co-operation in European crime prevention. Recently the Council of Europe has set up an expert committee to study early interventions, a developmental prevention strategy which is believed to be one of the most cost-effective ways of preventing juvenile criminality.

In the 1990s there were efforts to organise crime prevention in the European Union. European police co-operation already had a long history, a natural consequence of the Union's basic principles. The intention to organise crime prevention in a framework beyond that of police co-operation was first expressed in the 1996 Seminar on Crime Prevention in the European Union. Crime prevention was presented as a complement to police co-operation. The 1997 EU conference on Crime Prevention: Towards a European Level discussed surveillance, youth criminality and violence, city planning and residential safety, and administrative measures against crime. The third important meeting, the 1998 Partnership seminar organised by the British Home Office, witnessed a change: England, the Netherlands and Sweden opted to promote crime prevention within the European Union under the umbrella of police co-operation. The focus among subtopics of crime prevention had also changed. Earlier high priority topics such as urban crime, social exclusion, and city planning were displaced by the police perspective.

Conclusions of the European Council in Tampere 1999 may mark a new phase in crime prevention organised by the European Union. Conclusions 41 and 42 stress the importance of developing crime prevention in and between the member states, the need to define common priorities and to develop an interchange of best practices. Depending on which kind of organisational solution results from the Tampere conclusions, the European Union has the opportunity to take a leading role in European crime prevention.

The third co-operation organisation for European crime prevention is the independent SecuCities network of European cities. In 1987, France organised this network of direct inter-municipal co-operation, supported both economically and ideologically by the European Union and the Council of Europe. At present, some 150 cities participate in the network. Its prevention ideology follows the French model described below. The main topics of concern are urban social problems, youth marginalisation and drug problems. For cities in those countries where no special national agency has been set up, this forum is important in offering the possibility of participating in crime prevention co-operation.

Social Europe, repressive America

It is misleading to speak about European crime prevention as different from crime prevention in other parts of the world. The central ideas and methods of crime prevention do not belong to one continent. Also, there are variations among European countries in their crime prevention ideology, organisation and major fields of activities.

Michael Tonry and David P. Farrington dare, however, to state in their book *Building a Safer Society: Strategic approaches to crime prevention* that "Crime prevention strategies, program development, and research have received more sustained attention in Western Europe than in North America, and within North America have received greater emphasis in Canada than in the United States or Mexico. Governmentally funded crime prevention initiatives have been implemented far more extensively in England than in the United States, possibly because of the greater American emphasis in criminal-justice policy on individual responsibility and punishment."[55]

Francis Bailleau and Georges Garioud have characterised American crime prevention as "offensive" compared to the European defensive approach. According to them, this applies also to Canada in comparison with Europe, and even to England if compared with, for example, France.[56]

Countries with large differences in incomes and standards of living and with strong class conflicts seem to make more use of the penal law system and repression. In crime prevention, countries with strong class conflicts tend to favour methods aimed at excluding the threatening problem or the threatening group of people. According to David Garland,[57] a repressive approach dominates during weak governments. Strong governments do not need to strengthen their position by symbolic 'law-and-order' measures.

A European typology[58]

In this analysis, those countries where crime prevention is primarily understood as a concern of penal law, police and courts, will not be described, notwithstanding that this approach is very prominent in some European countries. It is also understandable in former socialist countries, where organising police forces, courts and prisons, and creating a whole new penal law system have been a demanding task of first priority. For those countries, punitive reforms are naturally loaded with high expectations.

'The British model'

During its entire history, British crime prevention has been based on criminological research. British crime prevention is project-based and evaluated. In crime prevention publications of the Home Office as well as in more academic literature, crime prevention is described as a five-step process starting from the collection of data on crime and progressing through crime analyses and the identification of preventive measures to implementation and finally to evaluation.[59] This model has produced a considerable number of successful crime prevention projects whose effects are evaluated by research. Some (like the Kirkholt project) are classics in crime prevention literature. In an American report,[60] a large part of non-American references to so-called evidence-based crime prevention originated in the United Kingdom. Even projects like the Safer Cities Programme – where evaluation problems are considerable because the project itself was not designed for evaluation – are studied. Nearly 300 single projects of the Safer Cities Programme resulted in 56 000 prevented burglaries according to the evaluation.[61]

In spite of the useful knowledge this model has produced, projects are short-term programmes, usually with a special temporary organisation. They are usually planned to produce short-term, evaluable effects. To see crime prevention in this manner is not to appreciate the continuing routine work in crime prevention carried out by different authorities and organisations. The outcome is difficult to evaluate in simple evaluation studies. This applies to a great deal of project thinking introduced in public administration.

Secondly, the British model has emphasised the situational approach, which has its roots in British criminology. The Crime Prevention Unit in the Home Office started with the mandate to develop "short-term measures which will have a direct impact on crime".[62]

A third characteristic of the British model, particularly when compared to the French one, is that crime prevention is strongly police-powered. Crime prevention is organised in the Home Office as a part of the planning of police activities in general. The Crime Prevention Centre in the Home Office teaches police staff crime prevention. The checking of building security, one application of crime prevention through environmental design, is done by police; in Denmark, where norms and recommendations for safe building and area planning have long existed, safe building norms and recommendations are addressed to architects and city planners and the checklist for residential safety is even addressed to residents, despite the secretariat of the Crime Prevention Council being administratively part of the police.

"Partnership in crime prevention" is understood in England as partnership with the police.[63] The UK is one of those member states in the European Union that are pushing crime prevention co-operation strongly under the umbrella of police co-operation.

'The French model'

In France, crime prevention was organised in 1983 on three levels: national, regional and municipal. French crime prevention is distanced from the police. On all levels, police are used only in an expert role. Local crime prevention is defined primarily as urban policy, where mayors have a leading role and are usually presidents of their local crime prevention councils. French crime prevention is intended to be a part of urban development policy.

Since 1989, the secretariat for crime prevention on the national level has been the Prevention Pole within the Ministry of Cities in the French central government. In proportion to the population, public expenditures on crime prevention in France are high, four times those in the UK.[64] However, the French system includes in its crime prevention costs state subsidies for city renewal, which in other systems are not defined as belonging to crime prevention expenditures.

It is difficult to find a single evaluation study on French crime prevention. Projects such as Decibel or the *Été-jeunes* Programme, which are described in international sources, are reported as activities without any evaluated results. When a French project is reported as "successful", references add that there is no research-based evidence. The International Centre for the Prevention of Crime in Canada reported in its publication *Crime Prevention Digest* (1997), 'Successes, Benefits and Directions from Seven Countries', that the only impact of French crime prevention was a decrease in registered crimes in some cities by 11% one year after local crime prevention councils were established.

The lack of evaluation studies follows the French scientific tradition, which, in contrast with the British one, does not favour empirical evaluations. Crime prevention in France follows a strategy where simple evaluations are difficult if not impossible. The main strategy is social prevention. Dutch experts have also concluded that, in the long term, the social prevention approach is the most effective strategy in spite of its weak short-term effects.[65]

The social prevention approach in France continues the earlier tradition of the *défence social* movement in criminal policy. There also seems to be a general difference between British and French culture in structuring social concerns. In Gallup polls regarding the main concerns of the population, 60% of the population in the UK see crime as the most important social problem, and 40% unemployment. In France, the situation is the opposite. According to victim surveys, however, crime is very similar in both countries, and unemployment is only slightly higher in France. Thus the French culture, more than the British, structures societal problems as 'social' problems.

Generally speaking, over the last ten years registered crime has remained almost constant in France. During this time, a large number of measures have been targeted at problems which play a central role in increasing crime trends in many other countries: crime problems caused by poor urban areas and marginalised immigrants, and crimes committed by narcotics addicts. In tackling the last problem, France has developed a system that includes a variety of substitute methods.

Especially characteristic of the French model are the systems of *contrat d'action de prévention,* introduced in 1985, and the *contrat de ville,* introduced in

1989. The state (Ministry of Cities) commits itself to finance crime prevention activities (often, it is a matter of improvements in housing conditions in the poorest areas or other social measures), provided that the city has analysed its crime problems and made a plan to tackle them. Such contracts are reported to have been entered into with some 170 cities. Belgium introduced a similar contract system during the 1990s.

'The Nordic model'

Nordic crime prevention councils have worked for some years together to articulate their common crime prevention ideology.[66] Denmark and Sweden led the way with their national crime prevention councils. Later, a council was set up in Norway, and finally, the Finnish council was established in 1989. Iceland has planned to establish a similar agency for a number of years.

These national councils co-operate closely with a division of labour between them. The mandate, organisation and resources of each council are different, and each has its own special areas of expertise. For example, the Swedish council is a strong criminological research unit where knowledge-based action and the evaluation of results are emphasised; the Danish council produces much practical information material and has been the leading Nordic expert in crime prevention through environmental design; Norway has been strong in crime prevention in schools; the Finnish council has mainly worked on situational crime prevention.

Living conditions and culture in the Nordic countries are relatively similar. They are small, wealthy welfare societies, socially very stable and equal. The state guarantees a high level of social security and equalises the differences in living standards through high taxation and considerable income transfers.

Crime problems are similar or lesser in comparison with other small European countries, but considering the extensive crime opportunities caused by wealth and freedom, crime is in a fact relatively low. According to the opportunity index, Sweden, Finland and Norway (Denmark and Iceland did not participate in the study) are among the top countries in Europe. In Nordic society, women and youth have a very similar degree of freedom as men and adults. Finnish youth scored highest in a European comparison in which youth were asked how free they felt from parental or other control.

Nordic societies are considered to be safe. According to standard questions on the fear of crime in the international victim surveys, Sweden and Denmark consider themselves the safest European countries, and Finland and Norway are also near the top. In spite of wealth, protection devices are used less frequently in Nordic countries than in Europe on average.

The Nordic model differs especially in comparison to crime prevention in the United States with regard to the point of departure, which in Nordic countries is the social and health policy of the welfare society. An equal division of welfare and the prevention of marginalisation are seen as values on their own, not as instruments of crime prevention. Several effective methods of crime prevention are implemented in the Nordic countries routinely as part of ordinary social service systems. Parental advice, free high-standard education and other such services are seen as the rights of every citizen in Nordic countries. They are guaranteed from principles of social equality, not offered because of their impact on crime.

The city planning policy of the municipality of Helsinki has been successfully working against social segregation of different areas of the city. The ideology behind this policy has not been the prevention of social problems and crime (in spite of the fact that segregation leads to them), but the ideal of promoting equal living conditions. Sometimes, non-Nordic descriptions of Nordic crime prevention claim that it is directed towards situational measures. These play a central role, and at least councils in Denmark, Sweden and Finland have strongly promoted this approach. This description does not, however, take into account the fact that the content of social prevention is in these countries not defined as crime prevention but as welfare policy. The existence of this policy is considered to be a precondition for more specific crime prevention efforts.

A second characteristic of Nordic crime prevention is the emphasis on safety based on human relationships. It is safety, not security, if the two are in conflict, which the Nordic model prefers to promote.

Accordingly, several methods of crime prevention borrowed from the United States have been given a softer content in the Nordic countries. In Denmark, Norway and Sweden, neighbourhood watch programmes are called neighbourhood co-operation or help programmes. Their aim is to activate social relations in neighbourhoods and to promote mutual care-taking, not to activate dwellers to report offences and to control suspicious events or people. The use of CCTV in public places is almost totally forbidden in Denmark, and in Sweden and Norway its use is limited by law. One reason behind such limitations is the idea that the new technology is used to compensate for the lack of social control created by human relationships, and in the long run, extensive use of this control method can weaken social relationships.

In crime prevention through environmental design, ideas of an open society and of the built-up environment as a facilitator of communication between people from different social and age groups are emphasised according to ideas that safety is created by people and their mutual relationships (also by relationships to those we don't know). The Danish norms, recommendations and checklists for safe building use "safe" and "pleasant" almost as synonyms.

Developments

During its short history, crime prevention in Europe has already changed. A few tendencies are highlighted here, some of them problematic.

The industrialisation of crime prevention

The most striking development has been the growth of the security industry. This is not a European tendency only. Neither is it less evident in countries where public investment in crime prevention has been high.

Industrialisation means the growth of enterprises producing, selling and installing security devices such as alarm systems, video cameras and identification systems. A second central section of the industry sells private surveillance, sometimes resembling private policing. On the market some enterprises also sell crime prevention know-how. We have poor comparative knowledge on the turnover or volume of persons working in this branch. Only the number of private guards is studied. In European countries it varies from one-third to two-thirds of the number of police staff and it seems to be higher particularly in those countries where public crime prevention is also highly developed.

The industrialisation of crime prevention is problematic from several points of view. Protection devices and services promote the idea that safety is created by technical devices, not by human relationships. However, it is also clear that in tackling modern crime problems there is a wide area where the most acceptable principles are 'instigator pays' or 'benefit-taker pays'. Public crime-prevention policy has tried to co-operate with the security industry rather than limit its growth.

Defining social problems as police matters

During the short history of crime prevention, there has been a constant tension between the view that crime prevention is mostly policing, its associate or a new method, and the view that crime prevention is mainly an activity of other responsible agents. The concept of crime prevention has traditionally included both these conflicting ideas.

The development from reactive policing to proactive policing, from measures concerning crimes already committed to measures for preventing future crimes, has emphasised the responsibility of police in crime prevention. In community policing, the police are primarily responsible for crime prevention initiatives. Often this implies other kinds of activities than those the police organisation is basically designed, empowered and trained for.

Localisation

In its early days, crime prevention meant activities on a national and state level. National crime prevention councils were established, and interdepartmental committees were set up. Now it is emphasised that crime prevention, to be effective, must focus on local problems and local needs and circumstances. Local communities have the right to define their own problems, and well-functioning communities can find solutions most appropriate for them.

Local crime prevention councils or other networks have been set up in several countries. If local crime prevention is not specifically organised, at least crime prevention activities are being implemented more and more locally. Localisation is very evident in countries where police forces are municipal, but also in countries where national social policy is weak compared with municipal actions. In the latter case, as for instance in some Mediterranean countries, local crime prevention often is almost synonymous with municipal social policy.

Comprehensive programmes or increasing symbolism

The establishment of crime prevention councils was in several countries preceded by national crime prevention programmes.

In recent years, several European countries have drafted comprehensive governmental or national crime prevention programmes, including both social and situational prevention measures. They allot the responsibility for actions between several state departments, between the state and the municipalities, and possibly also between the public and private sectors. The Swedish national crime prevention programme *Our Collective Responsibility* (1996), the Finnish programme *Working Together for Safety* (1999) and in the United Kingdom *The Government's Crime Reduction Strategy* (1999) are examples of the most recent programmes of this kind.

The drafting of crime prevention programmes may be seen by cynics as a symbolic action no different from other political programme work. In some countries, crime problems have given rise to political concern to such a degree that governments must demonstrate – at least verbally – their willingness to deal with them. On the other hand, some countries base their programmes on an analytic approach and, as is the case of Swedish and Finnish programmes, introduce the perspective of crime prevention in all public decision making. Thus, the impact on crime must be taken into consideration in all sectors of public administration, for example in area planning in the municipalities. Much modern crime is caused by public decisions in areas where the impact of policy on crime and safety is neglected.

Exclusion

The increased use of exclusion as a crime prevention method has been referred to when discussing industrialisation trends. In fact, the oldest methods in crime prevention, padlocks, moats etc, have been exclusive. Technological progress has created new, sophisticated ways of using old methods for keeping problems and threats outside. Some experts[67] have defined crime prevention as setting physical and psychological barriers to crime.

Methods of exclusion are in operation everywhere, so that few people question them: minors can be excluded from shopping malls as anticipated shoplifters, workers can be drug tested in their workplaces. If such methods do not create problems from the human rights perspective, they are easily accepted and, when available, used without considering the fact that they often weaken the problem-handling capacity of the community.

What are the results?

Is European crime prevention able to demonstrate results? Modern prisons were established a century ago with great expectations as to their rehabilitative effects. Most criminal law reforms have resulted in very little, if any, changes in crime in spite of great expectations. The lack of results from traditional methods of criminal policy has been a central reason to develop crime prevention. Will the future judgement concerning crime prevention be the same: great expectations, but weak results? We cannot expect to find final solutions to crime problems. Therefore, expectations must be realistic.

The easiest way to answer the question is to refer to success stories. There are successful examples from different countries, some of them scientifically evaluated: some kinds of crimes have indeed decreased in some places, and this has been due to preventive measures.[68]

There are no proper materials to analyse developments in crime in European countries or the possible effects of crime prevention measures on these developments. However, we may ask whether crime risks (and fear of crime) are lower in those countries that have been active in crime prevention as compared with less active countries.

In the following table, the establishment of a special national crime prevention agency is used as an indicator of crime prevention activity. Figures on crime risks and fear of crime are based on international victim surveys,[69] which are a more reliable source for evaluating crime prevention than statistics of registered crime. Crime prevention measures tend to increase reporting, and therefore trends in registered crime may provide a misleading picture of real changes. In international comparisons, the numbers of registered crimes are usually worthless because of differences in crime definitions and statistical practices.

Crime risks and fear of crime in some European countries (% of population victimised in one year and % of population who feel unsafe walking alone in their neighbourhood after dark)

Table 1: Countries with crime prevention agencies

	Burglary	Robbery	Assault	Fear of crime
England and Wales	2.7	1.1	3.9	26.2
Sweden	1.3	0.4	3.4	18.6
France	2.4	0.6	2.8	26.6
Netherlands	2.3	0.8	3.8	20.1
Belgium	2.2	1.0	1.9	19.6
Finland	0.6	0.7	4.0	19.4

Table 2: Countries without crime prevention agencies

	Burglary	Robbery	Assault	Fear of crime
Germany	1.3	0.8	3.1	32.3
Italy	2.4	1.3	0.8	38.6
Spain	1.6	3.1	3.1	23.9
Switzerland	1.1	0.7	2.1	27.0

As shown in Table 1, we cannot say that crime risks are generally lower in countries that have been active in developing crime prevention. They are not generally safer than countries without a special crime prevention agency.

Table 1 indicates a relatively clear tendency according to which fear of crime (which is largely independent of crime risks) is lower in countries that have been active in crime prevention. This is surprising, because crime prevention is often supposed to increase fear. There are, however, several interpretations. We may suppose that those countries where fear of crime is high tend to favour, instead of prevention, 'law-and-order' measures, harsh penalties and more police.

A non-repressive alternative

Has crime prevention offered an alternative to the repressive system of criminal law?

The best and simplest indicator for repressiveness of a country's crime policy is the number of prisoners. A system is the more repressive the more there are prisoners per capita, regardless of whether this is caused by long sentences or by the widespread use of imprisonment.

It should be noted that long, reliable and comparable time-series on prisoner rates are difficult to find.

Most striking is the development in Finland. Starting from an exceptionally high level, the prisoner number goes down to the lowest level among these six countries. The national crime prevention council was established in Finland only after the prisoner rate had decreased consistently for ten years. The decrease also continued after this agency was set up. A possible interpretation of the Finnish development is that the crime prevention council has not offered a non-repressive alternative, and its establishment was merely one logical step in a series of measures where the repressiveness of the Finnish criminal policy was reduced.

Imprisonment rates have increased in the United Kingdom and France, slightly more in the UK. The number of prisoners was slightly decreasing in France before the violence prevention council was established, but afterwards, it turned to a steadily growing trend. On the basis of these figures, we cannot find support for the hypothesis that crime prevention could have worked as an alternative to repression in either of these two countries.

The Danish imprisonment rate has remained almost constant from the beginning of the 1970s when the crime prevention council was established. In Sweden, the number of prisoners was slightly decreasing when their crime prevention council was set up, then remained stable on the same low level for ten years, and then turned upwards. In Sweden, the increase has, however, been relatively moderate.

Investments in crime prevention in the Nordic countries may be interpreted as representing one part of a criminal policy that has aimed to reduce repressiveness.

However, the rate of imprisonment in Germany (higher than in Sweden or Denmark) has remained constant, and Germany has not set up a special crime prevention agency. In contrast, in Portugal, Spain and Italy, all countries without a special crime prevention agency, prisoner rates have increased dramatically.

The intense growth of the prisoner rate in the United States proves that crime prevention does not need to reduce repression. Quite the opposite, since crime prevention in the USA may be seen as an essential part of a very repressive criminal policy and as operating to increase repression. In the Netherlands, the rate of prisoners has also increased in spite of large investments in crime prevention. However, the starting point there was the lowest in Europe and the Dutch development is therefore not analogous to the American one.

In general, it is not possible to say that crime prevention has represented an alternative to repression, not even in Europe. In some countries, investments in crime prevention may be seen merely as part of an increasingly repressive criminal policy. In contrast, the Nordic model of crime prevention seems to have played a role among many other policies in order to avoid increasing repressiveness, which can be seen as a general international trend.

Success stories

There are some fifty success stories usually cited in international studies, but most success stories are not widely known. They are local, not properly documented and, if reported, in European minority languages. A task for European crime prevention would be to collect these experiences for common use. Such a task is important also for balancing existing international expertise, which is dominated by the United States and therefore not always suitable for application to European cultures.[70]

Therefore, allow me to use a little known Norwegian success story:[71]

The small northern city of Harstad started a project to prevent health risks caused by accidents and violence. Violence reports were analysed, and it was noted that in almost one out of every two fights a conscript was involved. The fights occurred in and near popular restaurants. Minors also used to come together to drink alcohol in and near restaurants. Therefore, an action focusing on restaurants, the local garrison, and minors was developed: police personally contacted every conscript and paid regular visits to the restaurants in question urging them to improve their peace-keeping, and parents were contacted when their children were found drinking late at night.

Even after a critical reading of the project report, one has to accept that about one-third of serious violent acts (where clinical care in a hospital was needed; in this respect, hospital journals are more reliable sources than police reports) were prevented. Harstad received a World Health Organisation certificate as a "safe community" because of this programme.

Value choices

Crime can be prevented, and usually in several ways. Therefore, it has become an increasingly important question to prevent crime in the right way, where not only the harm done by crime is minimised, but also the negative consequences of preventive measures, including long-term consequences. There are problematic tendencies in crime prevention, referred to earlier. Therefore European work to develop international recommendations for crime prevention with the intention of protecting human rights is one step towards ethically strong crime prevention policy. Choices between alternatives are value choices. These must be made with a particular view as to the direction in which we want European societies to develop. European crime prevention must be developed so as to articulate and protect human rights and the finest values of European cultures.

Chapter 4: Emerging issues and new patterns of criminal legislation

Ernesto Savona, University of Trento, Adelmo Manna, University of Foggia and Giacomo Forte, University of Foggia, Italy

Introduction

The reform of both substantive and procedural legislation undertaken in recent years has been driven by two main sets of interacting variables: on the one hand, the structural, cultural, organisational and technological changes that occurred in Europe during the second half of the twentieth century, and, on the other, the close concern of public opinion and legislatures with key issues in the personal and social spheres, such as violence against women and children, the environment, corruption and organised crime. The changes made to criminal codes in Europe and the adaptation of criminal procedure codes may be interpreted as the result of a combination of these two factors.

Criminal law

The penal laws of the European countries are characterised by the two traditions of Common Law and Civil Law. While Great Britain's criminal law on the one hand and that of the countries of central and southern Europe on the other have distinct features, those of the Scandinavian countries contain certain elements that are more closely related to the traditions of the western countries.[72] During their transition from a socialist to a market economy, the eastern European countries introduced far-reaching reforms in their socialist legal systems, including numerous elements of other European codes, and in particular – as far as organised crime is concerned – of Anglo-Saxon law.

The distinction between codification and non-codification has lost importance in the face of the vast and complex production of laws, which, owing to the lack of changes in the codes, are placed among the special laws. The reforms that are undertaken by various countries have tended to focus less on the structure (the code or precedents) and more on what should be criminalised or decriminalised, what type of sanction should be applied, and the type of procedure to follow. In other words, they raise three issues: what legal good should be protected; how to improve the effectiveness and efficiency of sanctions by better safeguarding the rights of the offenders; and how to protect the victims.

As far as criminalisation/decriminalisation processes and penal sanctions are concerned, there is a general trend in penal legislation towards greater criminalisation of violent crimes, organised crime (especially drug trafficking), and economic crime – particularly corruption. By contrast, it is also possible to observe a progressive decriminalisation of offences related to individual morality. Furthermore, privacy has been given more penal and administrative protection.

The choice between long-term penal sanctions, including imprisonment, and sanctions geared towards the re-education and socialisation of perpetrators outside the prison system depends on a mix of variables. These include political responses to the need for security; greater concern with the protection of the rights of the perpetrators; and more attention to the victims' right to justice. Each of these elements, and others, must be taken into consideration and, according to the circumstances, has a lesser or greater weight than the others. For example, an increasingly widespread fear of crime, despite the generally stable crime trends, is leading to an increase in the number of penal sanctions and in the more frequent application of the prison sentence, which has brought the European welfare model closer to the American system.

There is still an open debate in all the penal systems that are undergoing, or have recently undergone, reform. Because of the differences in the common and civil law systems, these reforms have mainly concerned law enforcement agencies in the former and law codes in the latter. While the common law systems are more flexible and adaptable to new situations, the natural rigidity of legislative reform and above all the need to reform the codes mean that the reform processes of civil law systems are much longer and therefore require more time. This has produced a kind of anomaly in contemporary European penal systems: the constant but fragmentary expansion of special laws, which have nevertheless satisfied the new need for protection. It has been necessary to use this method, however, because of the rigid nature of the codes and the need for a vast political consensus regarding their reform. What follows is a brief description of the reforms undergone in some European countries.

During the reform of the German Penal Code, starting from the reform of its general part in 1975,[73] great attention has been given to the principle of re-education of the perpetrator by making sanctions for serious crimes harsher, while going back more frequently to alternative sanctions for lighter offences. This explains the wider space given to the pecuniary penalty. Thus, the payment of a fine calculated on a daily rate basis (§40), under the provisions of §47, has become the normal penalty for offences carrying a sentence of less than six months. The judge may only impose a custodial sentence for these cases if the circumstances and the perpetrator's personality make it essential to do so.

Another adjustment of the German Penal Code to respond to the needs for prevention was the introduction of *Absehen von Strafe.* This provision, which is foreseen in §60 of the German Penal Code, consists in waiving the sentence. In other words, the judge can waive the sentence when its effects on the offender would be so detrimental that its application would obviously be a mistake. The real aim of this disposition is to reduce the number of petty offenders in the penal system. The German depenalisation law of 1975 also worked in this direction by creating a general sub-system model of administrative penal procedures.[74] Thus, for example, section 29a of the penal code was abolished, resulting in the depenalisation of all those infringements punishable with a fine.

As far as the special part is concerned, this is being continually amended in response to new demands for protection and changes in society. This has resulted in the abrogation of crimes that have become obsolete (such as adultery or homosexuality among males aged eighteen or more). On the other hand, new crime types have been introduced (for example, in the field of computer crime, computer fraud [§263a] and computer sabotage [§303b], which consists in dangerously interfering in other people's data elaboration systems). Numerous by-laws have also been created outside the sphere of the code. Some of these are quite important, such as the law on drug abuse, which increases the number of crime types and applies much stricter sentences for them.

In Portugal, the 1982 reform of the Portuguese Penal Code[75] remedied the obsolete Code of 1852. Various principles inspired this new text, including the decriminalisation of some crimes and the criminalisation of others. This led to a significant reduction in the overall number of crime types (some crimes against public order and public authority were depenalised) although some new ones were also introduced (such as soliciting suicide (Article 139), disturbing the peace through the use of a telephone (Article 190.2), computer fraud (Article 221), and trading in influence (Article 335).

France's old Penal Code of 1910 was radically reformed in July 1992. The new French Code[76] appears to be aimed at improving functionality and efficiency without, however, neglecting the need to adequately protect individuals. It gives particular attention to the protection of privacy by introducing provisions that punish interference in people's private lives through the use of technical instruments (Article 226.8), harming a person's reputation by using audio-visual aids (Article 226.8), and sabotaging automated data elaboration systems (Articles 323.1-323.7).

At the sanctioning level, the French Code is marked by its pragmatism, as is testified by the vast range of sanctions that have been introduced as main forms of punishment, and by the wide discretionary power given to the judge in deciding which one to apply. The French Penal Code is one of the most innovative sanctioning systems because it attempts to compensate for its harsher penal sanctions by using alternative special preventive measures (for instance, "socially useful work"). The sanctions have also been divided according to whether the active subject is a physical or legal entity.[77] With respect to the latter, it should be pointed out that the current French Penal Code regulates the penal responsibility of legal entities. Thus, for example, the first clause of Article 121.2 states that "legal entities, with the exception of the state, are penally liable".

In the case of Spain, the new Spanish Penal Code[78] was finally approved by the Ley Orgánica on 8 to 15 November 1995. Developments in Spanish society since 1975 have modified the social perception of those legal entities worth protection. As a consequence, the Spanish Penal Code has attempted to protect new legal entities that might be harmed by technological and economic progress. Thus, for example, Section XII of the Penal Code contains specific provisions that protect the territory and its natural resources. Actions that are detrimental to human life have also been criminalised, such as behaviour that harms the human foetus (Articles 165-166), genetic manipulation,[79] and unauthorised artificial insemination. Nor is there a lack of new property crimes (like Article 252, which punishes computer fraud).

Important changes have been made in the sanctioning system. Significant limitations have been imposed on the length of custodial sentences (the maximum length is normally set at twenty years although this can be increased to thirty years in exceptional cases). There is also a tendency to abolish short custodial sentences, and new forms of sanctions have been introduced, such as weekend confinement in various non-penitentiary institutions (this type of sanction is used as an alternative to the payment of fines or to custodial sentences of less than two years).

Other European countries have not undertaken any radical reforms but are nevertheless introducing reforms in their national penal systems. A case in point is Norway, whose Penal Code dating back to 1902[80] has been modified in recent years. The changes include the abrogation of the life sentence in 1981, and the introduction of penal responsibility for legal entities and other commercial enterprises in 1991. In the same year, a new type of penalty was also introduced – "compulsory social service". Finally, in 1997, the provisions on guilt and on security measures were modified.

In Italy, changes to the Penal Code have been discussed and proposed for some time. Various noteworthy attempts have been made in this direction but without success. These include the draft law to reform the Penal Code drawn up by the Pagliaro Commission of 1992),[81] and the most recent proposal to reform the Penal Code drafted by the Grosso Commission set up by a Ministerial Decree of 1 October 1998.

The recent depenalisation law,[82] which transforms certain crimes into administrative offences and reforms the system of penalties, is particularly important. This law, like the 1975 German depenalisation law, has contributed towards creating a general sub-system model for administrative penal procedures. The depenalised crimes consist in: providing alimony to the spouse; navigation, traffic and transport offences; breaches of financial and tax laws, and infractions of regulations governing financial, stock market, banking and postal practices. None of these changes will significantly reduce the judicial work-load.

More substantial changes are being made in the countries of eastern Europe. It is worth noting the approval of the Slovenian Penal Code[83] which, like other Continental codes, enshrines the principles of legality, subsidiarity, non-retroactivity of the penal code, culpability, legality of punishment, and the general validity of the provisions set out in the general part of the Penal Code. The Slovenian Code is largely based on the German Penal Code. Article 14 is particularly interesting because its assertion that "acts of scant importance are not punishable" clearly aims to reduce penal responsibility by waiving punishment for offences that are obviously illegal but not serious enough to warrant their criminalisation. A further interesting aspect of the new Penal Code is its plurality of penal sanctions.[84] These are (Article 5): penalties, admonitory sanctions, and security and educational measures. Although detention is still the most widely applied form of punishment (it can be applied for all crimes, either on its own or as an alternative to the payment of a fine), great attention has been given to alternative forms of sanctions. It should be noted that the judges have been granted broad powers in deciding on the type of alternative sanction to be applied and on its length. Another important change, introduced by Article 104, is that short prison sentences can be replaced with "socially useful work" in order to reduce the burgeoning prison population.

The special part of the Slovenian Penal Code also has features that are similar to those of western penal codes: it contains specific provisions that protect basic goods, written in a clear and precise language. The section of the Code devoted to the protection of economic interests is particularly interesting. In fact, following the transformation of Slovenian society, penal protection is no longer targeted at social ownership, or at an allegedly self-managed economy, but rather at other values such as the economic market system, competition and the absolute equality of all forms of property.

Another country in transition whose legal system is worth noting is the Republic of Croatia.[85] In fact, the new Croatian Penal Code was enacted on 1 January 1998. It is similar in many ways to the Slovenian Code. For example, Article 1 enshrines the subsidiarity of penal repression, as well as the principles of legality and culpability. Another interesting element in depenalisation is the institution of the power to take legal action against a person, as well as of irrelevance of the fact. As far as the special part is concerned, this is based on criteria similar to those used in other eastern European countries.

Still on the theme of former socialist countries, it is worth noting the approval of the new Penal Code of the Russian Federation in 1996,[86] which definitively protects the rights of the individual (above all the principle of legality).

Criminal procedure

From a look at the new trends in criminal procedure in Europe, it is possible to observe that the push towards an accusatory type of trial has slightly weakened. This has produced accusatory systems with some inquisitorial elements and, where they prevailed, inquisitorial systems with accusatorial elements. In other words, greater attention is given to the rights of the legal parties as well as to ensuring their substantial and legal equality during the criminal-justice process, on the one hand, but also to the system's capacity to identify and incriminate the offender as soon as possible, on the other.

Some examples of this mix of systems can be found in various countries. Thus, for example, although German penal procedure has inquisitorial roots, it also contains some accusatory elements (*der Anklagegrundsatz*). Hence, for example, the Public Prosecutor has to respond to the Executive. German law prescribes that the Public Prosecutor must take action (obligation to take penal action) as soon as he/she becomes aware of the committal of an offence. This principle is mitigated when the power of prosecution *ex officio* is replaced by the power to take legal action against someone. As far as the probatory rules are concerned, although there is an investigative phase during which the Public Prosecutor gathers elements that may partially influence the judge's decision, the real evidence can only be produced during the trial. At the same time, however, the Public Prosecutor and the judicial police are granted wide-ranging powers during the investigative phases, such as the power to adopt measures to find evidence, that infringe on the liberty of the suspect. In fact, they can resort to a wide range of measures to identify the suspected person; they can intercept telephone calls when they are in the possession of serious and well-founded evidence regarding the committal of the offence and cannot use other measures; and they can effect house searches and personal inspections (although they must be performed with full respect for the dignity and sense of decency of the persons subjected to the inspection). A final interesting aspect worth mentioning is the close concern given by the law maker to guaranteeing the defence of the accused person and, if necessary, the provision of free legal assistance.

In France, too, the Public Prosecutor is responsible for following up crimes. He/she is flanked in this task by the investigating judge, whose main role is to co-ordinate the investigative phase and ensure that it is conducted correctly. In accordance with Article 81 of the Criminal Procedure Code, the Public Prosecutor must "carry out all the investigative acts deemed necessary to ascertain the truth", either directly or by delegating other persons to do so. The adjudicating judge is also given limited powers to carry out further investigation if this will help to discover the truth. These powers are particularly penetrating with respect to the investigation of the suspect. The only form of guarantee in this sphere is represented by the investigating judge who guarantees respect for legality. Thus, the investigating judge can order telephone interceptions in cases of crimes or offences (provided that they carry a custodial sentence of not less than two years), as well as house searches and personal inspections. It is not possible, without a proxy issued by the investigating judge, to carry out a search without the consent of the person being searched, unless the person is caught in flagrancy.

The fundamental guidelines of the Belgian criminal procedure system have a definite inquisitorial character during the investigative phase, but then tend to follow the accusatory model during the trial phase. Although different functions are assigned to different organs, the investigative phase – similarly to what happens in France – is carried out by the investigating judge who has wide investigative powers (to order telephone interceptions, on the basis of a law of 30 June 1994, searches and seizures). The only task assigned to the Public Prosecutor is to take legal action. A markedly more accusatory element is that the same judge can no longer intervene in the same case, as a prosecutor or as a judge, nor as an investigating judge or as a member of the adjudicating organ during the first instance trial or appeal.

The English criminal procedure based on Common Law is characterised by a triangular relationship. The parties confront one another under the arbitration of a judge and they all dispose of the same means to find evidence, on a perfectly equal basis. Both the accusing party and the defence must respect this equality. The police are obliged to provide the accused party with any evidence in its defence. If, in fact, the defence does not have the appropriate means to find evidence in its defence, it can use the services of the bodies responsible to the accusatory organs. Another feature of English criminal procedure is the presence of what can be defined as a 'dual-track system'. In fact, those procedures that grant the police the power to take action limit the victims' power, for the very reason that they are victims. Thus, for example, the victim has no right to be informed about how the process is progressing. The picture changes, however, when it is the victim who decides to take penal action. He/she then becomes a legal party and, as such, is entitled to all the powers linked with this position.

As regards Italy, the current Criminal Procedure Code that was introduced in 1988, when it substituted the Rocco Code of 1930, is orientated towards the accusatory model. Italian criminal procedure has been adapted to the principles of the constitution and to the international conventions ratified by Italy. The Italian system is a mixed one, although the accusatory model prevails, and is characterised by an equal position between the accusing party and the defence, as well by the impartiality of the adjudicating organ. The decision to adopt the accusatory system has been continually modified since the beginning of the 1990s, however, and has moved towards a more inquisitorial model following a series of interventions by the law-maker[87] and the Constitutional Court.[88] Two laws, Law No. 332/1995 and Law No. 267/1997, attempted to remedy this unbalanced situation. The first reform, which dealt with precautionary measures, involved the creation of a set of regulations on preventive custody to guarantee greater rights. The second reform reformulated Article 513 of the Criminal Procedure Code by providing that any declarations made during the investigative phase by an indicted person who does not appear before or respond to the court can only be utilised following an agreement between the two parties to do so.

Specific aspects: sexual violence

We will now take a closer look at penal legislation by studying the countries and legislative reforms that best express more general trends. Sexual violence has become an important issue in this respect because in recent years it has undergone substantial change following an increased demand for protection on the part of women. First the feminist movement and then a greater awareness among the population have resulted in greater attention being given by the lawmakers to the demands for protection of women and children. The main features of these transformations are: the passage to more direct penal categories such as 'offences against the person', an increase in the number of penal sanctions, and the *ex-officio* reporting of cases of violence against minors or of domestic violence.

The norms regarding sexual violence used to be aimed at protecting meta-individual rights such as public morals and decent behaviour. This solution gradually proved unsatisfactory, however, and greater emphasis has been placed on protection of the personal freedom and self-determination of individuals in making sexual choices. This protection is enhanced when the victim is a minor or in a condition of limited freedom that impedes self-determination.

The reform of the Italian law in 1996 moved violent crimes from the category of crimes against public morality, to the category of crime against personal freedom. It then established the principle of taking official legal action against a person when the victims of the crime committed were minors, or in cases of domestic violence, and increased the number of sanctions envisaged for them. The same solutions have already been adopted by numerous other European countries. For example, already in 1982, the Portuguese Code moved sexual offences from the category of "offences against the values and interests of society" to "offences against the person" where they are listed separately as "offences against freedom and sexual self-determination" (Articles 163-179).

It is possible, from the overview of the legislation described above, to identify two crime-type models. A more traditional model divides sexual violence into two different crime categories. These are carnal violence (punishable with more serious sanctions), on the one hand, and sexual harassment – that is, all those other acts of a sexual nature that are committed against and without the consent of the victim – on the other. Thus, in Germany there is a distinction between *Vergewaltigung* (§177) and *Sexuelle Nötigung* (§178). In France, the Penal Code punishes two different forms of sexual violence – *viol* (Articles 222-24) and *l'agression sexuelle* (Articles 222-28), as does the Portuguese Code (Articles 164 and 165 of the Penal Code). The 1995 Slovenian Penal Code also distinguishes between two types of sexual violence: "carnal violence" (Article 180) and "sexual violence" (Article 181).

The second model refers more generally to the concept of "sexual acts". This comprehensive term refers to any act whatsoever of a sexual nature that harms the freedom of self-determination of an individual. This model is currently in force in Italy, and Article 809*bis* of the Penal Code punishes "any one ... who forces someone else to perform or be subjected to sexual acts". Although this second model is certainly more effective in limiting the number of useless and humiliating investigations to which the victim has to be subjected, it suffers, nevertheless, from lack of precision and thus allows the judge greater discretionary power in applying the rules.

In order to enhance the protection of minors, penalties have been made harsher and, as is the case with the Italian law, legal action is now taken officially and not by the damaged party. In France, the statutory penalty envisaged by Articles 227-25 of the Penal Code regarding violence against minors has been set, by Article 18 of Law No. 468 of June 1998, at between two and five years of imprisonment, while the pecuniary penalty has been increased from 200 000 French francs to 500 000 French francs.

Environmental protection

During the second half of the century, an increased political awareness of environmental problems (promoted by the 'green' parties) has influenced penal law and forced it to speed up its modernisation process. The law makers have focused on identifying a type of offence that provides better legal protection to the environmental good. The inclusion of the category of environmental crimes in the penal codes by many countries has had a cultural and educational function. It has helped to underline the importance of the protected good.

In Germany, a specific category of "crimes against the environment" (*Straftaten gegen die Umwelt*) has been introduced. These are divided according to the natural elements that are being harmed (water, air, soil), as well as by the polluting activity. They are contained under Title 28 of the *StGB* in §324 ff. These offences, which were introduced in 1980 with the aim of unifying the matter so as to increase people's awareness of the social danger represented by pollution, were further modified during a reform in 1994.[89] The Slovenian Penal Code also dedicates an entire paragraph to environmental protection: "offences against the landscape, the environment and the natural heritage" (Articles 333 ff.).

Other countries have preferred, instead, to modify the common danger crimes. In particular, already existing crime types that protected other goods have been reformulated in an ecological key. Thus, for example, the Spanish Penal Code of 1995 lists environmental offences under Title XVI, which covers "protection of the landscape, and the cultural and environmental heritage". This, in turn, is divided into five paragraphs, dealing with territorial planning; the cultural heritage; natural resources and the environment; protection of flora and fauna; and general dispositions.[90] The Austrian Penal Code dedicates a whole section to environmental crime (it was reformed in 1989 in order to make the fight against pollution more effective).[91]

The Portuguese Penal Code goes in the same direction. It does not contain a specific section dedicated to environmental crime, but has instead introduced this type of crime among "crimes of common danger". This category lists crimes that represent "a threat to nature" (Article 278), "pollution" (Article 279), "pollution that threatens the common good" (280) and "threat to animals and plants" (Article 281).[92] Finally, in the new French Penal Code, environmental protection is considered a fundamental national interest. In fact, it includes "ecological terrorism" among its terrorist-related crimes, in other words, the act of "individually or collectively, and with the aim of seriously disturbing public order by intimidation or terror, introducing in the soil, subsoil, or in the water – including that of the territorial sea – a substance that places at risk the health of men, animals or the environment".[93]

The situation in Italy is different in that there is a huge number of laws related to the environment. This makes it even more difficult to understand each law in depth, whether they are respected, and therefore their level of effectiveness.[94] The Pagliaro Project of 1992, and more recently the Ronchi Project[95] attempted to remedy this situation by creating a homogeneous set of environmental norms to substitute the numerous disorganised norms disseminated all over the various law texts.

Another characteristic of environmental criminal law is that it uses a model that refers to crimes of an abstract danger[96] or, moreover, of an abstract-concrete nature.[97] This latter model is the one adopted in Germany. Its first category of crimes in particular – referred to under §330 ("serious threat to the environment") – grants the penal law great autonomy with respect to administrative law. Thus, for example, "disobedience" is punished when it contains particular offensive elements specified by the law itself. A second category of crimes comprises, instead, crimes whose level of threat in the economy has a much more abstract dimension. This is the case, for example, of §327 (unauthorised running of industrial plants). There is, finally, a third category of crimes (for example §330a) which – given the seriousness of the crimes – lacks any reference whatsoever to 'lack of respect' for the administrative rules.

In order to avoid difficult probatory problems, above all at the causation level, the law-makers in the various countries have made the penal law 'administrative'. The government is 'delegated' to balance beforehand the interests at play, in other words production requirements on the one hand, and respect for the environment, on the other. This avoids an effective confirmation of the threat posed to the protected good. The third fundamental characteristic in the subject matter of environmental protection refers to the model of crime utilised, that is, whether it is an infringement or crime model. The systems diverge on this point.

The main European penal codes adopt the crime model. It should, in fact, be noted that the German Penal Code has completely removed the infringement model, as has the Portuguese Penal Code, which puts environmental crimes under a category of "crimes that represent a common threat" (in other words, like Germany, infringements are not envisaged). As far as the Spanish Penal Code is concerned, although it has retained the crime-infringement dichotomy, it has also included environmental crime in the crime sphere, obviously because the environment is expressly mentioned in Article 45 of its constitution.

Other codes, like the Italian one, use the infringement model. However, although this model facilitates the collection of evidence from a psychological point of view[98] and is the most appropriate when using the abstract threat parameter,[99] it has not proved very effective because, above all, of its limited prescription terms. It was for this reason that both the Pagliaro Project[100] and the Ronchi Project proposed to adopt the crime model, also to highlight the serious harmful nature of these infringements. The last interesting element on the issue of environmental protection is the punishability of the legal person. It should be noted, in fact, that since environmental pollution is often the result of an entrepreneurial policy, simply punishing a physical person would be useless and of scarce effect. In order to overcome these difficulties in Italy, the Ronchi Project proposed to introduce real penal sanctions for the legal persons. These have already been introduced in other codes such as those of England[101] and France. There are also other systems –

like the German one[102] – which have preferred to opt for direct responsibility only at the administrative and pecuniary level.

The situation in England is somewhat different in that these property-related measures are also used to fight drug-related crimes. In particular, the Drug Trafficking Offences Act, enacted in 1986 and successively reformed in 1994, provides a complex set of laws aimed at striking at the patrimony of the offender.

Conclusion

It is possible, from the above analysis, to present a picture of more or less homogeneous changes. This can be observed, first of all, with respect to the types of goods that are protected. Protection of the person has certainly been given high priority (as is testified by the attention given to sexual violence) and the law-makers have adopted a tough stance with respect to these crimes by making them punishable with harsh prison sentences. The same tough approach has been adopted for organised crime.

This picture changes with respect to other crimes. In the field of economic crimes, too, attempts have been made to adapt penal law when necessary, but keeping well in view the requirements and developments of society and technology. Hence the introduction of new forms of property crimes, for example, computer fraud, insider trading and breach of trust. Great attention has been given to ensuring the effectiveness of these forms of protection, as is confirmed by the new prospects of penal law (punishability of the legal person) and the increasing use of alternative sanctions.

Another interesting common element regards sanctions. There has been a growing need to introduce new forms of sanctions as major penalties. These sanctions are directly applied by the judge in substitution for, or in addition to, the prison sentences. We have therefore witnessed the introduction of sanctions whose main objective is to re-socialise the sentenced person (this explains the growing focus on penalties to be carried out within a social context).

A final, but no less important element, regards the depenalisation of so-called petty offences. In fact, it is felt that alternative measures should be applied for those offences traditionally considered not serious enough for the application of a penalty. This would reduce both the legal work-load and the prison population, as well as the harmful social effects that short custodial sentences can produce on the offender, and solve the problem of the scarce consideration given to the goods harmed by the offence, or the scarce offensive capacity of the incriminated act. This has led to more or less widespread depenalisation and the greater use of pecuniary penalties (often instead of short custodial sentences), to the introduction of alternative measures, to the wider use of confiscation and of sanctions directly targeted at the illegal profits.

From the picture painted so far, we can conclude by stating that substantive penal law now pays more attention to effectiveness than to guaranteeing the rights of the legal parties, which has moved into the background. This is also partly true with respect to criminal procedure, which, as has been seen, gives great emphasis to the need for rapidity and effectiveness, and economic factors, but at the same time guarantees the rights of the indicted person. This is further highlighted by the excessive formalisation of the crime types, which seem almost as if they were created to serve criminal procedure. This is demonstrated by the various environmental protection laws, in which single crime types refer to an abstract threat in order to avoid serious difficulties in proving the causal nexus that would otherwise arise if the crime types adopted were to refer to damage or to a concrete threat. This also partially applies to corruption where the trend (already mentioned above) is to avoid difficult probatory questions related to official duty, without considering the link with a specific official duty.

Chapter 5: Policing the new Europe

Amadeu Recasens I Brunet,
Director of the Police School of Catalonia, Barcelona

Police and social change

Over the past 30 years European police forces have kept pace with social, economic and political change. Immense pressures have left them in a critical situation, which must be considered in its context. The crisis within the police is part of the relative, but generalised, breakdown of institutions and of the concept of the state. At the same time it must be recognised that a crisis may be provoked as a reaction to expansion.

The evolution of social reference points, from the parameters of social consensus to those of conflict and subsequently to the complexity of society, has brought about a crisis of values and a questioning of beliefs within police forces. Consensus theories have clearly led to a confrontation between law and order and lawlessness, and placed the police in one of the two fields as a legitimate user of violence[103] and as an upholder of the law.[104]

These conflict theories present an important element in the debate concerning lawlessness wherever police were displaced from the task of keeping law and order to that of protecting the interests of certain groups (the powerful) in conflicts. The notion of the police as a state machine, placed within the state instruments of control ("within the frame proposed by the new criminology"), has been a hard blow for traditional beliefs.

Thus, the police force is another actor in a complex system where "a great many independent agents are interacting with each other in a great many ways".[105] From this perspective the police are seen as yet another component and an integrated element within a complex social system, one that must be integrated into its surroundings, exchanging matter, energy and information. The police should not be a separate alien body.[106] Over the past 30 years the police have gone from being (and wanting to be) a separate entity to becoming (willingly or unwillingly) a partner in a game where there is no place for absolute convictions. Today, the police are in a state of uncertainty. They are searching for a new model, in which citizens, the state and the law all play a role.

This situation has generated an apparent paradox. The breakdown of the traditional police ambit and the profound changes in the notions of law and order (in its broad sense of social order), far from marginalising the police into exclusion or oblivion, have done quite the opposite. New demands and new security control spaces have emerged, giving way to a growing need to manage situations and conflicts, as well as different ways of carrying out police tasks. But all these demands differ from those the police were used to controlling in the past. This drives the police towards the assumption of a relevant social role, and increasingly complex surroundings are forcing them to constantly adapt to new requirements. This implies constructing new instruments, new resources and new management systems as well as a new corporate culture. This is a crisis of growth and not of breakdown.

The breakdown of the sovereignty concept and undefined objectives

Europe has a problem of definition. One the one hand, the Council of Europe considers European states to be those countries with a national territory contained totally or partly within the European continent and whose culture is closely linked to the European tradition.[107] On the other hand, we have the 'European Community', later known as the 'European Union', formed by countries that belonged to the European Economic Community (EEC) and that have come together in an unfinished unifying process, making up most of what we call 'western Europe', but certainly not all of it. Finally, the countries of central and eastern Europe are undergoing a political transition from a system known as 'real socialism' towards constitutionally democratic and social states.[108]

This triangle is based on three complementary, often overlapping, entities moving at varying paces in creating links and connections, and finding common ground. All these issues affect security to a considerable degree, as well as affecting the police forces, which are immersed and integrated within the dynamics of European evolution.

If these three entities share a common feature, it is the will and the need for integration into supranational areas. This does not necessarily imply the disintegration of nation states, but it obviously reflects a certain degree of crisis in the concept of states within Europe in that states form geo-economical subdivisions which are increasingly less competitive. This affects the traditional concept of the sovereign state, defined by Max Weber as "a human community within a given land – the concept of land is essential to the definition – that claims (successfully) the monopoly of a legitimate physical coercion".[109]

The necessary assumption of security areas (for operative or analysis purposes or for co-ordination and co-operation) on the part of supra-national instances, is the best indicator of the move towards a new police model in Europe.

Defining a new policing space in Europe

The formation of the European Union is the result of a number of economic needs and is a natural continuation of the European Economic Community. The Treaty of Rome (1957) reflected the political will to overcome the traumas suffered by Europe in the second world war, but it reflected even more clearly the need also felt by some of the smaller European states to go beyond their borders for trading purposes and to face the resulting economic upsurge of the great powers.

The passage of time and global social and economic development have together pushed these European countries one step further. The international situation, with increasingly globalised economies and the pressure of states bordering on the Economic Community (made more acute by the end of the cold war, the breakdown of the communist bloc and the countries under its influence) initially brought about the signing of the Single European Act (SEA) in 1986, and later the Treaty on European Union in 1992 (TEU). This evolving political process is guided by strong economic trends.

For the citizens within this economic area the process has helped define four basic freedoms – the free circulation of citizens, goods, services and capital. All four are essential to economic development, but at the same time they are liable to political interpretations and therefore they are also essential in any political convergence towards the European Union. The common ground shared by the four freedom areas is geographical mobility – a key element in all trade and labour exchanges. Thus, these freedoms are ambiguous. Either they are real rights for citizens of the European Union or they are a means to favour the economic need of moving goods and labour. This exchange of trade and labour also generates mistrust, an anxiety that lies at the root of all political schemes on law enforcement in the European Union and in all 'free-circulation-compensating measures.' These questions arise not only in the European Union. In fact, they were already contemplated in the Single European Act, and even in the European Economic Community as far as goods are concerned.

The idea of establishing an area of law enforcement in the Europe of the EEC and the EU is even older. It is the result of three 'motive powers' or 'ghosts' which have been cropping up since the 1970s and have led to more powerful police co-ordination,[110] basically made legitimate by the fight against the four major problems outlined below.

Terrorism

Terrorism has been a transnational problem throughout Europe since the early 1970s, and includes the rise of the Red Army Faction (RAF) in Germany, the Red Brigades (RB) in Italy, the Irish Republican Army (IRA) and the Euskadi Ta Askatasuna: Freedom for the Basque Country (ETA), to cite the most important organisations. In the transnational setting, attention has been focused mainly on the Middle East conflict, which has manifested itself in Europe by such acts as the massacre of Jewish athletes during the Munich Olympic Games of 1972.

Drugs

The problem of drugs also emerged in the 1970s, gathering strength during the 1980s when it was perceived as drug-trafficking. This brought about the formation of the first European Police Unit.

Organised crime

Fears arising from the law controlling citizens' free movements reached a peak when the Single European Act came into force, and they were tackled in the second half of the 1980s. This last problem is much more complex since it affects many more people and is much more widespread since it has an effect on the four aforementioned rights. In fact, it has repercussions on many issues including the rights of foreign citizens and related problems (usually in the administrative area) as well as organised crime, both of the Mafia-type and of a criminal nature, from the legal point of view. This includes money laundering, large-scale drug-trafficking movements of criminals and large-scale fraud, the theft of works of art and cars and environmental damage.

Social violence

Gradually a fourth generation of motive power emerged, which has been related to the more widespread concept of violence (for example among urban tribes, in sports and against children) or problems derived from multicultural and multi-ethnic societies, such as racism and exclusion.[111] This situation has generated a first line of responses such as the European agreement on violence and spectators' invasions in sport events, particularly in football matches, which in 1985 gave way to the 'Rotterdam Charter' on a police force for a multi-ethnic society and efforts to promote non-aggressive mediation in conflicts.[112] But most of these initiatives are still at an early stage of evaluation.[113]

While awaiting the development of this 'fourth generation', we can make reference to three elements that generate law-and-order breakdowns throughout Europe, and to three waves of law enforcement, which have attempted to fight them. This struggle has provoked an important exchange of experiences and information between the police and those working in the field of research and criminal enquiries. Without such an exchange it would have been impossible to contemplate police co-operation within the European Union today. Previous experience and the formation of a transnational élite police force have established relevant contacts and relationships over the years, both on a technical and a personal level, thus creating a network reaching beyond Europe's limits.

Out of the recurring elements of security in the EU framework we can conclude the following:

- They arose mainly in the 1970s, following several isolated precedents (the Pompidou Group, the Vienna Club, the Bern Club) and a transnational organisation – Interpol, setting itself up as a 'rival referent.' The use of motive powers as catalysts of police co-operation has grown out of strategic moments; at the same time it tends to generate a frame of reference for western Europe.
- The various elements are not exclusive or excluding; they tend to integrate, accumulate and thus blur the limits between them. The underlying concept is becoming increasingly vague and more subjective, and has ever more social repercussions. Thus, there is a fragmentation of law-breaking that goes beyond the legal concept and inevitably manifests itself in violence, which with its wide spectrum (schools, sports, cities) speaks with many voices. It has not yet been determined what role these

motive powers play in objective facts, and what magnification they potentially hold when used as an instrument of fear, social alarm and a perceived decline in law and order.

- Such a sequence of recurring elements has led to the development of a supra-state police space, which has also exposed the shortcomings of the European nation-state. At the same time a well-defined and more progressive area of police co-operation has been generated out of the need for immediate operational needs before those of the European judiciary or a political space within the framework of the European Union. The supra-state law enforcement area that has thus developed has grown in tandem with citizens' growing needs and demands for a closer police presence in their day-to-day activities.

Police and transition: the Spanish case

Spain's shift from a totalitarian political regime to a democratic state from 1975 onwards labelled it a non-typical case within the European Union. After forty years of dictatorship, the country faced several internal and external challenges, which constituted a complete transition. Modernisation, democratisation and social change were not the only important phenomena of the moment; there were now the prospects of membership in international fora, previously vetoed because of the antidemocratic features of the old Spanish political system.

During the 1980s, which constituted the first decade without dictatorship, security issues required a great effort of theoretical reconstruction of both political and social ideas and images. It was not easy to interpret and understand the social feeling towards security or the judicial meaning of the constitution (especially Articles 104, 126, 149.1.29) and its agreements.[114]

The political will reiterated by citizens through all their means of expression (from demonstrations to the voting ballot), by political parties in their programmes and finally by those who interpreted the constitution, revealed that it was time to change the old-fashioned Franco concept of public order. This order had been based on a simplistic and blunt structure, which relied on strict compulsory obedience and submission to restrictions on rights and liberties (Public Order Act). Thus, the state had to defend itself from its own citizens. The protected good was the established order, more particularly in the public arena.

Such a formula could no longer be applied in a democratic and constitutional state. Nor could it be part of a mature and developed society that resembled other European states. Hence, it had to be dispensed with and even its name had to be replaced in order fully to accomplish its new mandate.

It also created a new concept, that of the security of the citizen, a fundamental element in the coexistence of citizen and state. Consequently, security became not a right in itself but a guarantee for the exercise of rights and liberties. This point is crucial in order to avoid interpretations that identify security as a right that encroaches on other rights. Such an argument may have led to perversions based on the claim that the restriction of certain rights, allegedly put forward as the 'right' to security, would actually repeal those rights it was intended to protect.

The concept of 'security of the citizen', however, has a less defined profile than that of public order. Allegedly public order can be objectively measured by statistical data (albeit often manipulated), allowing us to quantify whether the level of obedience to the state has increased or diminished. Alternatively, the concept of 'security of the citizen' (public security) involves a certain amount of subjectivity, the 'perception' that citizens have of their own capacity to exercise their rights and liberties. It is, therefore, harder to provide a strict definition of security because it would have to include data regarding feelings, fears and impressions; also, it could not dismiss the communication factor of such sensations, whether they were transmitted or not; and finally because it deals with an area of social relations. The concept appears to be divided into 'objective' (supposedly existing and real) and 'subjective' (perceived as existing by citizens, whether real or not).

The 1980s were a confusing period with regard to police forces as the principal agents guaranteeing security. The administrations entrusted by the Spanish Constitution to carry out these tasks (that is, the state, autonomous communities and municipalities) were independent of each other and developed different policing models, which in many instances provoked inevitable clashes.

As a result, it could be argued that during the 1980s there was a certain immobility of state administration, which stubbornly pursued the centralist model. At the same time, autonomic police forces were restored in the Basque country, Navarre and Catalonia. These police forces, which were directly dependent on autonomous governments, began a process of deployment over their respective territories. At the same time there was a resurgence of the 'local' police. So far, these forces had merely played an auxiliary role but in the new environment (and always dependent on the mayors), they began a process of renewed development. This process was partly due to the will of the new democratic town-hall meetings, which wanted a police force close to their citizens.

Neither the effort to co-ordinate these three levels nor the timid attempts at state decentralisation were sufficient. This was mainly due to the lack of development of Articles 104 and 126 of the constitution and their corresponding laws. In fact, the incomplete and pre-Constitutional Police Act 55/1978 of 4 December was applied for several years. This law was promulgated a few days earlier than the constitution, probably in order to avoid dealing with constitutional issues such as the development of autonomous police forces and unions within the police. It took eight years to bring into force Organic Law 2/1986 of 13 March on "Security Forces". This law, which remains in force, implied a considerable move forward by its mere existence. Yet it was also the loss of an excellent opportunity to establish a flexible and diverse model of policing (Recasens, A., 1986). Many points of distrust, gaps and non-fulfilment that can still be detected in the law, such as the definition of the different functions among the police forces, the role of the judicial police, the organs of co-ordination, and so on, should be urgently reformed.

Enmeshed in its own restructuring process and its search for an identity, during the 1980s the Spanish judiciary was characterised by its inability to modify its own fundamental regulations. As a result, there was a need for widespread reform of laws such as the Criminal Code, the Prosecution Criminal Act and the Organic Law of the Judicial Power. The latter, enacted in 1985, introduced several reforms dealing with the judicial police, even though one year later the Organic Law of Security Forces restrictively modified this regulation. This step raised serious doubts as to the coherent and harmonious development of Article 126 of the constitution. Despite the valuable task carried out by the president of the Constitutional Court, Francisco Tomas y Valiente, the work of the courts did not contribute to rationalising the situation.[115] Hence, it could be argued that the problems and evolution of the security of the citizen during the 1990s were to a great extent the product of what had occurred in the previous decade.

The 1990s certainly had a stabilising effect. Although not the best solution, the balance of interests relating to the range of issues mentioned above tended to remain stable through the will and effort of citizens, the contribution of administrations and simply because of the unavoidable and obstinate forces of reality. New elements, new phenomena and sensitivities that highly affected the field of security needed to be taken into account. In post-Franco Spain, the development of a complex society generated a sentiment of permanent evolution, change and transformation that has strongly marked the field of security and its study. This new trend has shifted towards a more precise interpretation of the objective data and the search for methodological instruments needed to understand fully the extent of criminality and its social perception. On the other hand, a new phenomenon has been identified which is related to urban violence. The link between Spain and the European Union on matters of security has also been able to provide a new perspective on this problematic issue.

To summarise, the evolution of the police over the last decades has tended towards a federalist model in three regions, while decentralisation of police forces has been maintained in the rest of the territory. The great challenge to security during this Spanish transition has been the modernisation of the police and the intention to establish bridges between the police and other social elements. Everything has been carried out within the framework of protecting the security of citizens.

Today, the police model is well defined. Furthermore, security policies have been more clearly defined from the point of view of their foundations, concreteness and final evaluation. Nonetheless, despite a change in generation, both the police and the Spanish security system still feel the effects of an inconclusive state model in terms of its political and territorial definition.

The police and transition in central and east European countries (CEEC)

The European Union does not comprise the whole of Europe, and other European countries are undergoing a political economic and social transition that generates its own particular difficulties with regard to police and the enforcement of the law.[116]

Up to a point, the recurring elements emerging in western Europe are the result of worldwide interaction and globalisation. Thus they can be generalised, as they also affect central and east European countries. However, they do not lend themselves to identical interpretation nor are their solutions and experiences directly transferable. In central and east European countries (CEECs) the social and economic situation, as well as the chosen means of transition, have generated problems that require structural and statutory reorganisation of their police forces and the control of criminality to a degree previously unknown. The thorough reform of the concept of law and order, the breakdown – even greater than in western European countries – of the state model and new forms of old problems, such as organised crime, corruption and so on,[117] require specific solutions. There is no evidence that the formulae adopted by western countries could or should be applicable to CEECs.

This situation begs questions on European police co-operation that can only be effective when recognising the differences in their full dimensions and complexity. The entry of the CEECs into the European Union, although carried out step by step, will not be problem-free in the field of police co-ordination and integration.

The common ground of all European states is, beyond doubt, the Council of Europe. Together with the European Parliament it is an ideal forum for investigating common issues, providing elements for reflection, training and meetings capable of setting the foundations for greater future co-operation among Europe's police forces. Some parameters must be established within this framework so as to allow police forces to join other agencies and projects in a future Europe. However, so far no agencies or controls capable of setting pan-European guidelines have been created. Moreover, the role of an international judiciary system has not yet been decided. The goodwill of states and international law tribunals is not yet sufficient to fill the gaps in this area. To this we must add the need to develop clear and specific policies regarding the role and limits of private security forces. As a whole, too much is still undefined to assure citizens' safety and law and order in Europe.

Policing spaces

The policing macro-space

Throughout the last decade there have been important changes in areas of policing, whilst at the same time, an important dichotomy has developed. It could be defined as 'tension between macro- and micro-areas'.

The macro level is closely linked to the aforementioned powerful issues, which have appeared over the last few years, together with their international evolution. Although police co-operation in Europe can be traced back to the end of the nineteenth century, the history of police structure as we know it today is much more recent.[118] As mentioned above, between the 1970s and mid-1980s a great number of police co-operating groups emerged, but they were highly unstable. They had no statutes and did not sign international treaties or agreements. What remains of them lacks transparency and only a number of names and acronyms remain, if anything at all. These groups, whose components were not all police forces, contributed to the creation of an important network of personal relationships based on a limited number of policemen and specialists.

The beginning of a convergence towards more solid police structures came about in December 1975 in an EEC meeting of Council of Ministers of the Interior in Rome. Its main purpose was to exchange information on the evolution of terrorism in member countries. The outcome was a Ministers' agreement to hold such meetings regularly. Thus the Trevi Group was born and for several years remained a simple structure for the exchange of information. The signing of the Single European Act in 1986 gave the Trevi Group new responsibility. The reluctance of some governments and police forces, when faced with the prospect of free circulation of citizens and the elimination of border controls (contemplated in the Single Act), gave way to the so-called 'free-circulation-compensating measures'.

The Trevi Group's responsibilities were increased between 1986 and 1990. They were provided with stronger structures, they intensified their meeting frequency and formed a framework document to regulate their activities – the Trevi Action Programme. Moreover, they extended their limits beyond the EEC member countries, co-operating with countries such as Austria, Canada, the United States, Morocco, Norway, Sweden and Switzerland, and at the same time forging links with other organisations such as the Federal Bureau of Investigation (FBI).

Trevi symbolised a great qualitative change in police co-operation in Europe. Its ministerial status and its powerful structure (despite an evident lack of statutory backing and its status as a non-institutional group of officials) made it a more powerful force than anything that had existed until then in Europe. Despite all this, it never became a specific police operation framework. Its mission was to produce strategies and common objectives for member countries and it became an experiment for the policing area laid out later in the Treaty on European Union. For this very reason, it was abolished when the treaty came into force.

Overlapping Trevi, another policing area was set up in Europe. On 14 June 1985 five states (France, Germany, Belgium, the Netherlands and Luxembourg) signed the Schengen Agreement on gradually reducing controls of common borders. These signing countries expressed their will to go further in police co-operation, moving at a faster pace than the other member countries in the Trevi framework. The initial agreement covered 33 items that were of greatest concern to the signing states: abolishing custom controls, only visual monitoring of tourists, producing a list of countries whose citizens should bear a visa when entering the Schengen area, and the problems arising from drug trafficking and organised crime.

The agreement was opened for entry to other countries. It was a clear invitation to police co-operation and for police forces to co-operate with justice authorities. Schengen was gradually extended to other European countries (Spain, Portugal, Italy, Austria, Sweden, Denmark and Greece). The agreement, as laid down originally, represented a framework that was to be provided with operating elements. This required five years of negotiations, after which the Implementation Treaty of the Schengen Agreement was born. This treaty is a document containing 142 items and offers a set of provisions and measures aimed at co-ordinating and orienting police action within the Schengen area.

The last few years have brought about changes that have affected the development of the Schengen Agreement. On the one hand, the unification of Germany and, on the other, the coming into force of the European Union Treaty put Schengen to the test. In the first case, this was because the Schengen area was expanded to include a former east European country and in the second because there was some overlap between the Schengen Treaty and the European Union Treaty.

The main Schengen concerns focused on the free circulation of people and its implications for facilitating the unchecked movements of drug trafficking and other types of crime and delinquency. Nevertheless, in relation to previous structures, the qualitative step taken with the Schengen Agreement is considerable, particularly in the fight against money laundering and organised crime. Although these are not new ideas, at least they are seen in a new light and are given a greater relevance. However, the lack of judiciary definition of organised crime has been the object of criticism.[119] A main technical innovation was the setting up of an information network comprising all member countries. This is known as the Schengen Information System (SIS) and provides information exchange to facilitate the search for wanted people, objects, cars, asylum requests, identification papers, inadmissible foreign subjects, expulsions, extraditions, missing persons and so on.

The main objections to Schengen have come from the European Parliament, particularly from the Committee on Public Freedoms and Interior Affairs. They point out the democratic shortcomings and the lack of international judiciary control (since it is a non-community intergovernmental regulation) as well as a lack of police cohesion and legal aid for affected subjects.[120]

In short, Schengen is a relevant step towards the construction of a policing area in Europe. It is not only the first area with full judiciary legitimacy (international agreement) but it is also the first to allow police operations, thus generating a very powerful information system. However, it must be stressed that it suffers from the aforementioned deficiencies.

A further step in the development of a European policing area took place in February 1992 with the signing of the Treaty on European Union, known as the Maastricht Treaty. Its basic structure has three pillars – the first includes matters under the jurisdiction of community laws and institutions as such; the second, which is not part of community laws, is common foreign and security policy (CFSP), while the third one deals with co-operation in law and interior affairs. The last one is the least subject to community discipline.

Thus the European policing space laid down in the TEU attempts to make progress in co-operation, yielding as little state sovereignty as possible. The main co-operation points are: political asylum; crossing external borders (as marked by the TEU); third-country nationals and immigration policies; the war against drug abuse and that against international tax evasion; judicial co-operation on penal and civil matters; customs and police co-operation in preventing and fighting terrorism; unlawful drugs traffic and other serious international crimes, including certain areas of customs co-operation related to organising an information exchange network within the European Union under the European Police Office (Europol).

This policing area makes the most of the Trevi legacy, since it was Trevi that prepared most of the third TEU pillar, and disappeared shortly after the TEU was implemented. That replacement was a giant step forward because for the first time police and judiciary co-operation was gathered in a formal well-documented agreement and included all European Union members. This accelerated communication process within the European policing area must be considered a positive one on the condition that it take place in a clearly-operative democratic frame and is subject to controls.

Item K.1:9 of the TEU envisages a European police office with the fundamental mission of fighting terrorism, drug trafficking and other international crime, as well as customs co-operation (unspecified) in the organisation of an information exchange network.

Nevertheless, the project was born even before the TEU itself. In a meeting held in Luxembourg on 28 and 29 June 1991, the Council of Europe, in response to a proposal from Germany and with considerable reluctance from the United Kingdom, undertook the "commitment" within the Treaty framework to create and fully develop a European Central Office for crime police (Europol) with responsibilities in the areas mentioned above, setting a deadline of 31 December 1993.

The Trevi Group had been at work since August 1991. With a specific working group, called Trevi IV or the *Ad hoc* Working Group on Europol (AHWGE), they were also responsible for designing a specific unit, the European Drug Unit (EDU), whose working guidelines were laid down by a Ministers' agreement in June 1992.

The EDU came about because the European Union member states, always cautious, opted for an exploratory approach before launching Europol. This was reflected in the development of a central core formed by EDU (formally established in April 1993 in Strasbourg). The initial purpose was information exchange and analysis of drug traffic, money laundering in the European Union and criminal networks involved in those crimes. But from its very beginning the EDU went beyond its drug-trafficking duties, and demonstrated an expanding strength within a structure that had the will to become the core of Europol. The Essen Summit enlarged the Unit's role to areas such as clandestine immigration, illegal car trafficking, threats to security and money laundering related to the latter.

Since February 1994, all EU member states have at least one liaison officer working in the EDU. These links are backed by the departments of each state to work on drug-related issues. The EDU operates at three levels: the 'macro level', where several agreements have already been signed on the exchange of information; the 'middle level' developed from co-operation among liaison officers; and the 'micro level' with various specific duties.[121]

Europol's objectives are conditioned by those set by the EDU, although there are other main lines, such as terrorism, which are included among Europol's objectives in response to strong pressure from Spain as of 1993. Finally, the EU Justice and Interior Ministers' meeting held in Paris on 26 January 1995 agreed to include terrorism among the responsibilities of Europol. Other matters included trafficking of nuclear materials, drugs and human organs, and money laundering.

A decisive step in the development of Europol was the Council Act of 26 July 1995, when the EU Council established a real framework, including descriptions of functions, structure, bodies, information and filing systems, data processing, legal status and responsibilities. From that moment on, Europol can be considered a truly operative body.

On 2 October 1997, fifteen European Foreign Affairs Ministers signed the treaty known as the Amsterdam Treaty. This was the long-awaited reform of the Maastricht Treaty. Not all objectives and expectations previously set for that reform have been fulfilled. With regard to the third pillar (Justice and Interior), progress has been observed particularly in decisive areas such as the process of community creation and the integration of Schengen issues into the European Union.

A great deal of co-operation on justice and interior issues (issuing of visas, residence permits, asylum procedures, judiciary and civil co-operation) comes within the Community framework. More relevance is thus given to the Court of Justice of the European Community, and in general to European Union institutions. Without doubt, this implies considerable progress in the construction of a European space, and, therefore, can be considered positive. Shortcomings can be found, once more, in the policing area.

Once again, criminal justice and police co-operation are kept at the intergovernmental level (including Europol). Nevertheless, advancing in European policing-area matters is not enough without parallel development of justice and common legislation. The outcome of the Amsterdam Treaty confirms once more the impotence and mistrust, or lack of willingness, of the member states to provide a true policing space. Certainly, this is not an issue to be developed in a hurry or in isolation, but a snail's pace is not favourable either for a European Union in which a properly-framed policing space emerges as a necessity of the first order.

Integrating the Schengen space into the EU framework must be seen as the continuation of a harmonising process of the European policing space. It means going one step further in creating the variable mechanisms and in the tentative attitude that, in this and other matters, is a constant feature of EU behaviour. In its time, Trevi was subsumed into Maastricht, and it is now the Schengen space that is taking over the higher areas of the EU. At the same time, it is worth pointing out that this 'reinforced co-operation system' has not always worked among the subscribing states. Is this dissent going to be passed over to the newly created space? Despite all this, the existence of a policing area within another area is coming to an end. This has been encouraged by Schengen and Europol and should be construed as positive. Again, the reluctance shown by certain states (United Kingdom, Denmark, Ireland) is impeding full harmonisation.

Some time will be needed before we can see whether the positive and negative aspects of the Schengen experience are passed on to the European Union.

The policing micro-space

As stated above, the division of policing spaces is moving away more and more from the nation-state and is creating tension between supra-state macro-spaces and infra-state micro-spaces.

Police intervention in micro-spaces, nowadays known as proximity policing or neighbourhood policing, is not new and includes the zero-tolerance policing mode. During the eighteenth and nineteenth centuries various modes of 'proximity policing' emerged, coinciding, to a greater or lesser degree, with their respective state patterns.

Already in 1749, M. Guillaute, an officer of the Maréchaussée de l'Ille de France proposed to the king the creation of a 'kind of officer' who would control twenty families and all their movements, wealth and relations, filling up a file that had to be sent to their superiors, and had to include items such as name, age, origin of the subject, trade, exact address, earnings, belongings, and so on. The professional callousness of this full report precedes Orwell by two centuries, but a good part of its directives is nowadays unquestionably implemented.[122]

In England, Robert Peel became the architect of the 'New Police', in London from 1829 and covering the whole country from 1856, with a clear remit to be preventive and identify closely with citizens.[123]

To a greater or lesser degree, this issue of proximity policing has recurred over the last hundred years, but the latest upsurge can be placed at the beginning of the 1990s.[124] Briefly, it consists of finding a professional community model based on a shared association relationship (partnership) among citizens, police forces, private security, public services (education, employment, health) and justice (police, courts of law, referees), for prevention and repression, with a view to the solution of problems (problem-solving or problem-orientated policing).[125]

This model has been extended throughout Europe to countries such as France,[126] Italy (Cittá Sicure in Emilia Romagna), or Spain (Barcelona's Project, Plan Policía 2000 de la Dirección General de la Policía).

To sum up, the idea is to have a police force that is close to citizens, capable of sorting out problems related to every-day life and which can provide a feeling of security.

From this standpoint, it should be the duty of the police to search for solutions to problems in the community or neighbourhood. And this search should be in harmony with local citizens' organisations or groups and should create a partnership, negotiating between the various actors of law and order. This micro-integration should favour a decrease in the breakdown of law and order at objective as well as at subjective level, based on principles such as:

- systematic police consultation with the community and their representatives and associations;
- the interactive attitude and behaviour of the police (police-community);
- a considerable part of police energy focused on conflict/problem-solving;
- the main aim being to improve quality of life;
- continuous police presence through neighbourhood patrols;
- police organisation to become more decentralised with a higher level of self-responsibility and independence of police agents;
- mandatory reporting to the community or elected political representatives;
- creating prevention schemes;
- establishing consultative citizens' committees to create schemes.[127]

As long as there is a legal framework to permit it and adequate professional training of policemen responsible for carrying out this kind of work, more advanced proposals could formulate mediating models (always limited) in which the policeman, beyond solving primary conflicts, acts as a referee in solving problems. Such options should be closely linked to a level of justice geared towards swift sorting-out of these type of events which can be classed as minor but which generate upheaval in the life of the community.

This brings us to the new conception of the police role. The main mission of the police ceases to be maintaining law and order, understood as preserving authority as a principle aimed at perpetuating pre-set norms and whose main mission is to force citizens to obey those norms. The change lies in the concept of a police role connected to the objective and subjective idea of law-and-order breakdown. The main mission is to preserve rights and liberties through the exercise of a public service with the aim of protecting citizens' safety for the sake of obtaining a considerable improvement in society and citizens' quality of life.

As a counterpoint to proximity micro-policing, over the last few years the so-called 'zero-tolerance' model has been developed. Without ceasing to be a micro-vision of the police role, it is situated in an area clearly differentiated from community policing (although not necessarily contrary to it).

These theories became well known around the mid-1990s when they were backed by the City of New York, its Mayor Giuliani and his former Commissioner Bratton. During the last decade, this idea has gathered strength in American cities and has enjoyed some prestige in Europe.

The development and implementation of these theories and theses was conceived by two conservative criminologists[128] in an article published in the *Atlantic Monthly* review of March 1982 and disseminated as the broken-window theory, although in view of its limited scope, lack of corroboration and limited scientific content, it should be classed as a hypothesis rather than a theory. In their unoriginal argument, these criminologists propose that "if the first broken window in a building is not repaired, then people who like breaking windows will assume that no one cares about the building and more windows will be broken. Soon the building will have no windows".

Needless to say, this is not a new argument and shows a short-sighted view. The criminologists do not seem concerned with finding the root causes of a problem. They should start by asking why people break windows. Wilson and Kelling conclude that some people like breaking windows, an argument close to the one maintaining that if someone is poor it is because they want to be, and they make no effort whatsoever to improve their situation – an argument that was popular among extreme conservative sectors in the nineteenth century and part of the twentieth. It is, therefore, a question of visualising a problem and its symptoms. This is obviously much more rewarding from the political point of view, precisely because it has immediate effects.

Nevertheless, from the point of view of results, serious doubts have been raised regarding the cause-effect ratio between the implementation of the zero-tolerance formula and a decrease in crime, as the Mayor and police of New York claimed. There is a marked danger of "mistaking a relationship of concomitance in time (...) for an effective correlation, and *a fortiori* a causal-type relationship".[129] In fact, the New York case and its zero-tolerance policing are provided as an example.[130]

The applicability of this theory to Europe is cast into serious doubt by several authors and police chiefs. Thus, the deputy commissioner of the London Metropolitan Police, Brian Hayes, maintains that despite its appearance of being based on common sense, the broken-window hypothesis and the implementation of zero-tolerance methods are not practically applicable in the United Kingdom because neither the resources nor the objectives are the same. Therefore, "it would not be realistic to expect a general and sustained application of operation tactics linked to the zero-tolerance strategy without it having a really strong impact on other lines of action that are very important to us".

Another sad but proven fact is the translation of the zero-tolerance implementation into police brutality.[131] Thus, we have recently seen how New York policemen were charged and condemned for brutal aggression (Volpe's case). They had acted under the protection of this very policing model. In that sense "some police actions perceived as unnecessarily brutal, the use of police powers of appeal, searching and identifying seen as undiscriminating and arbitrary may yield results in the short term, but at the same time they endanger law and order for the future". In other words, and by the same author, "certainly, our men do not play in the same league as the New York police".

In fact, zero-tolerance theories stem from proximity-police theories, but it is a derivation taken to extremes by deforming the basic elements of common sense and subjecting them to a deeply élitist and reactive reading. The positive results have not been factually proven, and their counterweights advise at least keeping these hypotheses under wraps while awaiting future – and unavoidable – eclectic theories attempting to match up the new community police with zero-tolerance actions.

Conclusions

The police response to the challenges raised by the evolution of Europe has been translated into an important effort to meet demand. All European countries have undergone political change, at functional as much as territorial levels. The old – and in my opinion misguided – strongly Manichean proposal that confronted two alleged models (the one repressive, the other preventive) has been losing descriptive value. On the one hand, it was a false relationship, since its terms do not even constitute a model, but mere functions. On the other hand, such distinctions establish the merely descriptive field of a profession and of professionals who act according to either the preventive or repressive model, depending on the time and situation they find themselves in. The fact that police interventions can be mostly preventive or repressive will generally depend on socio-economic and political factors.

In order to meet micro-social needs, police forces have made an effort to adapt their structures and functions to their territory. Thus the last few years have seen a real 'accordion' movement in which some police forces have started to decentralise or de-concentrate (France). Other police forces have tended to concentrate their structures, as is the case in England. Yet other police forces have been transformed, like the Dutch or Belgian police, or have adopted federal structures, as the Spanish police have done.

The task of restructuring police forces in Europe has affected spearhead institutions such as the Council of Europe or the European Union, which, within their scope, have attempted to analyse and restructure the police of the future. A new police space has emerged at macro-social level with a clear supra-state vocation, which is making progress but is not without obstacles. The disparities in European structures and ambits require a homogenising (between the police, the judiciary and penitentiary services) and a converging process.

The hazards of turning citizens' Europe into fortress Europe in the face of a socially more open and politically more democratic process must be a warning to all European states and institutions. Each one must create a fitting framework in which to develop a policing space based on strict observation of human rights, on deontology, and on an operating capacity fitting to the most advanced social and legal democracies.

In this future that we refer to, we cannot forget the imminent incorporation into western European structures of the changing central and east European countries. Probably one of the greatest challenges to police forces on a macro level are, on the one hand, the construction of Europol, with responsibilities and standards of efficiency, and on the other hand, the undistorted incorporation of countries from central and eastern Europe.

At the micro-social level, a response must be provided to the growing demands for a proximity police, whose function in their everyday work should be the preservation of rights and liberties, translated as quality of life. Thus, citizens' participation through associations must be encouraged, as well as the incorporation of municipalities and European regions along with the states in order to establish security policies capable of protecting within their boundaries the objective and subjective security of European citizens and acting as an instrument for free exercise of their rights and liberties.

The future of policing functions is being decided in the new Europe that is being built. Not only the new policing model but also the social co-existence model for European citizens depend on what has been done up to now and what will be done in the immediate future. For this reason, it is absolutely necessary to follow closely the progress of a development that, in a an uncoordinated fashion but with unflagging determination, affects the present and future society of the entire continent.

CHAPTER 6: THE PROSECUTION PROCESS AND THE (CHANGING) ROLE OF THE PROSECUTOR

Alenka Šelih, Faculty of Law, University of Ljubljana, Slovenia

In recent years, the position and the role of the prosecutor have been much discussed and written about in the area of criminal justice.[132] There are many reasons for this increasing interest. With globalisation in general, globalisation of crime control has become indispensable; this has intensified efforts to compare analyses in criminal law. International co-operation in this field has also increased, both in quantity and in quality.[133]

On the surface, these processes have emphasised the differences between Anglo-American and civil-continental views on criminal law and criminal procedure as a whole, and on prosecutorial bodies in particular. In almost all European countries codes of criminal procedures have been changed over the past ten or twenty years; the changes referring to the role and/or position of the prosecution have been the most noticeable.

Delays in criminal proceedings all over Europe have led researchers, professionals working within the judiciary or within the prosecution, and governments to look more closely into the structures of prosecuting bodies as well as other agencies involved in criminal procedure.[134] Efforts to find new, alternative ways of solving the 'conflict' represented by the criminal offence have also led to new roles and new competencies of the prosecutorial bodies.

The enormous political and social changes which shook Europe at the end of the 1980s have provoked enormous activity in the field of criminal justice in order to learn about the criminal-justice systems in the eastern- and central-European countries and to find ways to adapt them to the demands of democratic political systems and the rule of law.

At present, the position and the role of the prosecutor in criminal procedure is being studied in depth and, in many countries, the prosecution office has either already changed or is undergoing change. On the other hand, the outcome of this change and adaptation is not certain or clear. It is, therefore, very appropriate to take a closer look at the problems in this area in order to better define the prosecutor's role and its importance within crime policy today – and that of tomorrow.

The status of the prosecutor

Internal organisation

Organisational hierarchy

Historically, prosecution has always shown a hierarchical structure in continental Europe. It is generally accepted that France was the first country to have such a service, originating in the middle ages.[135] The procureur du roi was a centralised organisation with an individual at its head. This has remained the case until today, although in some instances a collegiate body represents the head of this service (as in Belgium and the Netherlands).[136] It is an exception to have the minister of justice as head of this service (as in Austria, France, Poland, Turkey) and even more so to have no such top hierarchy (as in Italy).

Development in England and Wales followed a different path: prosecution was based upon *actio popularis* and made up part of the everyday life of the police until it developed into the prosecuting service. Although since the last quarter of the nineteenth century the service of the Director of Public Prosecution contained certain elements of a specialised prosecutorial service, it was only in the 1980s that a Crown Prosecution Service was established and has since acted as a prosecuting service.[137]

It has often been said that a hierarchical structure is necessary to carry out the prosecutorial function. Nevertheless, examples of somewhat more horizontal structures (especially in the United States) suggest that a hierarchy is not indispensable but may have other origins, such as a more hierarchical societal structure in Europe in general, especially if viewed historically.

A prosecution office is composed of the prosecutor and his/her deputies (their job titles vary) and the powers of each member of the unit are based upon the law; only exceptionally do these powers originate at the top of the hierarchy or even with the minister of justice.

The hierarchical structure has always been deemed necessary to implement a co-ordinated and, above all, efficient crime policy. This basic organisational principle has of course various consequences on the performance of the service. It is closely connected to the powers vested in the top of the hierarchy. These powers amount to control, co-ordination, instructing, ensuring uniform crime policy and uniform prosecution. The power of control gives the superior prosecutor the right to control the actions of those prosecutors under his/her control. In many countries, provisions of statute laws explicitly provide for such a power. On the other hand, the subordinated prosecutor as a rule enjoys the right to recourse in cases where he/she believes the instructions are against the law.

The head of the hierarchy has as a rule the power to delegate cases to another prosecutor and to revoke or call in a particular case, that is, to deal with it at the highest level. The head also has the power to direct crime policy and to co-ordinate the work of subordinates.

Specialised units

The usual organisational form of the prosecution service follows that of the court system and the levels of the prosecution offices correspond to court levels. The hierarchical principle as described above applies to any unit within the system. Historically, the powers of a prosecutor have referred to prosecuting all criminal offences (at a certain level) without exception. There has been a general power to prosecute. As a rule, exceptions referred to special offences, such as treason. One should also note that a specialised service – that for juvenile delinquency – has existed for a relatively long time. Whether within the general prosecution service or outside it, this service has been the most specialised prosecutorial (and also judicial) service for almost a century.

In the latter part of the twentieth century, however, the complex nature of crime, especially economic and organised crime, contributed to setting up specialised prosecution services.[138] These can be found for different criminal offences, especially those related to the many facets of economic crime – such as business crime and money laundering – to organised crime such as terrorism (France) and trafficking in arms and drugs. In some systems environmental criminal offences are included (Norway). Although information on the issue is scarce, it is fair to conclude that these specialised units are, as a rule, based on statute law provisions, which give details of their powers and responsibilities. When this is not the case, the special units are part of the general structure of the prosecution service.

As a rule these specialised units do not have power to act outside their territorial jurisdiction. In systems in which this is nevertheless possible (Belgium, France, Norway, Poland), such extraterritorial powers refer to specific offences, such as terrorism, money laundering environmental crimes, economic crimes, fraud and war crimes. Unless the legislation provides for clear solutions on the organisational structure of such units, on their competences, powers and accountability, problems may arise. It is extremely important to secure these parameters in the statutory provisions and leave no room whatsoever for a difference of interpretation.

While there is no doubt that prosecution for complex crimes demands specialised expertise on the part of law-enforcement agencies, such units of experts should not be outside the general system of accountability and control.

Relations with the judiciary and the executive power

Relations with the judiciary

There are two dominant patterns. In the first one, the prosecution service forms a professional body in itself and is not considered a part of or dependent on the judiciary. In the second pattern, it is considered a part of the judiciary. The first model is the dominant one. In the first model, a prosecutor usually remains within this service but he/she can also step out of it and pursue a career as a magistrate. In the second model, typical for example in Belgium, France, Italy, Romania and Switzerland, members of the prosecution service form a united body with the magistrates (*corps unique de magistrats*) but enjoy organisational and functional independence from the courts. It has been noted that the unity of the judicial and prosecutorial services is most pronounced in Italy, and France is also tending to go this way.[139] This model can be best explained by historical development since the two services have been closely connected for a long time.

In the eastern and central European countries the two services were conceived as part of the judicial authority in a broader sense. Each of them had their organisational and functional independence, but a marked difference was that the prosecution, especially the *Prokuratura* in the Soviet or Russian type of organisation, had the power of the so-called "general control of legality" over all areas of social life including the judicial (court) system as well as the economy.[140] These special powers resulted in the disproportionately powerful position of the prosecutor.

Relations with the executive

Relations with the executive are of particular importance (and difficulty) as they also contain a political dimension. The relations of the prosecution service with the executive reflect the degree of (in)dependence of the service itself; in principle, the influence of the executive on the prosecution body is smaller in systems where the two are separated and the former has no power over the latter. However, over the years, in those systems where the executive has powers *vis-à-vis* the prosecution service, rules on how and when to use them have also been developed. The systems have a great variety of ways of regulating the relationship. Different solutions can be distinguished: in many countries the prosecution is part of the executive or submits to the ministry of justice; in a second model, it is independent of the executive; the third model is a mixed one, in which the prosecutor is appointed by the executive but is thereafter considered independent.[141] In the case of France, where prosecution depends on the executive, the famous rule of *si la plume est servie, la parole est libre* enables the prosecutors to be fully independent in particular proceedings.[142]

In principle and as a rule, the prosecutor is bound by the constitution and by statute laws; in some countries, the minister of justice has the power to give instructions and has the power of supervision. It is, nevertheless, generally accepted that prosecutors are neither representatives of the government, nor unilateral defenders of the government's point of view. The prosecutor is also bound to ensure that the defendant is treated fairly.

The independence of the prosecution is of such paramount importance because there exists almost no other legal recourse in cases in which a prosecutor's decision (especially not to prosecute) can be controlled.[143]

The problem of (in)dependence of the prosecution office has special weight in eastern and central European countries where, in the past, this service was *de facto* dependent on the executive (dominated by the party) and could be used for political ends. It is therefore important for these countries to reform the prosecution service to serve a democratic system and the rule of law.

Appointment procedures

Appointment procedures show the functional (in)dependence of the prosecutor and are therefore very important. Different ways of making appointments have existed, which have common traits. As a rule, appointment of the prosecutor general (supreme state prosecutor) differs from the way other prosecutors are appointed. The prosecutor general – the post also bearing political weight – is often appointed by supreme state authorities. The systems differ as to which authority this is – it may be the parliament (as in Hungary, Poland, Slovenia), the head of state (as in Austria, Finland, France, Norway), the government (as in the Czech Republic, Spain) or the minister of justice (as in Denmark). While it is perhaps too early to speculate, one cannot but note that the eastern and central European countries seem to rely on the parliament for these appointments and try to avoid the influence of the government in charge. Another generalisation that can be made is that in almost all systems the proposals for nominations are made by a collegiate body composed of prosecutors themselves and sometimes enlarged with professionals from other legal fields.

Prosecutors of the lower ranks are appointed either by the supreme state prosecutor, by the government (or minister of justice) or by the boards of prosecutors (or mixed boards) – as a rule upon the proposal or recommendation of a professional collegiate body. Nominations for prosecutors are formed in three ways: by competition, by professional collegiate committees or by the government. In practice, the terms of appointment are another important feature, one which determines the position and status of the prosecutor. The prosecutor general is very often appointed for a fixed term (the term differs from five to seven years). The subordinated prosecutors are either appointed for an undetermined period of time, which is the dominant method, or are appointed for a fixed term (as in Turkey, England, Wales and Northern Ireland, and in certain cantons of Switzerland). In systems in which prosecutors are appointed for a fixed period of time they can be re-appointed an unlimited number of times.

Appointments for a fixed period of time bear the inherent threat of instability and insecurity of the prosecutor. Although in this respect the legal culture, democratic tradition and an appropriate system of checks and balances play an important role, I believe that appointments for an undetermined period of time provide a better warranty for an independent and impartial prosecutor.

The initial qualification and in-service training of prosecutors

The initial qualification required is a degree in law. Prior to any appointment, in-service training within different judicial bodies (courts, prosecutor's offices, bar) and sometimes services closely working with them (police) is required. As a rule a special professional exam is required.

In-service training is an ongoing activity carried out regularly every year. Several countries have specialised "magistrates' schools" which organise and implement such training. The eastern and central European countries that are members of the Council of Europe have been beneficiaries of different programmes in the legal field organised by the Council of Europe, such as Demosthenes and Themis.

Disciplinary matters

Disciplinary matters are as a rule dealt with within the prosecutor's service. In most systems, the prosecutor general disposes of disciplinary powers. The second method of dealing with disciplinary matters within the service is to entrust them to the prosecutor's line superior. When these matters are dealt with outside the prosecution service, it is usually the minister of justice or the judicial committee (or equivalent body where it exists) who deals with them. Some systems require the consultation of the judicial committee.

The role of the prosecutor

The role of public prosecutor can be seen from various angles and contains a variety of problems. We shall restrict the discussion to four main points: some of the underlying principles governing the role of the public prosecutor; some of the dilemmas connected with the role of the public prosecutor as a state authority and/or a party in the proceedings; the relationship between the public prosecutor and the accused under the perspective of 'equality of arms', and, finally, we shall touch upon developments in eastern and central European countries with a special look at the Russian *prokuratura* as an institution apart.

Principles underlying the role of the public prosecutor

With the development of the services of the public prosecutor, some basic principles have been developed and although their list may differ, there is a consensus about the fundamental ones. The first is that of independence (which has been mentioned in a different context under the topic of appointment procedures). The core role of the public prosecutor is prosecuting criminal offences and bringing indictments before the courts. To do so, the prosecutor must enjoy such a degree of independence that he/she may act in implementing the law without any interference or constraint and in a way that other parties could consent to. The independence of the prosecutor's role must be understood within the principle of the separation of powers – it should secure the prosecutor independence from the government in deciding about prosecution. Several international documents, notably those of the United Nations and the Council of Europe emphasise this principle; the draft recommendation of the Council of Europe on the role of the public prosecution in the criminal-justice system is the most recent of these.[144]

Another principle governing the public prosecutor's functions, and which became prominent in the second half of the twentieth century, is that of respect for human rights. Dealing almost exclusively with problems where human rights are at stake – whether those of the offender or those of the victim – the prosecutor must orientate the work so as to respect these rights whenever and wherever his/her work touches upon them. It is around the concept of human rights that the Council of Europe and especially its European Court of Human Rights have built up a new outlook on man, state and society in which respect for human rights is the fundamental element.

The prosecutor as a party in the proceedings or as a (state) authority

Within a historical perspective, the role of the prosecution office in continental Europe has been closely connected with its authority as a state body, since it was the state that organised it and conferred upon it the right and the obligation to prosecute criminal offences. It was the gradual development of democratic political systems and ensuing reforms within the judiciary that, over time, caused this office to be restructured in such a way as to exercise – above all but not solely – those functions which pertain to a party in criminal proceedings. Its functions, which centred around the judicial process, had achieved a relatively high level of independence, reflected in the ways of appointing prosecutors, in the right to discretion in instituting criminal procedures, and in the indeterminate terms of the prosecutors' position, among others. It is a recent development in western European countries that prosecution offices are regaining certain functions (especially in administrative, customs and environmental matters), which may give them back some of the prerogatives they once enjoyed.

Apart from the continental systems, the United Kingdom developed its own system of prosecuting authorities; there are, however, differences in the organisation of the prosecution services. In England and Wales (and some areas of Northern Ireland), the police developed into a body entrusted with prosecution of criminal offences and a specialised prosecution service (Crown Prosecution Service) was introduced as late as 1986. Scotland, however, follows the continental pattern.[145]

The 'equality of arms'

The role of prosecutor as a party in the proceedings is closely connected with the demand that both parties, the accuser (prosecutor) and the accused, have equal position and equal rights. These are the basis for a fair trial, an achievement of the adversarial system, which has been considered the cornerstone of criminal procedure in a democratic state system based on the rule of law. All fundamental United Nations and Council of Europe international law instruments point to the importance of a fair trial as a prerequisite to ensuring all other human rights standards in criminal proceedings. Legal norms of the European Convention on Human Rights have also been elaborated in the case law of the European Court of Human Rights. The 'equality of arms' refers, on the side of the prosecutor, to the fact that the prosecution cannot have any other rights than are enjoyed by the accused; the latter has the right to a defence, which should – among other measures – ensure equality.[146]

Special problems faced by eastern and central European countries

The institution of the public prosecutor, the *Prokuratura,* in the Russian (and Soviet) system has had a different beginning and development than in continental Europe, or England and Wales. According to new information, the *Prokuratura* was at the beginning (during the reign of Peter the Great) conceived as a state body of universal supervisory power.[147] It was shaped by the specific needs of Russian society. Whatever the reasons and causes for its structures and powers in a non-democratic state, over time it evolved into an institution with a general and all-encompassing right to exercise control in any field of social life, including the judicial system.

The concept of *Prokuratura* had been taken over – to a lesser or greater degree – by all countries in eastern and central Europe. It was, therefore, a very demanding and sensitive task to restructure the prosecution service in these countries into a prosecutorial service that could correspond to the prosecution service of a democratic state ruled by law according to all criteria. The Council of Europe invested much energy, knowledge and funding to prepare the professionals and legislators in these countries to find new solutions adequate to their domestic situations. Restructuring and reform continue to be an ongoing process.

When contemplating the role of the public prosecution service, one can observe that there exists a certain *rapprochement* between the systems that developed in different ways.[148] While the eastern and central European countries are trying to remodel their prosecution service, especially in accordance with the provisions of the European Convention on Human Rights, the continental system has taken over some of the solutions and achievements of the common-law system, especially achievements originating in the adversarial concept which provide better equality of arms; on the other hand, the common-law system seems to have come closer to a statutory prosecuting service with the Crown Prosecution Service, and modifying the *actio popularis* principle which has prevailed for so long in the English legal tradition.

The functions of the public prosecution in criminal proceedings

It is obvious that the primary function of the prosecution is to prosecute criminal offences – to accept *notitia criminis* (report) and to prosecute offences, to monitor proceedings and to appeal criminal judgments. Historically, these functions have shifted – some have been omitted, others have been added, but the essential point has remained – it is the public prosecution service that is responsible for criminal prosecution. This task has been implemented within the framework of different, slowly emerging principles on the one hand and, on the other, in a constant interplay with other participants in the criminal proceedings. These include, above all, the police and the courts. The following analysis will deal with the most important of these questions.

Underlying principles of the proceedings

The prosecutor can act upon two different principles after the prosecution office has received a report on a criminal offence. The legality principle, which is dominant in continental systems of criminal procedure, binds the prosecutor to prosecute the offence if there is sufficient proof for the commitment of the offence and if the offence is being prosecuted *ex officio*. Hence, the principle does not refer to those offences in which the victim has the right to prosecute. The opposite principle is that of opportunity (discretionary principle) which is also known in some continental systems of criminal proceedings (such as in Belgium, Denmark, France, Netherlands, Norway, Sweden). It gives the prosecution office the right to dismiss a case.[149]

Some systems provide the public prosecution with discretionary powers, but only for certain (usually minor) offences. This discretion is based on criteria which take into account factors such as the public interest, the seriousness of the offence, and reasons not to prosecute. The first of the two principles (legality) may sometimes be inflexible, especially in the case of minor offences; the disadvantage of the second (opportunity) is, however, that it may lead to disparities in prosecuting: it may become more important who has not been prosecuted than who has. Today, these two principles have been relaxed by allowing prosecution offices to apply different alternative ways of dealing with criminal offences and offenders. So-called 'diversion' procedures, including mediation, will be dealt with below.

Since the mid-1980s, the Crown Prosecution Service in England and Wales fulfils the role of prosecuting but also has some filtering (diversion) powers.

Relations with the police

The work of the police and the prosecution office is closely connected by its nature: the police detect criminal offences, gathering information on them, recording offences, trying to find perpetrators. It is on the basis of this information that the prosecution can later prosecute a case. A Council of Europe survey shows that many countries reported that there existed no organic links between the police and the prosecution even though working links existed in almost every system.[150] Because of the nature of the work, relations between the two services are often dynamic and not always smooth. Although in some systems the prosecution office may issue instructions to the police in a particular case, the general supervision of police work and its performance is entrusted to the administrative branch (ministry of the interior).

While from a legal point of view the prosecution is entrusted with a crucial role in the preliminary proceedings, in reality the police being more operative and first to react often have greater powers which may lead to tensions between the two services.

Initiating criminal proceedings

Initiating criminal proceedings is one of the most vital functions of the prosecution office. Before doing this, the office usually has the possibility of diverting a case to an alternative procedure.

The prosecutor is the true *dominus litis* of the preliminary investigation, especially in systems with no examining magistrate. The prosecutor's powers in particular systems may range from inspections, personal and house searches, to seizures and even the interception of telephone calls. However, as a rule these measures need either a judicial decree or may only be applied jointly by the two bodies (prosecutorial and judicial). In systems which treat the prosecutors as a judicial body their position *vis-à-vis* these measures gives prosecutors more power than in systems in which the prosecutors do not enjoy such status.

In recent developments in some countries (such as France) special attention is being paid to the demand expressed in the case law of the European Court of Human Rights referring to the right of the accused to be tried in reasonable time. To prepare conditions to better meet this criterion the statute in France provides for a new way of processing, called "direct processing" – in this system the prosecutor decides whether to prosecute or not on the basis of a telephone call from the police. This system has deeply changed the working methods of prosecutors as well as their relationship with the police. According to data, prosecutors' offices dismiss about 70% of all cases brought to their attention.[151]

One of the main aims of preliminary investigation is the collection of proof: the prosecutors must prove the facts and the guilt; this burden of proof is on the side of the prosecutor. In continental law systems, the prosecution is as a rule bound to collect proof also in favour of the defendant, as it is bound by the principle of finding out the truth.

Recent developments have attributed new competences to the prosecution, that of taking care of victims' rights and that of supporting the victim's claims in a more active way than before. These developments clearly reflect the growing importance of the victim's position in the proceedings, which is partly due to the changing views on the criminal offence as 'property' and a 'conflict' as well as to the need to solve it.

Relations with the courts

Here, two different situations should be distinguished: in the preliminary investigation the prosecutor is the decisive authority, therefore, the prosecutor's relations with the investigating magistrates (where these exist) differ from relations with the trial judges during the trial period.

In the first case, the prosecutor has powers for fact finding and it is the state's demand for prosecution that the prosecution office is implementing. However, there are measures – especially those representing limitations or infractions of personal rights and freedoms – which by law remain in the hands of the magistrate. As a rule the magistrate is entitled to test their legality and not their adequacy.[152] On the other hand, as a rule the magistrate does not have the power to issue instructions or orders to the prosecutor – the investigating magistrate is regarded as a constitutionally designated assistant in the preliminary investigation. While the magistrate's powers may differ according to the seriousness of the criminal offence, he/she is as a rule obliged to act on the initiative of the prosecutor, who is at the same time bound by the principle of truth-finding in many (continental) systems.

In continental legal systems, the powers of the prosecutor as a state authority were in the past strongest in the preliminary investigation. Reforms in the 1980s and 1990s referred especially to this role of the prosecutor and changed it to be more consistent with the principle of equality of arms, which is most pronounced during the main hearing where *dominus litis* is clearly the trial judge (or the equivalent). Besides other rights that the prosecuting authority enjoys as a party, the prosecutor can propose sanctions in specific proceedings and, sometimes, the level of their severity.

The prosecutor's office and crime policy

The importance of the prosecutor's powers in directing crime policy has been growing over the past twenty years. Two main factors have contributed to this: the increase of cases to be dealt with on the one hand and the growing importance of the victim on the other. Among the different developments, two have been predominant: diversion procedures as a form of 'conflict solving' and as examples of a procedure now called 'restorative justice'; and different forms of 'negotiated justice', as plea bargaining is referred to in Europe.[153] In both procedures, the public prosecutor plays a key role.

The role of the public prosecutor's office in diversion and mediation procedures

The public prosecutor being the deciding authority in preliminary proceedings, it is natural that the prosecutor's office should be entrusted with diverting cases from criminal proceedings. The prosecution's powers in this respect are larger in systems that apply the discretionary principle of proceedings. However, in systems using the principle of legality of prosecution, under certain circumstances the prosecution enjoys considerable powers at present to divert certain types of offences from the criminal procedure. Today, these discretionary powers of the public prosecutor are increasing – one reason being to discharge the judicial system of less important offences and to entrust them to other forms of control. Overburdened judicial systems and the ensuing delays in criminal proceedings form one of most serious problems facing modern judicial systems, which must find ways and means of relieving the pressure on the courts, a problem ever since the 1980s.[154]

Diversion procedures, which entitle the public prosecutor to reach a consensus with the offender in order not to prosecute, as a rule refer to mediation. There exist, however, other forms of diversion, such as a conditional discharge in the German system, the "take no further action" (*classer sans suite*) in the French system and other forms. These forms seem to be of great importance from a practical point of view, as in some systems a substantial number of cases (up to 70%) are dealt with in such a way. The main aim of these procedures is practical (but nevertheless very important) – by discharging the judicial system of less serious cases the system can concentrate on the serious ones. However, one should mention that criticism has been expressed arguing that it is only the judge/magistrate who is entitled to decide *in merito* on the case and not the prosecutor.

The second development affecting the role of the prosecutor has been the concept of 'restorative justice' aimed at finding consensus between the victim and the offender; mediation procedures resulting from this development are another recent innovation which has changed the role of the public prosecutor considerably. This process started in the early 1970s with many contributing factors.[155] An extensive survey of the mediation procedures states that it started with developments of 'informal justice' – programmes such as citizens' dispute centres, small claims courts and the like – and was strengthened by growing scepticism of the use of non-custodial penalties in some cases as well as a general trend towards new types of sentences together with the growing support for victims. This idea emerged in the

United States, and was transplanted to Britain and soon to other western European legal systems.

In contrast to many other new ideas, it was introduced into the majority of these systems not by legal provisions but rather by empirical projects introduced as a rule before an adequate legal basis had been provided. Experiments in introducing mediation projects and schemes seem to be a general pattern followed almost everywhere where mediation has been introduced. It seems especially noteworthy that many of the eastern and central European countries have started introducing mediation in the same way (in the Czech Republic, Poland and Slovenia).

The main idea of mediation is that the prosecutor has the power, during the preliminary investigation or before it, to select cases (according to certain criteria fixed in advance) and entrust them to a special service of 'mediators' who try to find an agreement between the victim and the offender concerning the offence committed. Although there are several problems within mediation procedure as a whole – presumption of innocence of the offender, the offender's freedom of decision to enter the programme, fact-finding of the offence, to name only a few – the mediation procedure seems to be gaining in practice and is strengthening its theoretical framework, since some of its advocates question whether it represents just a technique or rather a full-fledged alternative to existing models.[156]

The public prosecutor's role in plea-bargaining procedures

Plea bargaining has been connected with the American system of criminal justice for a long time. But it seems that the old continent's criminal procedures have recently also been "afflicted by this lingering disease".[157] According to some, elements of this form of case-solving have been accepted in the procedures of continental legal systems for a long time – *Gestandniss* (admission of guilt) by the accused is cited as a *de facto* mitigating circumstance whenever it has occurred.

But the first step towards negotiating with the accused was accepted for the first time in 1988 in Italian procedure with the introduction of *patteggiamento,* which in its final consequence brings the accused a reduced penalty. In the 1990s, other western European legal systems have also at least embarked on analysing and searching for possibilities of similar "negotiations". It is obvious that plea bargaining contradicts the very foundations of criminal procedure as it has been developed in particular legal systems in Europe. In spite of this, practitioners in some countries have accepted its introduction without much hesitation – it has been rather the doctrine that provoked scepticism and criticism in the majority.[158]

The position of these two groups is not surprising, taking into account the fact that negotiating with the accused serves expediency in criminal proceedings. The negotiated justice may increase the (already) existing inequality, decrease the criminal law's predictability, and is in conflict with the principle of guilt as well as that of legality. It may nevertheless happen that an overburdened judicial system might opt for such an alternative. In such a case all precautions should be taken so that certain fundamental rights and principles not be lost, and two of them should be mentioned: the freedom of decision in entering negotiations and the presumption of innocence. Today, the concept of negotiated justice poses more questions than it gives answers. In an effort to introduce it, the legislation should be guided by the demands of the European Convention on Human Rights, especially those of equality and a fair trial, in order to avoid the pitfalls that can befall this concept.

'Europeanisation' of the public prosecutor's function

The second half of the twentieth century witnessed the growth of a body of international legal instruments aimed at harmonising national criminal law systems. Whether they are binding United Nations instruments – such as the International Covenant on Civil Rights and Liberties and the European Convention on Human Rights – or the non-binding legal norms contained in international standards, rules, recommendations and so on, criminal law, once the essence of national sovereignty, is gradually being harmonised and standardised on an international level.

The more the borders between states disappear, the stronger are the demands for eliminating borders in the co-operation of law enforcement agencies, demands for designing common standards for legislation in particular areas and demands for direct and swift co-operation among different criminal-justice systems. International legal norms have a double effect on the national criminal-justice systems: solutions provided for by the conventions must be taken into account by national legislative systems thanks to their binding power; while those contained in non-binding documents persuade with the power of their arguments.

Another increasingly important source of influence for legislation as well as case law in the member states of the Council of Europe has been the case law of the European Court of Human Rights and also the case law of the International Court of Justice of the European Communities. The former especially has strongly influenced recent changes in legislation in western European countries, and even more so in eastern and central Europe.

Both categories of international norms refer, among others, to the status and the position of the public prosecutor. Instruments dealing with human rights inevitably touch upon the prosecutor's position and role, with a tendency to limit them to the powers of a party. While particular decisions of the European Court cannot be dealt with within the framework of this work, it should be noted that some of them have triggered changes in national legislation concerning the public prosecutor's role.

The most recent of these developments touching upon the prosecutor's role has been the special endeavours of the European Union to protect its financial interests. These activities were started in the early 1990s by setting up expert groups studying administrative sanctions for violations of a financial nature and in particular legal systems. These studies finally resulted in the preparation of a common project on the protection of the European Union's financial interests.[159] This project represents the first attempt to introduce supranational norms in the field of criminal law – substantive, procedural and organisational at the same time.

Although the scope of the field to be protected may seem narrow – the financial interests of the Union – the project, besides setting up a list of criminal offences in the field, also provides for some fundamental substantive and procedural principles (for example, *mens rea,* responsibility of the head of a business and of organisations, sanctions to be imposed, principle of European territoriality, principles of proceedings called *contradictoire* – among others, burden of proof, admissible evidence, exclusion of illegally obtained evidence, subsidiarity of national law with regard to the *Corpus iuris,* and so on).

However, the most far-reaching proposal in the whole project is the one referring to the role and status of the public prosecutor: the project proposes the introduction of a European public prosecutor sitting in EU headquarters and having substitutes in each member country. These substitutes are considered European officials and should represent the Union before national justice systems in cases in which its financial interests have been infringed. This was certainly a novelty, which at the outset raised many doubts. It was obvious from the beginning, of course, that its future depended on a political decision. In fact, in August 1999, the first political steps for instituting this new European institution were taken. It will also take much time and energy to make such an institution work.

Conclusion

Although it is difficult to obtain a clear picture in a comparative perspective of changes taking place in the public prosecutor's office, it is worth trying to identify at least some of their common traits. There is a strong tendency to limit the prosecutor's function to that of a party in the proceedings and towards respect of the equality of arms principle. This means *de facto* limiting the prosecutor's powers. Taking into account many other new agencies (such as offices for the prevention of money laundering, for example) dealing especially with organised crime, suggestions might be made for the transfer of these powers to these new agencies. Such a development would be most regrettable and retrograde – in fact it would contradict some very elementary principles of fair trial.

Another new feature, which emerges from analysing the development of the prosecutor's role and position, is that of increasing the prosecutor's powers in the very early stages of criminal proceedings in the form of diversion and mediation procedures. In a way, it is a contradictory development: the prosecutor is given powers of deciding on cases in a definitive way, *in merito,* which has always been the realm of the justice authority. It seems therefore that appropriate checks and balances should be set up to see that the *ratio legis* of statute laws empowering the prosecutor are respected.

These developments seem to prove an interplay and influence between the two previously distinct legal systems – the common law and the continental one. The *rapprochement* of these two systems seems to have been brought about with changes of political structures as well as those of crime. The same could be said of ever more important developments on the supranational level where, for the first time in Europe, a 'European' official in crime prosecution has been proposed.

Last but not least, in the European context the changes brought about with the 'fall of the Berlin Wall' (to put it in a symbolic way) have influenced both groups of legal systems, those starting to change their political, economic and legal structure, but also those building a European community of democratic countries. Both groups are now faced with the great challenge of together building a modern, efficient and well-organised prosecution office based upon the demands of a democratic legal system and respect for human rights. It is a heavy task considering the fact that human rights and the liberties of individuals are at stake.

Chapter 7: Sentencing

Andrew Ashworth, All Souls College, Oxford

In view of the diversity of legal traditions and socio-political orientations among the various countries of Europe, one might not expect to find great convergence in sentencing policies. On some matters, such as the use of imprisonment as a sentence, there are different trends in different groups of countries (see also Chapter 9 on Prisons in Europe) – and the countries that appear to be pursuing similar policies have no close connection with one another. There is also divergence in the use of parole and early release from prison, which has been expanded in some countries and restricted in others.

There are also some discernible trends: this is not surprising where there has been explicit European co-operation (such as in dealing with terrorism, drugs, and money laundering), but it is also evident in the tendency to divert more offenders from the formal sentencing process, to deal less severely with theft, and to develop non-punitive responses to youth crime. Considering sentencing policy more widely, many countries have adopted and expanded the use of community service orders and suspended sentences (see Chapter 8 on Community Sanctions and Measures).

This survey is not only descriptive but also evaluative: it will consider possible explanations for the various trends, and it will also assess them in the light of the Council of Europe's Recommendation No. R (92) 17 on sentencing.

Trends in sentencing policy

Probably the most common trend in sentencing policy[160] is the introduction of sentencing procedures to ensure the forfeiture or confiscation of assets or of proceeds of drug trafficking and other serious crimes. The origins of this are to be found in the United Nations Convention against Illicit Traffic in Narcotic Drugs and Psychotropic Substances of 1988, which called for the comprehensive criminalisation of money laundering and the expansion of confiscation and mutual assistance arrangements as part of a global strategy against the drugs trade. Although some countries had introduced such laws before the UN convention, most countries either introduced or extended the availability of such measures in the 1990s, further encouraged by the Council of Europe Convention on Laundering, Search, Seizure and Confiscation of the Proceeds of Crime (1990), the European Community directive on money laundering (1991), the Schengen treaties and the Maastricht Treaty.[161] Thus new legislation has been introduced in Germany, the Netherlands, Austria and Spain; in other states, such as the United Kingdom, the law has been tightened.

Questions of principle are raised by the distinction between criminal and civil sanctions, as well as on the relationship between criminal sentences and other measures that are intended to amount to confiscation, deprivation, reparation or restoration. Similar questions arise from the relationship between criminal sentences and civil disqualifications or other civil measures.[162] These questions have a particular relevance to commercial crime and corporate offending (see Council of Europe Recommendation No. R (88) 18 on Liability of Enterprises for Offences).

Another trend for which there is considerable evidence is the expansion of diversion from prosecution in the 1990s. Some of the new policies may be connected to the increasing attention being given to victim concerns (see Chapter 2 on victim issues and concerns), whereas others may have their origins in attempts to re-socialise the offender (or, at least, not to 'de-socialise' the offender by subjecting him or her to the formal criminal process, unless the case is a serious one); still others may reflect the economic savings to be made from non-prosecution in times of fiscal constraints in many countries.[163]

Thus the Netherlands continued to use prosecutors' transactions widely in the 1990s, with the result that the great increase in reported crimes resulted in only a small increase in the number of cases sentenced by the courts.[164] Similarly in England and Wales the procedure of cautioning offenders was used increasingly in the 1990s, while the numbers sentenced in the courts fell significantly – a fall that cannot be attributed entirely to the slight fall in the level of recorded crime in the later 1990s.[165] In Germany a law of 1993 increased the powers of prosecutors to discontinue cases where the offender's guilt did not necessitate a penalty, a development that was in direct response to the economic pressures on the criminal-justice system following reunification.[166] The new power is in addition to Section 153a of the Code of Criminal Procedure, which since 1975 has permitted the diversion of offenders on payment of a sum of money. A similar development took place in Slovenia, with the enactment of the new Law on Criminal Procedure in 1994. This provided (in Articles 162-163) that the state prosecutor may under special circumstances discontinue the prosecution of a minor offence, in which the penalty would be less than one year's imprisonment; this procedure is being used increasingly. In Greece the draft of a new Code of Criminal Procedure (1996) made provision for prosecutors to discontinue certain types of case if the offender admits guilt and pays an administrative sanction: such diversion already takes place informally, but there is no legal framework.

In the context of diversion, the growth of victim-offender mediation as a response to crime should also be mentioned. For many years there were some small mediation schemes in several member states, and it is apparent that these initiatives increased during the 1990s. For example, in Finland there are voluntary mediation schemes in the three largest cities, and the number of offenders participating in mediation is only a little smaller than the number sent to prison in any one year. Mediation remains outside the criminal-justice system, but in practice its results are taken into account in decisions on non-prosecution.[167] In Belgium the number of offenders participating in mediation has risen to around one-half of the numbers sentenced to imprisonment, and the number of mediations in 1997 rose over 20% on the 1996 figure, although there appear to be different perceptions of mediation between French-speaking and Dutch-speaking citizens.[168] In Norway the position has been formalised by a law on conflict resolution commissions in 1991.

New legislation in Germany requires a court to take account, when sentencing, of any compensation and of victim/offender reconciliation. In Austria, too, there have been experiments with victim/offender mediation. In the United Kingdom the new English law on juvenile justice, introduced by the Crime and Disorder Act 1998, is designed to include elements of 'restorative justice'. These developments, discussed more fully in Chapter 2 above, have an effect on the flow of cases into the sentencing system, and raise various questions about fairness between offenders committing similar offences. Many of the innovations can be viewed as part of a trend towards restorative justice that has its modern roots in the writings of Hulsman[169] Braithwaite[170] and others. But it is important to recognise that a form of community justice was also practised in several of the central and eastern European states that were formerly in the communist bloc, and that in some forms this was non-restorative and tended towards severity.[171]

Diversion is one possible response to offences by persons of any age. However, diversion from the criminal courts remains the foremost policy in dealing with young offenders in almost all European countries. In most countries there is no possibility of a young offender appearing in a criminal court until the age of 14, although there are some well-known exceptions to this (such as Ireland, where the minimum age is 7, and England and Wales, where it is 10),[172] and there are some states in which it is possible to prosecute children under 14 for grave offences (such as the Czech Republic and Slovakia, where there is a lower age limit of 12 for certain serious offences).[173]

However, where a young offender is convicted in a court, there are manifest differences among countries in their willingness to use the sanction of imprisonment. A small survey of central and eastern European states by Šelih (1996) showed that the Czech Republic and Hungary used imprisonment for juveniles at the relatively high rate of 12% to 13% of those convicted in court, whereas Poland's rate was 2% and Slovenia used custody hardly at all. However, all these statistics must be viewed in the light of the legal and political heritage of those states: some of them started from a relatively punitive baseline, and what could be observed in the 1990s was a trend towards greater emphasis on the re-socialisation of young offenders and the introduction of a greater range of educational and community-based measures for juveniles. Another part of the context in states such as Poland and Russia was the considerable rise in recorded crime by juveniles, particularly in the early 1990s.[174]

In western Europe, the direction of movement is less clear because the baselines are often different. Thus in England and Wales around 85% of offenders aged 10 to 14 are cautioned and not prosecuted; but in the 14 to 18 age-group only around 55% are cautioned and, of those convicted in court, the proportion sentenced to custody increased from 9% to 14% in the 1990s. The latter figure, like the others mentioned earlier, must be considered in the light of the widespread diversion of young offenders from court. But in the late 1990s there were more young offenders receiving custodial sentences in England and Wales than there were in the early 1990s, which marks a contrast with states such as France, Belgium, the Netherlands and Germany.[175] The United Kingdom parliament introduced new measures, in the Crime and Disorder Act 1998, which regulate more tightly the diversion of young offenders from court and which provide for more severe penalties in court.

Turning to the general sentencing system for all ages, one change that appears to have taken place during the 1990s in many western European states, whether deliberately or otherwise, was an increasingly lenient response to theft. In France the proportion of convicted prisoners serving sentences for theft continued its steep decline, from 37% in 1985 to 16% in 1998.[176] A similar but less spectacular decline is evident in Finland, where the percentage use of custody for theft went down from 44% in 1980 to 36% in 1991 and over the same period the average length of sentences declined from 3.4 months to 2 months.[177] Further reductions took place in the mid-1990s, so that by 1997 the vast majority of persons convicted of theft were fined or given a suspended sentence. The maximum sentence for theft in Slovenia was reduced from 5 to 3 years in 1994.

In England and Wales the Criminal Justice Act of 1991 reduced the maximum sentence for theft from 10 to 7 years, but this signal to the courts was not followed by a reduction in the use of custody: between 1992 and 1997 the proportionate use of immediate prison for theft and handling stolen goods rose from 7% to 14%, an increase that probably reflected the growing emphasis on recidivism in English sentencing practice as part of the general hardening of English penal policy. To this extent England and Wales may be out of line with many other countries, where theft appears to have been re-evaluated as a less serious offence. For example, in Switzerland average custodial sentences for theft were over 16% shorter in 1992 compared with 1984.[178] In Norway a law of 1990 introduced fines as an alternative to imprisonment for property offences. However, the above remarks relate only to western European states, and it seems that in several central and eastern European states the punishment for theft is more severe, with a relatively high proportionate use of imprisonment for theft offences.

The transition between these mostly lenient sentencing practices and more repressive sentencing policies is provided by sentencing for drug offences. Despite the "war against drugs", it remains true that many countries regard the possession of a small amount of a soft drug as requiring nothing more than a small penalty. The effective decriminalisation of soft drugs for personal use in the Netherlands is well known, if not always well understood; less well known is the Polish law that regards the possession of drugs as lawful, thereby effectively preventing the police from intercepting consignments within Poland.[179] Belgium has new alternative measures for drug offenders, such as mediation and community service orders. In the United Kingdom the sentence for possessing a soft drug for personal use would usually be a fine and not a prison sentence. Several states have introduced treatment orders for drug abusers, including England and Wales, and Denmark.[180]

However, all these approaches change when the person to be sentenced has been convicted of supplying drugs to others, importing drugs, or otherwise trafficking in drugs.[181] The United Nations and Council of Europe conventions noted earlier form part of a global movement towards harsher sentences for drug traffickers. Perhaps the clearest example of the effect of this global movement may be found in the Netherlands, a state which until the late 1980s had one of the lowest incarceration rates in Europe. But prison capacity more than doubled during the 1990s, and one factor was the enormous increase in the number of drug offences, although the average length of sentence for drug crimes fell slightly between 1985 and 1995.[182]

The general European trend has been towards more severe sanctions.[183] In Belgium, research at the Brussels court revealed that the number of drug offenders had risen by some 350% between 1986 and 1996.[184] One phenomenon reported in many countries is that the prison population contained a higher proportion of offenders with long sentences in the 1990s than in the 1980s, and the more severe sentencing of drug offenders has been offered as the main reason for this both in France (in relation to sentences longer than five years)[185] and in Germany.[186] Even in Switzerland, where the overall stability of the prison population masks changes in its composition, the largest increases (comparing 1991-92 with 1984-85) were in drug trafficking generally (up 38%) and serious forms of drug trafficking (up 65%[187]). In Italy there have been increases in the statutory penalties for drug trafficking, and the new criminal code in France introduced similar increases.

Concerns about drug trafficking have been high on the agenda of western European states that have offered 'expert advice' to the new central and eastern European countries and it is recognised that some of the growth of organised crime in these states derives from the drug trade. Nonetheless, at least one of those countries (Poland) has declined to ratify the European Convention on money laundering, largely because a prohibition would have adverse effects on the economy,[188] although various measures have been taken in Poland to combat organised crime.[189]

There is also evidence that sentences for sexual offences became more severe in some states during the 1990s. The average length of sentence served by sex offenders doubled in the Netherlands between 1985 and 1995,[190] putting them higher than drug offences in terms of average sentence. A similar trend is evident in France, where the number of rape convictions increased by some 50% between 1984 and 1992, and the proportion of prison sentences for rape that were for 10 years or longer doubled from 17% to 35%.[191] The result is that offenders serving sentences for rape or other sexual offences constituted 18.3% of the prison population in metropolitan France in 1995, compared with only 7.9% in 1985.

In England and Wales the pattern is less clear: average sentence lengths for sexual offences increased from 34.5 months in 1987 to 39.7 months in 1997, but the number of convictions declined slightly. In Belgium there were at least six new laws and royal decrees on sexual crimes between 1989 and 1995, most of them prescribing higher penalties and legislation on sex offences, and new laws in Sweden introduced higher penalties.[192] In some countries, such as Norway, particular attention has been focused on sexual offences against children.[193] Even in the relatively stable sentencing system of Switzerland, average sentences for rape increased in length by some 24% between 1989 and 1992.[194] Increased sentence levels for crimes of violence are also reported from some countries: in the Netherlands average sentence lengths increased by some 60% between 1985 and 1995.[195]

Racially motivated crimes have become a growing preoccupation of some sentencing systems. In Spain a law of 1995 extended the provision on aggravation of sentence for racist, discriminatory or anti-Semitic motives to all forms of crime.[196] The Swedish Criminal Code was amended in 1994 so as to provide for aggravation for racial motivation (Chapter 29, section 2.7); new laws against racist propaganda and racial discrimination were enacted in Switzerland;[197] and provisions for the aggravation of racially motivated offences were introduced into the laws of England, Wales and Scotland by the Crime and Disorder Act of 1998. 'Hate crimes' became a particular source of concern in post-reunification Germany, and, because many of the perpetrators were young, this also turned attention towards policies on youth crime.[198]

Difficulties of racial integration in some countries have also manifested themselves in other ways. There is a distinct suggestion, to put it no more strongly, that sentencing practices may operate unfairly against members of certain racial groups. Sentencing statistics from France show that, for the most serious types of offence in 1991, the imprisonment rate for French nationals was 17% but for foreign defendants 44%[199] A detailed study of the sentencing of drug offenders in a Brussels court showed only a slight disparity between white Belgians and Moroccans in terms of average length of prison sentence but a distinct disparity in decisions to implement such sentences immediately (33% for Belgians, 48% for Moroccans) rather than to suspend or use probation.[200] This disparity is explained by reference to the prevalence of certain negative evaluations of the attitude and social ties of Moroccan offenders, which incline judges towards custody and away from re-socialisation.

A sophisticated study of race and sentencing in England and Wales identified significant differences in the sentence levels for white defendants and those from an Afro-Caribbean background, but concluded that 80% of the difference was attributable to the greater seriousness of the offences of which Afro-Caribbean defendants were convicted, 13% to the fact that fewer Afro-Caribbeans pleaded guilty and received the sentence discount for doing so, and only 7% was not explained by objective factors.[201] Such detailed studies have not been carried out in most countries, but there are statistics suggesting that the proportion of aliens among people convicted of serious offences, most especially drug offences, is rather high in many countries.

Perhaps related to 'hate crimes' and to apparently discriminatory sentencing are the various increases in penalties for offences connected with illegal immigration. Thus in Sweden the penalties for trafficking in illegal immigrants were increased in the mid-1990s, as were the penalties attached to the immigration laws in Germany. In turn, German concerns about illegal immigration have led to a more repressive attitude towards immigrants in Poland.[202] Generally speaking, the effects of opening the frontiers between western and eastern European states and of the wars in the Balkan region have led to considerable migration, and correspondingly to various fears among native populations, to which legislators have found it prudent to respond.[203]

What conclusions may be drawn from this brief survey? At the most crude level there is no evidence of a single sentencing movement across Europe in the 1990s. In terms of trends towards more severe or more lenient sentence levels, there is no clear pattern either: some states have increased the use of prison sentences (for example, Sweden, Netherlands, Spain, Portugal, England and Wales, Scotland), whereas others have not pursued more repressive policies (for example, Germany, France, Denmark, Finland, and Czechoslovakia until secession in 1992). Moreover, references to increases and decreases can only be interpreted in the context of the different baselines: for example, while the Netherlands has shown great proportionate increases in its use of custodial sentences, its prison rate remains below that of many other countries.

However, it is possible to identify certain pressures towards severe sentences for some types of crime – for example, European initiatives against drug trafficking and money laundering; the widespread re-evaluation of the seriousness of the crime of rape; the greater reporting of child abuse in recent years, with many more cases coming to court; the growing concern about terrorism in some states; various initiatives, such as by the European Union against racism; and even the move away from the use of the death penalty, urged by Protocol No. 6 to the European Convention on Human Rights, which leads to more long-term prison sentences.[204] These pressures towards severe sentences have been felt in many, perhaps most, countries – either directly, or by giving greater resources to the police which then leads to more arrests and more offenders to be sentenced.[205] Moreover, in some central and eastern European states there have been other pressures in the same direction, arising from the spread of organised crime.[206]

Generally speaking, however, pressures towards severity have not always led to overall changes in sentence severity because of what is called *la politique de dualisation* (bifurcation or twin-track sentencing). Thus in several states there has been a simultaneous pressure towards diversion of certain types of offender – particularly young offenders and those who commit minor thefts. Policies of diversion usually operate at the stage of prosecution, but they sometimes occur in court sentencing and in policies of release from custody. There are many possible reasons for pursuing policies of diversion, ranging from strong beliefs in re-socialisation or restorative justice, through to simple economic judgements about the least controversial method of controlling the costs of criminal justice. Some states have had one or more amnesties, for example, France and Hungary.

The pressure towards diversion is felt in most countries, whereas it appears that the pressures towards severity are felt much more strongly in some countries than in others – perhaps because of legal tradition, social stability, the power and inclinations of the newspaper and television, and the emergence of crime and sentencing as political (rather than merely 'legal') issues.[207] To attribute these pressures towards severity to increasing globalisation might not be persuasive: several European countries appear not to have been affected by these pressures, and certainly Japan – with its long tradition of relatively low use of imprisonment – has remained unaffected.[208]

How do these trends relate to the principles declared by the Council of Europe? Recommendation No. R (92) 17 on consistency of sentencing sets out in Annex A, a number of fundamental principles for sentencing. These principles are necessarily fairly general, but they do raise questions about some of the trends noted above. Thus principles A5 and A6 call upon each country to re-evaluate its sentencing laws from time to time, in order to avoid excessive severity and to have proper regard to the need for humane penal policies, for example, in the use of imprisonment and in the use of diversion and mediation. Although there is evidence that some member states are pursuing policies compatible with these principles, others seem to have opted for greater severity without much regard for the principles. Similarly, principle A8 states that penalties should not impose unnecessary suffering on offenders and should not inhibit their return to civil society: some states clearly give little weight to this principle, notably in their extensive use of life imprisonment and other long prison sentences. Principle A7 promotes non-discrimination in sentencing, as an application of Article 14 of the European Convention on Human Rights, and we have seen that there is a suggestion that in some states this principle is not being pursued with sufficient vigour.

Perhaps the most important point to emerge from this brief comparison is that some European states regard a certain approach to sentencing as natural and unavoidable, whereas other European states – which are not dissimilar in many ways – regard the same approach as unjustifiable and wrong. Legal, social and political explanations for these divergences can be offered, but the key question is whether countries are willing to re-think their approaches according to the principles recommended by the Council of Europe. This may suggest that issues in sentencing should be considered only in terms of consistency, whereas some will warn of the danger (as they see it) that any Europe-wide reconsideration of sentencing is likely to lead to greater severity rather than to any overall lowering of levels of punishment. If that opinion is adopted, what is the proper response – to cease all discussion of sentencing policy, lest the result should be greater repression? Surely the better approach, in terms of European policy, is to emphasise the principles set out in Annex A to Recommendation No. R (92) 17, which give priority (A6) to the progressive reduction of the use of custody in favour of community sentences, and to diversion and even decriminalisation in respect of minor wrongs.

New initiatives in sentencing guidance

One of the purposes of Annex A to Recommendation No. R (92) 17 was to encourage member states to adopt new methods of guidance in order to enhance the consistency of sentencing practices. Recognising the diversity of legal traditions among countries, different forms of guidance were proposed and five possible methods of giving effect to the guidance were set out (paragraphs B3-B4). There is little evidence that member states have adopted any of these suggestions since 1992, except insofar as legislation remains a primary method in most member states for introducing changes to sentencing policy.

Those countries that previously adopted other and different methods have continued to use those methods. Thus in Greece there have been further ministry circulars on sentencing policy which have been sent to judges, and in the Netherlands new prosecutorial guidelines have been created by the Assembly of Prosecutors General – guidelines which bind the prosecutors, and which courts usually adhere to (although they are not bound). However, in many other member states these methods of guidance would not be regarded as appropriate. The same might be said of the guideline judgments used increasingly by the English Court of Appeal: in recent years, for example, the use of judicial discretion in sentencing drug offenders has been restructured in several detailed guideline judgments on the various types of drug, but in many other member states this would not be regarded as an appropriate function of an appellate court.

General principles of sentencing

In some states there have been legislative re-statements of general sentencing principles. A reformulation of the sentencing chapters of the Swedish Criminal Code took place in 1988, based on the principle that the sentence should be proportionate to the penal value of the crime, and including lists of aggravating and mitigating factors and other general principles.[209] English law took a similar course in the Criminal Justice Act of 1991, based on the principle that the sentence should be commensurate with the seriousness of the offence, but the legislative structure has not been applied faithfully in the courts and sentences based on general deterrence are frequently upheld by the Court of Appeal, even though the 1991 Act was intended to exclude such sentences.[210] This contrasts with the position in Finland, where the law also makes proportionality the basic principle and where deterrent sentencing seems to have ceased because the courts recognise, as criminologists have shown, that it has little effect and that other approaches have a greater impact.[211]

The law in England and Wales also contrasts with the situation in Scotland, where there is no equivalent legislation and where "the clash [between the ideologies of welfare and punishment] makes a major contribution to the continuing lack of a coherent philosophy underlying sentencing".[212] In Slovenia the new Criminal Code of 1994 states the principle of just punishment (Article 41), but that principle does not apply to juveniles, in respect of whom the main aims of intervention are education, protection and control (Article 73). Until the 1990s, at least, the tradition in many central and eastern European countries was to rely on sentencing as a form of crime prevention.[213]

Individualisation of sentencing retains a prominent place in several countries, sometimes within limits, sometimes with no limits. The English law of 1991 provides for individualisation when a court has decided on a 'community sentence' and has to choose which one is most suitable for the offender.[214] In the Netherlands, the courts have wide discretion in the choice of sanction: the legislative aims of sentencing are retribution, individual or general deterrence, rehabilitation, protection of society and reparation, and the court may choose which aim it will adopt in each case. This allows considerable individualisation of sentences, taking account of the 'needs' of offenders, but it also leads to inconsistencies of approach by different judges.[215] It was in order to avoid those inconsistencies that the Council of Europe's Recommendation No. R (92) 17 proposed a firmer structure for sentencing principles: that the leading rationale(s) for sentencing should be declared, that if more than one rationale is declared the order of priority should be made clear, and that in all events the system should avoid disproportionality between the seriousness of the offence and the sentence (A1, A2, A3 and A4).

Developments in judicial training and research

Programmes for the training of judges are in place in many countries. In Finland a special programme of seminars for judges was arranged in connection with the 1990 reform of criminal law, and discussions on sentencing were held. The statistics show that the intended changes did occur, most clearly the reduced sentence levels for property offences, but it may be relevant that the courts had already begun to move in that direction before the 1990 law was passed.[216] In England and Wales a special programme of seminars for judges was arranged in connection with the sentencing reforms introduced by the Criminal Justice Act 1991. However, for a variety of reasons, the statistics do not suggest that the 1991 Act was widely successful in changing sentencing practice: indeed, judicial resistance was one factor in the repeal of certain provisions in 1993.[217] In Belgium several judicial seminars have been held, in conjunction with the universities and the correctional agencies, on such matters as community sanctions.

To some extent the question of judicial training is linked to the legal and political context in which judges are selected and hold office: one might expect that young judges intending to make a career in a judicial office (as in most western European countries) would be more likely to accept and follow their training, whereas the process of judicial selection in common-law systems (such as, England and Wales, Scotland, Ireland) relies on the appointment of experienced lawyers who may be more likely to have independent views and considerable self-confidence. Yet in many central and eastern European states the development of a principle of judicial independence has been a struggle: for too long, judges were regarded as functionaries and as state officials rather than as independent and impartial arbiters, but the signs of change are now clear.

There is relatively little evidence of new research into sentencing of a kind that involves observing and interviewing judges. There is, of course, a large amount of criminological research in many countries and some of it consists of detailed statistical studies of sentencing, which are particularly important for assessing practices and trends. But research projects that scrutinise the judicial approach to sentencing remain relatively rare. One example is a small project on the sentencing of drug offenders in the Brussels court,[218] which involved interviews with judges. An English sentencing survey was enhanced by interviews with magistrates about their approach to sentencing non-serious cases, but there were no interviews with judges about the sentencing of serious cases.[219] As long ago as 1974 the Council of Europe report on sentencing stated the importance of detailed research into the motivations and practices of judges in the sentencing process, but there is still considerable resistance to this among the judiciary of most countries.[220]

Perhaps the most striking innovation, relevant also on the question of sentencing guidance, is the development of the Scottish High Court Sentencing Information System (SIS). This incorporates a computerised database of all High Court sentences passed since 1993, subdivided and categorised so that a judge who consults the SIS can specify the key facts of a particular case and will then be informed of sentences passed in materially similar cases by other judges.[221] The SIS was used by half of the judges in the Scottish High Court in 1998, and will soon be extended to all judges. The system is for information only, but it has the potential to supply guidance that may assist in the development of consistent sentencing practices.

Influences on the development of sentencing practice

Where debate exists about changing the sentencing laws in particular states, is reference made to the sentencing laws of other European countries, to Council of Europe standards, or even to wider international reforms? It is fairly clear that experiences in sentencing reform in the United States are not generally regarded as a good example to follow: proposals for numerical sentencing guidelines have not met with enthusiasm in Europe, but the introduction of certain mandatory and minimum sentences into England and Wales by the Crime (Sentences) Act 1997 was modelled on American laws. Recent reforms and reform discussions in Greece and in Slovenia have paid particular attention to German sentencing laws and also to the Council of Europe standards. The Swedish reform of 1988 developed an approach that had been adopted in Finland in 1976; and the English sentencing reform of 1991 had some similarities with the new Swedish framework, although this connection was little discussed in public. Probably the best example of intra-European influences is the development of the community service order, which has spread through several member states within a relatively short period of time (see Chapter 8 on Community Sanctions and Measures).

The main purpose of the Council of Europe's recommendations on consistency in sentencing was structural: although it does contain some recommendations on the substance of sentencing policy, it was also concerned with certainty and consistency in sentencing. It seems that its recommendations on the rationale(s) for sentencing, in states that have considered them seriously, have often foundered on the rocks of legal tradition and (in many jurisdictions) judicial discretion. Such matters of principle seem to be treated as far less important than the war against drugs, money laundering, economic crime and child pornography where the level of government commitment is greater, and where European co-operation is much easier to achieve.

This brings us to a difficulty that has received insufficient attention in these times of political upheaval and growing 'European' identity. On the one hand, the Council of Europe has consistently made declarations, endorsed by the Committee of Ministers, in favour of the lowering of penal severity, reductions in the use of imprisonment, the diversion of minor offenders, etc. On the other hand, there has been increasing concern about forms of wrongdoing which have been either ignored or under-valued in the past – for example, rape, sexual harassment, child abuse, racially motivated crimes, corporate crimes, and so on. These are justifiable concerns and, if they are taken seriously, they are likely to result in the greater use of criminal sanctions, sometimes relatively severe sanctions.

It seems, therefore, that at the beginning of the twenty-first century we find ourselves in a state of transition towards a different ranking of criminal wrongs. The consequence should not necessarily be a greater overall severity, because part of the re-evaluation of criminal wrongs is to reduce the seriousness with which certain other crimes are viewed, notably some offences of theft. Although we have noted that in some states there was a trend towards treating theft less seriously during the 1990s, there remain several states, many of them in central and eastern Europe, in which the proportion of the prison population serving sentences for types of theft other than robbery is 35% or higher. This may, however, be nothing more than a further demonstration of the close connections between criminal-justice systems and social problems, and of the political context of sentencing laws in many, even most, countries. In that context the prospects for greater 'rationality' and 'consistency', in accordance with the Council of Europe's recommendations, may be somewhat impaired.

Chapter 8: Community sanctions and measures in Europe: a promising challenge or a disappointing Utopia?

Anton Van Kalmthout, Tilburg University, the Netherlands

Introduction

Rising crime rates, an overburdened judicial apparatus, overcrowded prisons and changing patterns of criminality – since the 1970s virtually all criminal-justice systems have been preoccupied with the search for efficient but non-custodial responses to crime other than the traditional pecuniary sanctions and non-intervention or non-prosecution policies based on conditional or unconditional discharges. Most of these efforts have been devoted to the search for alternatives to imprisonment (especially short-term), which – despite its laying a heavy financial burden on the state – did not live up to expectations. That is, imprisonment did not act as an effective deterrent to crime or reduce recidivism.[222]

One hundred years after the process of reducing short-term imprisonment was first initiated on a large scale, the issue is again a topic of discussion in political, social and scientific spheres, at both national and international levels.[223] The development and implementation of these non-custodial sanctions and measures has been strongly influenced and stimulated by studies carried out by the European Committee on Crime Problems and by the resolutions prepared by the Committee of Ministers of the Council of Europe.

An important stimulus was the adoption by the Committee of Ministers of Resolution R (76)10, on some alternative penal measures to imprisonment, in 1976. In this resolution, based on the report "Alternative penal measures to imprisonment", member states were asked not only to spare no effort in developing such existing alternatives as probation and fines, but also to study various new alternatives to prison sentences and investigate the advantages of community work and – more especially – the opportunity such work provides. The promising alternatives explicitly mentioned were deferment of sentence, community service and semi-detention.

Some years later, the United Nations made similar recommendations. In 1990 these recommendations were concretised in the UN Standard Minimum Rules for Non-Custodial Measures (Tokyo Rules),[224] followed in 1992 by the European Rules on Community Sanctions and Measures.[225]

Stimulated by these resolutions, almost all European countries reformed their sanctions system, sometimes as part of a comprehensive reform of the penal code (for example in France, Portugal, Switzerland and Spain), and sometimes mostly limited to the sanctions system as such.

General features of the new non-custodial sanctions

In almost all countries, the simple sanction system which can be imposed – with imprisonment, fine and conditional or suspended sentence – of thirty years ago has disappeared. The list of penalties and measures has been expanded with the addition of a series of such non-custodial sanctions as community service, compensation and restitution, victim-offender mediation or community mediation, withdrawal of licences, training courses, cognitive-behaviour-orientated learning and training programmes, treatment programmes (especially for drug and sex offenders), supervision and attendance orders, placement in probation hostels or day centres, intensive supervision or probation orders, curfew orders, house arrest and electronic monitoring, deferment of sentence with supervision, family custody, and many others.

This search for new non-custodial sanctions has had an enormous impact on the pre-trial and post-trial phase. In many countries (for example Austria, Belgium, Germany, the Netherlands) the public prosecution service or examining magistrates – or sometimes even the police – now have sentencing powers that formerly belonged exclusively to the courts. In many countries, conditional waiver or discharge, financial settlement or transaction, compensation, mediation and restitution, conditional pre-trial release, community service and training courses can be applied as part of out-of-court settlements to reduce pressure on overcrowded prisons and the overburdened judicial apparatus.

But the effort to minimise the damaging effects of a prison sentence and reduce the actual period to be spent in prison has also led to a wide variety of sanctions and measures that apply after completion of any sentence. Many are simply modifications of such existing judicial sanctions and measures as semi-liberty, electronic monitoring, semi-detention, conditional release, penitentiary programmes, assignment to the probation service and community service. However, an essential difference is that the decision to apply these sanctions is not taken by the trial judge, but by the prison authorities or a specialised sentencing judge after the trial (Italy, France, Portugal, Spain). These powers can be so extensive that a custodial sanction imposed by a trial judge can be transformed into a non-custodial sanction or measure with a character completely different from the one the trial judge had in mind when passing sentence.

However, this new category of sanctions is only meaningful if the offender is willing to co-operate. Thus, they differ essentially from traditional penalties. Because they require the offender's co-operation, almost all penal codes require his or her consent. Another important aspect is the commitment of society. Community service, social training courses and victim-orientated sanctions need society's involvement; after all, that is why they are called 'community sanctions' or 'community-based sanctions'. According to Recommendation No. R (92) 16, community sanctions and measures (CSMs) are to be understood as "sanctions and measures which maintain the offender in the community and involve some restriction of his/her liberty through the imposition of conditions and/or obligations, and which are implemented by bodies designated in law for that purpose". The term, furthermore, "designates any sanction imposed by a court or a judge, and any measure taken before or instead of a decision on a sanction as well as ways of enforcing a sentence of imprisonment outside a prison establishment".

In this definition, the place and role of the community in the enforcement of community sanctions is unclear, as it focuses only on the non-custodial aspect of the sanction, and not on the involvement of the community. However, the intrinsic value of sanctions must be more than the simple fact that the offender can stay in the community during its enforcement.

The real value and meaning of community-based sanctions or measures must be sought in the fact that they contribute to the reintegration of offenders into society by stimulating and improving offenders' sense of responsibility and their social skills by confronting them with the consequences of their offending behaviour and by asking them to perform resocialising activities. Because community-based sanctions put emphasis on the offender's inclusion in, rather than exclusion from, society, the involvement and commitment of the community – in particular the local community – is indispensable. Community-based sanctions and measures can only be applied within a community-orientated infrastructure geared to the specific requirements of these sanctions.

It goes almost without saying that the implementation of these community sanctions is to a large extent dependent on the existence of an organisation like the probation service. With a certain independence from judicial or governmental organs, this service organises (and also prepares, enforces, supervises and controls) the community-based sanctions in close co-operation with private, semi-public and public organisations or institutions. The reason community sanctions have not gained a firm footing in, for example, Spain (excepting Catalonia) and Portugal must be mainly ascribed to the lack of a well-functioning implementation system.

How successful are attempts to reduce imprisonment rates?

In spite of the fundamental reform of a number of penal codes – and even the introduction of completely new (draft) penal codes – there have been few attempts to depenalise, decriminalise or down-penalise, or to bind judges to strict sentencing criteria and to more stringent requirements regarding the provision of reasons behind their decisions.

The same disappointing result can be observed regarding the many alternative sanctions introduced into most penal codes over the last decades. Although in several reports of the Council of Europe the conclusion has been drawn, with some satisfaction, that since the 1976 resolution on some alternative penal measures to imprisonment over twenty alternatives have been introduced into the different sanctions systems, a closer look at the nature and application of these alternatives reveals a less rosy picture.

A number of these alternatives are not so much replacements for the short prison sentence as an alternative form of implementation of a short prison sentence already imposed. Although periodic detention, semi-detention, semi-liberty, weekend detention, work release and the (partly) suspended sentence represent methods of implementing a custodial sentence in the majority of western European countries, they are not a real alternative to imprisonment, since they only substitute a part of the prison sentence.

Other alternatives to custodial sentences mentioned in the reports of the Council of Europe and in studies by national research centres have been laid down in penal legislation with a view to offering judges greater choice in sentencing; in practice, however, they have been used only on a very limited scale. One such alternative is to restrict or take away rights or licences. The most frequently applied sanction of this kind is the suspension of the driving licence. Other examples of alternatives to unconditional imprisonment, as introduced in France in 1975, are the confiscation of one or more vehicles owned by the accused, a prohibition on the possession of weapons, the withdrawal of a hunting permit and refusal of a new permit, and confiscation of one or more weapons owned by or at the disposal of the accused.

In contrast to many other countries where these types of sanctions can be applied, in France the regulations leave it entirely up to the judge to choose the sanctions. A connection between the nature of the criminal offence and the type of sanction is not necessary. So, for example, a simple theft could be punished by withdrawing the offender's driving licence. If the convicted person does not comply with a prohibition or duty imposed upon him or her, this is considered a new offence punishable by a prison sentence of between two and twenty-four months, irrespective of the seriousness of the original offence.

The French legislature had high expectations of the effects of these new sanctions, that is, they should have made a real contribution towards reducing the number of short-term prisoners. However, research in France and in other countries where similar sanctions have been laid down in the penal code demonstrates that these new sanction modalities are not deemed by judges to be sufficient and practical alternatives to a prison sentence. Furthermore, even where they are imposed, it is questionable to what extent they replace unconditional prison sentences. In almost all countries these types of sanctions are being used not instead of but in addition to the prison sentence and/or a fine. The same can be said of the other alternatives, such as reprimand, deferment of sentence, conditional or absolute discharge and compensation for the victim. Until now the impact of these alternatives on the rate of imprisonment has been only marginal.

Are community service and other new community sanctions a better alternative?

Of the alternatives to custodial sanctions recently developed in a large number of western European countries, only community service seems to be applied on a greater scale. In many countries the penalty of doing hours of unpaid work for the community is third on the list of alternatives to imprisonment (after fines and a suspended sentence or probation), and the number of such community service orders is increasing annually.

This is especially the case in England, France and the Netherlands, where yearly over 39000, 14000 and 16000 community service orders, respectively, are being imposed on adult offenders, either as a principal sanction or as a special condition attached to a suspended sentence. The Czech Republic also reports an increasing application of community service orders since they were introduced in 1996; in 1997, this new sanction was imposed more than 1 300 times.[226] In Switzerland community service is also gaining more and more ground, despite its experimental stage and the limited scope of its application. Although originally only applicable as a substitute for the last part of prison sentences of up to one month (since 1996 up to three months), in 1997 more than 2000 of roughly 9000 prison sentences were commuted to community service.[227] In such other countries as Germany, Italy, Poland, Portugal, Spain and Switzerland, community service functions mainly as an alternative to default detention, weekend detention (Spain) or as an obligation attached to the penalty of liberty limitation (Poland), and hardly as an alternative to the principal prison sentence.

Along with the traditional alternatives – fines, suspended sentence or probation – community service seems to be the only new substitute sanction that has played more than a marginal role in reducing the number of short-term prisoners. In many European countries, 'short-term' means a sentence of between 3 and 6 months; in others, it means a sentence of up to 12 months. In only one country (Greece) does it mean a sentence of up to 3 years.

In theory these short, unconditional prison sentences can be replaced by community service or by other community-based sanctions. This last category includes – besides the conditional or suspended sentence and probation, whose roots go back to the beginning of this century – sanctions that have only recently been developed, such as intermediate treatment, non-residential treatment programmes, social training courses, courses for drunken drivers, compensation and several forms of supervision. This is the case in Portugal, France, Luxembourg, the Netherlands, the Czech Republic, England, Scotland, Ireland, Germany, Norway and Denmark. These community-based sanctions can be imposed under conditions comparable with the imposition of a community service sanction.

The popularity of and belief in the viability of these community sanctions is also demonstrated by the fact that some years ago the United Nations and the Council of Europe published a series of standard minimum rules on non-custodial community sanctions and measures.

Statistics concerning the number of unconditional prison sentences imposed during the last decade, especially in countries where these community sanctions have been applied on a very large scale, show that there has been no major reduction of prison sentences or of the prison population. In fact, the contrary is the case if we take into account the enormous increase of prison capacity in such countries as England, Wales, France and the Netherlands during the last decade.

Limits and shortcomings

Although community sanctions are not necessarily ineffective they still rank low on the list of sanctions imposed. It is important to investigate why, in spite of their (quantitatively) successful application, they have not succeeded in reducing the number of prison sentences to a greater extent.

What are the limits and shortcomings of these alternative sanctions? And what is the impact of these alternatives on prison conditions?

Community sanctions are playing only a marginal role as substitutes for custodial sanctions because their nature and sentencing aims are still very unclear and questionable. Should they be seen primarily as punitive sanctions with a repressive-retributive aim, like imprisonment and fines, or should they be aimed more at the rehabilitation and re-socialisation of the offender, as is the case with parole, suspended sentence and probation? Or should they be considered from a victim-orientated perspective? In most countries, the judiciary and legislature tend to prefer the first option, while probation authorities and community organisations involved in the implementation of these new sanctions put more emphasis on the rehabilitative and victim-orientated aims.

This lack of distinction is illustrated by French legislation where, for example, a sanction such as community service can be imposed as the principal penalty, as a special rehabilitative condition attached to a suspended sentence, as the execution modality, or as a supplementary penalty, which can even be combined with an unconditional prison sentence. In other countries, too, the combination of a community sanction with an unconditional prison sentence is not uncommon, which of course does not favour its application as a real substitute.

A striking example of this conceptual confusion is provided by the Model Law on Juvenile Justice, drawn up by the United Nations Centre for International Crime Prevention.[228] While in many countries community service is classified as an educational sanction, the Model Law classifies it as a punitive sanction. In the Netherlands, social training courses for adults and juveniles are regarded as sanctions that fall between imprisonment and a fine; in such countries as Belgium, Denmark, Germany and Spain they are seen as rehabilitative conditions attached to a suspended sentence or parole.

This lack of clarity in the law, the lack of clear and uniform objectives, and the different rationalities surrounding community sanctions undermine both their credibility and their application. Owing to this incomplete ideological base, in most countries community sanctions are still considered as alternatives, which means that they are subordinated to the real sanction (that is, imprisonment) rather than being a sanction in their own right. Consequently, many judges who could impose this penalty have serious reservations about its punitive character. If the characteristic feature of a penalty is that it inflicts punishment, this aspect has been given very little exposure in legal and political discussions. This is all the more strange in view of the fact that in the legal regulations of many countries community-based sanctions are substitutes for quite long prison terms. This is in spite of

Rule 6 of the European Rules on Community Sanctions and Measures, which states that the nature and duration of CSMs must not only take into account the personal circumstances of the offender but also be "in proportion to the seriousness of the offence".

Given the relatively low maxima for hours of community service and comparable community sanctions – 200 (Finland), 240 (Belgium, Denmark, Ireland, Luxembourg, Sweden, United Kingdom), 300 (Scotland), 360 (Norway, Switzerland), 380 (Portugal), 384 (Spain), 400 (Czech Republic), 480 (Italy, Netherlands, Poland) – it is understandable that the judiciary tends to consider these alternatives only as a special favour to those who commit certain types of non-serious crime (mostly property crimes and traffic offences), which are normally punished with a very short prison sentence, a fine, probation or a suspended sentence. These community sanctions are actually substituted for prison sentences only in roughly 50% to 60% of cases. In other cases, they are used as substitutes for other non-custodial alternatives.

A lack of belief in the punitive character of community sanctions, the perseverance of the traditional orientation towards retribution and deterrence, a lack of adequate education, information and interest in other ways of dealing with offenders amongst prosecutors and judges, combined with the growing tendency towards a more repressive sentencing policy, means that the judiciary accepts less and less the obligation to impose such activities as community work or social training courses for a period of 240 hours – or, in some countries, 360 hours – as a real alternative to prison sentences of more than 1, 2 or 3 months. This can be demonstrated by the fact that:

- in practice few longer prison sentences are actually commuted to these new alternatives and
- more and more community-based sanctions are being combined with other sanctions, such as conditional sentences, fines, probation, electronic tagging and even unconditional sentences.

Another important reason why community sanctions have so far only partly fulfilled their purpose is the lack of a well-equipped financial and organisational infrastructure. In spite of what is said in the European Rules on Community Sanctions and Measures (Rules 38 and 42), implementing authorities in most European countries do not have adequate financial means provided from public funds to create the necessary infrastructure for the implementation of community sanctions. In contrast to Rules 39 and 40, there is an obvious lack of financial funds and trained professional staff. Even when sufficient budgetary means have been provided they are mostly financial means that have been taken away from other activities of probation services rather than additional means. This is the case in almost all European countries. It shows that politicians' belief in the viability of non-custodial sanctions is not very high – at least, not as high as their belief in the viability of the prison system, into which they are willing to pour budgetary allocations measured in hundreds of millions each year in order to expand capacity.

Of course, probation services and social-work units within the criminal-justice system have been extended considerably since the 1960s, mainly due to the development of these community-based sanctions. However, this trend came to an end in the 1990s, a decade during which the general policy was drastically to reduce budgets. As a result, most probation officers and social workers in the criminal-justice system are weighed down by a huge caseload and have to cope with this problem by simplifying the community sanctions procedures. Instead of being 'custom-made' sanctions, community sanctions are increasingly becoming 'ready-to-wear' sanctions that are not adapted to the personal and individual needs, skills and circumstances of the offender – thus neglecting some of the core aims of community sanctions, which are to enhance the offender's skills as much as possible and to develop his or her sense of responsibility to the community in general and his or her victim/s in particular, as laid down in Rules 67, 71 and 30 of the European Rules.

In order to reduce transport and accommodation problems, probation services are giving highest priority to facilities that are close to the offender's home. Because searching for new reception facilities consumes too much time and energy, probation services tend to offer the same organisations where the sanction can be carried out. For reasons of efficiency, there is an increasing tendency to let the sanction be carried out in as short a time as possible.

Although community service and other community sanctions are meant as 'fines on people's time' – they require the offender to perform his or her activities during leisure time – research has shown that in many countries, not only the probation service but also many (especially unemployed) offenders prefer to work during the day and on a full-time basis. However, this jeopardises the original concept of a community sanction being 'a fine on time' devised in order to oblige the offender to perform his or her tasks over a relatively long period of time in a community-orientated environment. As a consequence, the community sanction is losing its formative and reintegrative character, because the way it is carried out does not give the offender the required time to make a real commitment to the community.[229]

An understaffed probation organisation and too high caseloads also have consequences for the supervision of the offender during the performance of the sanction. Several research studies have shown that there is an obvious relationship between the failure rate and the quality and intensity of supervision: the less control and supervision, the higher the drop-out rate.[230] Apart from the lack of sufficient staff and financial resources, many probation officers are still notoriously reluctant to take breach actions because they consider a failure to complete the imposed sanction as a breakdown of the therapeutic relationship or as the consequence of the offender's chaotic lifestyle.[231] In several countries, probation officers still consider the supervision of a penal sanction difficult to bring into line with their professional principles. The different approach by probation officers is partly due to the fact that in many countries, in spite of Rule 24 of the European Rules, strict and uniform rules with respect to breach criteria and procedures are lacking.[232]

Probation officers, public prosecutors and judges do not respond to breaches in a uniform way. Not only is this questionable because of the principle of equality, but it also creates mistrust and resistance on the part of public prosecutors and the judiciary. This is especially the case in countries where a professional relationship between magistrates and social work (probation work) agencies is lacking or does not function well. Because of this lack of mutual co-operation and trust, there is a risk that judges and public prosecutors will lose their confidence in community sanctions. This has also contributed to the disappointing result that in many cases community sanctions no longer function as substitutes for imprisonment, but as substitutes for fines or other non-custodial sanctions.

That community sanctions are only partly successful is also due to the fact that no social inquiry reports are requested, especially with respect to minor crimes. This means that very often the offender, when standing trial, will not have had any contact with a probation officer or counsellor. As a consequence, the chances of receiving an alternative sanction instead of a short prison sentence will be very small. Only in a few countries (the Czech Republic, Denmark, Finland, Sweden, the United Kingdom) must the probation service draw up a pre-sentence report concerning the suitability of the offender for a community sanction, including his or her consent to such a sanction. But even then, this does not mean that the consent is informed and explicit, as is stipulated by Rule 36 of the European Rules. Nor is this the case when consent is sought during trial. In most countries, asking the offender's consent is only a formal ritual maintained in order to preclude the presumed violation of forced or compulsory labour regulations.

Especially in countries where persons can be convicted in their absence, a high percentage of such convictions are of persons who have committed a minor crime. In such cases, a community sanction cannot be imposed because of the absence of the required consent. Only in France is it possible (since 1989) to request the tribunal to commute a prison sentence to an alternative sanction afterwards. In practice, however, this possibility is very seldom used because of the inconsistency and deficiency of the legal regulation and the reluctance of many judges to commute prison sentences.

Counter-productive effects

The second category of limits and shortcomings comprises so-called counter-productive aspects of these community sanctions, in the sense that the mere existence of these community sanctions stimulates and provokes custodial sentences. This can happen in several ways.

Investigating judges (who do not like the 'soft option' of community sanctions) sometimes try to avoid these sanctions by imposing pre-trial detention in cases where this is not necessary, or no longer necessary from the point of view of the investigation. However, these pre-trial decisions, which are intended to be a 'short, sharp shock', mean that a later, non-custodial sentence cannot be passed, because the judge can only impose a custodial sentence of the same length as the time already spent in pre-trial detention. The existence of non-custodial alternatives also stimulates the (ab)use of pre-trial detention for this purpose.

Thus, the concept of community-based sanctions also points to the need to develop strict criteria which will help prevent the (ab)use of pre-trial detention as a form of pre-trial custodial penalty. It also underlines the need not only to develop alternatives in the sentencing phase but also to search for non-custodial alternatives in the pre-trial phase, or at least to use to a larger extent the existing alternatives, such as bail, controlled freedom and house arrest.

The second way that non-custodial alternatives can lead to an increase rather than a decrease in the rate of imprisonment is when, because of non-compliance with the community sanction, the case is brought back to court to be punished with a custodial sentence. The increasing effect is very obvious when the original community sanction is imposed as an alternative not to a prison sentence but to another non-custodial sanction, or when a community sanction is combined with a suspended sentence. This happens in almost 50% of all community sanctions.[233]

Although both the United Nations' and the Council of Europe's Standard Minimum Rules (Rule 86) on non-custodial sanctions explicitly reject the idea that a decision to revoke a community sanction or measure necessarily leads to a decision to impose imprisonment, this is the general policy of the judiciary in most European countries. In spite of the Standard Minimum Rules (Rule 84), countries such as France, Ireland, Luxembourg and Portugal have even laid down in their penal code that non-compliance with the obligations of the community sanction must be considered a form of contempt of court, which can be punished as a separate crime with a prison sentence that can be much higher than the one that could have been imposed for the original crime. A special problem is that, contrary to the standard minimum rules (Rule 13), in many jurisdictions no appeal is possible against a prison sentence imposed after a breach of a community sanction.

In this respect, it is also of paramount importance (in particular as regards the acceptance of CSMs by the judiciary and the public) that there be clear and rational conversion rates between the various penalties incorporated in the system of criminal sanctions.

Intermediate penalties and community-based sanctions on the one hand and financial and custodial sanctions on the other hand must be related to each other and be made comparable on one or several levels. This is one of the weakest points in many jurisdictions. For example, it does not seem very logical that a 12-month sentence that has been commuted to 240 hours of community service should, because of the individual's refusal to comply, be converted to a prison sentence of no more than 120 days; such a legal provision, which allows calculating offenders to gamble, is certainly doomed to failure.

The third way in which community sanctions can have a counter-productive effect is what we call the net-widening or inversive effect of non-custodial sanctions. The popularity of these types of sanction and their broad acceptance by society can seduce politicians and legislators into using them also for crimes which previously resulted in fines, suspended sentences or probation, or for which a conditional or unconditional waiver was the normal procedure. CSMs are welcomed as gap-fillers between such 'soft options' as conditional waiver, fine and suspended sentence on the one hand, and imprisonment on the other hand. This tendency is most obvious at a time when repressive justice and neo-classical ideas are gaining ground.[234] Although both the UN's and the Council of Europe's Standard Minimum Rules (Rule 86) on non-custodial sanctions explicitly reject the idea that a decision to revoke a community sanction or measure necessarily leads to a decision to impose imprisonment, this is in most European countries the general policy of the judiciary. In spite of the Standard Minimum Rules (Rule 84), some countries – e.g. France, Ireland, Luxembourg and Portugal – have even laid down in their penal code that non-compliance with the obligations of the community sanction must be considered a form of contempt of court, which can be punished as a separate crime with a prison sentence that can be much higher than the one that could have been imposed for the original crime. A special problem is that contrary to the standard minimum rules (Rule 13), in many jurisdictions no appeal is possible against a prison sentence imposed after a breach of a community sanction.

Also, in countries where penal mediation is increasingly applied there are clear indications that it is primarily used as a substitute for an unconditional waiver and much less as an alternative to prosecution.[235]

Two other negative effects

When discussing the counter-productive effects of community sanctions, attention must be paid to two other effects that are generally neglected in the literature.

Where community sanctions are used as an alternative to prison sentences, they are in principle only imposed on 'normal, decent' offenders or less serious criminals who lead a more or less stable life. Rule 20 of the European Rules prohibits discrimination in the imposition and implementation of CSMs on grounds of race, colour, ethnic origin, nationality, gender, language, religion, political or other opinion, economic, social or other status, or physical or mental condition. However, this rule seems to be very difficult to comply with, considering that many community sanctions require the offender to live under relatively stable conditions and to be capable of fulfilling the demanding obligations attached to a community sanction.

When we look at the characteristics of offenders sentenced to a community sanction, we must conclude that very important categories of offenders (such as drug addicts, foreigners and homeless persons) are highly under-represented. Also, some types of offences (such as drug crimes, violent crimes, drunken-driving and sexual crimes) are under-represented in many countries, because formal regulations or sentencing practices exclude them from the application of a community sanction. Not infrequently, offenders with a previous criminal conviction are also excluded. This corresponds with the characteristics of the prison population, which is changing dramatically and becoming more and more the refuse dump for certain categories of offenders for which no community projects are available, due partly to lack of financial means and partly to lack of political will.

In this sense the application of non-custodial alternatives not only has very discriminating and stigmatising effects, but also negatively affects the rest of the prison population by implicitly or explicitly excluding these categories of offenders from community sanctions. Thus the remaining prison population is increasingly being seen and treated as a group of dangerous, unmanageable and incorrigible criminals, who have to be locked up in special units or prisons and whose former prison rights are more and more restricted. This changing attitude towards prisoners on the part of society and politicians is partly caused by the fact that as a consequence of the absence of 'small-time' criminals, the effectiveness of imprisonment in terms of recidivism and re-socialisation is becoming weaker and weaker.

There has also been an apparent change in the role and attitude of the social services (such as the probation service): they are neglecting and seem to be giving up on the prison population. For several reasons (lack of financial resources, pressure from politicians and the ministry of justice, burn-out symptoms, increasing desire to achieve higher success rates) these services are giving the highest priority to community-based sanctions and consequently withdrawing from probation work for prisoners and released prisoners.

The recent trend towards extending the scope of alternatives to detention into the post-trial phase, by giving prison or executive authorities the power to fully or partly substitute non-custodial execution modalities for prison sentences, should also be seen from this perspective. The lack of adequate judicial control and fixed criteria means that this can lead to an aleatory and subjective use of discretionary powers. It can also result in "undue manipulations of the sentencing system and render the criminal sanction too flexible, thus nullifying the principle of equality and the rule of law and delaying the general reform of the whole criminal sanctioning system".[236]

Conclusion

If we look at the results achieved with the new types of community sanctions over the last three decades, we cannot draw too optimistic a conclusion. However, this is no reason to use the expression 'nothing works' with respect to these new sanctions. What we can learn from the experiences gained is that community service and other community-based sanctions play only a modest role in reducing custodial sentences, and in so far as they are successful one must also take into account the counter-productive aspects in other areas.

In order to provide community sanctions with a broader perspective and more viability in the long run, it is necessary to take into account not only the positive aspects inherent to them. By being aware of their shortcomings and counter-productive effects, one will be better able to avoid them during the further process of renewing, inventing and implementing existing and new ones. More energy must be invested in evaluation research, especially with respect to the items mentioned in Rule 90 of the European Rules.[237]

Research is particularly needed because the dearth of independent empirical evaluations of community sanctions impairs their viability and credibility, especially now that the call for tougher and more deterring sentencing practice is gaining approval amongst politicians and mass media. However, contrary to what is commonly suggested by politicians, mass media and criminal-justice authorities, there are clear and sufficient indications (derived from opinion surveys) that, generally speaking, society supports the use of CSMs. The majority of the public prefers community service, restitution and intensive treatment or training programmes to imprisonment and other custodial sanctions.[238]

But without reliable evaluation studies, community sanctions will soon lose this support, especially now that the response to crime is increasingly being characterised as 'populist punitiveness'. The same will be the case unless lessons are learnt from the experiences with CSMs and measures are taken to counterbalance their limits, shortcomings and negative side-effects. One encouraging factor is that most of the important obstacles to and problems concerning CSMs are more secondary than primary, as they derive not from the CSMs themselves but from the circumstances that surround them.[239]

Chapter 9: Prisons in Europe

Frieder Dünkel, Ernst-Moritz-Arndt University, Germany and
Sonja Snacken, Free University of Brussels, Belgium

Introduction

Prisons face paradoxical expectations in our society. They are traditionally supposed to protect society through retribution and deterrence, but at the same time they are to reform prisoners into law-abiding citizens. However, experience and research results since the 1960s have described prisons as total institutions, implying a detrimental effect on the personal and social situation of prisoners and their families, thus reducing rather than enhancing their chances to lead law-abiding lives. The dependency of prisoners in traditional, authoritarian prisons is also known to increase the risk of inmates being victimised by other prisoners or staff, becoming institutionalised, unable to cope with freedom and responsibilities upon release, or engaging in deviant prisoners' subcultures, such as resistance or riots to compensate for the loss of their social identity.

International standards, including Council of Europe conventions and resolutions, thus promote the use of imprisonment as a last resort, when other reactions to delinquency are no longer possible, together with better protection of the human rights of prisoners inside prison (European Convention on the Prevention of Torture and Inhuman or Degrading Treatment or Punishment, 1989; case law by the European Court of Human Rights) and an active regime fostering the preparation of the social re-integration of prisoners (European Prison Rules, 1987).

However, imprisonment remains the most important penal sanction in many European countries, and prison populations have soared in some countries since the 1980s. This chapter therefore first looks into the quantitative differences and evolutions in prison populations in Europe, later discussing more qualitative problems and good practices in prison policies.

Prison populations

Evolution

The importance of imprisonment and the use of incarceration vary considerably from country to country, and also between regions or states in federal systems. Among European states, a range from 30 to 679 prisoners per 100 000 of the population was noted in 1998. Certain countries have very low or low prison populations (up to 60) such as Slovenia (40), Croatia (49) or Iceland (37) and the other Scandinavian countries (Finland and Norway with 54 and 57, Sweden with 60); some countries have up to 100 prisoners per 100000 of the population such as most western European countries (Belgium: 81; Netherlands: 85; France: 88; Germany: 96, Austria: 86 and Switzerland: 85); countries with somewhat elevated imprisonment rates between 100 and 150 (Spain: 112; England and Wales: 126; Portugal: 147; Hungary: 142; Slovakia: 138; Poland: 148) and countries with double, treble or more times as many prisoners as in the average of western Europe. This group includes only central and eastern European countries. The Baltic states range between 332 (Estonia) and 389 prisoners (Latvia); the highest prisoners' rates can be seen in the Ukraine (415), Belarus (505) and the Russian Federation (679).

The statistical data collected by the Council of Europe indicate that in the fifteen years up to 1999 prisoners' rates in most western European countries increased. The Netherlands, Portugal, Spain and the United Kingdom especially faced strong increases, as well as Italy since 1992. However, there were important exceptions such as the Scandinavian countries and particularly Finland, which considerably reduced its prison population (see Mechanisms of change below). In central and eastern European countries, following vast political change and widespread amnesties the prisons were nearly empty. However, within short periods of time the prison populations increased again, partly due to the increase of more serious (violent) crimes. On the other hand, some countries succeeded in stabilising their prison population (Bulgaria, Hungary, Moldova, Poland) or even reducing it (Slovenia).[240]

Mechanisms of change

Changing prison populations are often seen as the direct result of changing criminality, especially by politicians and penal practitioners. However, international literature shows this to be an oversimplification. Many illustrations show examples where prison populations increase while crime rates remain stable or even decrease, and vice versa (increasing crime rates with decreasing prison populations). For example, western European and North American crime rates remained more or less stable from the mid-1980s to the late 1990s, and central and eastern European crime rates were stable from 1992-93 to the end of the century. Even studies limiting such a comparison to 'serious' crimes, which are more likely to be punished with imprisonment, or counting clear-up rates by police fail to find a consistent relation with prison populations.[241]

Analysis of the international literature shows that prison populations are not determined by one factor, but are the result of a complex interaction of several mechanisms: external (structural changes in society: demography, economy), internal (criminal justice and policy) and intermediate factors (public opinion, politics, media).[242]

Demographic influences work through the relation between age and criminality: youngsters and young adults are over-represented in both crime statistics and prison populations. The relation between age and criminality is supposed eventually also to influence the prison population in the case of major changes in the age structure of a given society, especially affecting the younger categories.[243] This relation is often used to forecast future prison populations. However, whereas the link between age structure and criminality is generally confirmed, its influence on prison populations is corroborated much less often.[244] Criminal policy plays a key role in strengthening or weakening the effects of demography.

Other factors are migration and ethnic minorities: migration directly affects demography through the officially recorded number of e/immigrants, and indirectly through a different birth/fertility pattern (and hence age structure) with immigrants. Although this aspect has scarcely been studied, we know that in some countries non-European Union immigrants have a higher birth rate (for example, Belgium: 3,72 versus 1,42 for Belgians) and therefore present a different age structure. However, the link between ethnic minorities and criminality is very controversial. Ethnic minorities or foreigners are often over represented in prison populations, but this may also result from selectivity of the criminal-justice system itself. It is important to realise that many western European countries face an increasing group of second- and third-generation 'immigrants', who continue to constitute a socio-economically deprived category of citizens.

As for the relationship between the economic situation and criminality, empirical research finds contradictory results concerning possible links between unemployment and criminality. More consistent results are found concerning increasing income discrepancies and property offences, supposedly following feelings of relative deprivation.[245] Both western and eastern European countries are facing an increasing 'dualisation' of society, in which the display of wealth is combined with increasing income discrepancies. However, other studies demonstrate that deteriorating economic circumstances lead to rising prison populations independent of crime rates.[246]

Hence the importance of attitudes and decisions within criminal-justice systems. Prisons are situated at the far end of criminal-justice systems and are thus influenced by decisions taken and policies developed at the previous stages: legislation, policing, prosecution, and sentencing. Previous chapters of this book outline the latest developments in these areas. Of special importance for the prison populations is without doubt a growing 'bifurcation policy' in many western countries since the 1970s, with more alternative sanctions for petty crimes but more and longer prison sentences for violent, drug-related and sexual offences, resulting from more repressive legislation and sentencing (for example, France, Belgium, Germany, England, the Netherlands). More generally, the introduction of minimum terms of prison sentences that have to be served has also considerably extended the average time to be served in prison ('Truth in sentencing' in the United States, Canada and England and *peines incompressibles* in France).

In many countries, the repression of drug-related offences has led to higher imprisonment rates for foreigners and ethnic minorities, including women and juveniles. Several empirical studies have also found evidence that unemployment and race as an individual characteristic do influence decisions by criminal-justice practitioners to deprive a person of his liberty, both before trial and after sentencing, and even more so when both characteristics are combined. This apparently results from a more negative prognosis on their risks of recidivism.[247]

The emphasis on punishment for sexual offences grew during the 1990s and repression was further fostered by the political and media attention given to the Dutroux scandal in Belgium. The result was more stringent legislation, sentencing and parole policies even outside Belgium (for example in Germany in 1998). This illustrates the importance of intermediate factors such as public opinion and the political climate, both influenced by the media. Similarly the Bulger case in England influenced criminal policy towards juvenile delinquents.

However, it should be noted that there is no such thing as a single 'public opinion', and that its effect on a prison population depends on the interpretation of public demands by politicians and policy-makers and on the latter's view on whether they must follow or influence "public opinion" (consider the example of abolition of the death penalty despite public support in Europe versus the United States). Moreover, empirical research has shown the interaction of public opinion with criminal-justice professionals to be a case of 'multiple ignorance': the public demands harsher sentences, but underestimates the severity of sentencing, professionals assume the public is not in favour of non-custodial sanctions, while international and national surveys show results to the contrary in several countries (such as community service orders). 'Public punitiveness' has proven to be less linked to individual experience of victimisation than to the over-rating of serious violent crime (by media coverage), the socio-economic status and the political views of the respondents and the interview techniques used.[248] An important obligation to inform hence rests on politicians, academics and the media.

Changes in prison populations are thus more connected with changes in penal policies and philosophies than with changes in crime rates. It is interesting to see that no longer are political parties of the right supporting increased penal austerity and 'get-tough' sentencing, but neither are middle-ground, left-leaning parties.[249] The Scandinavian countries are a good example of a conscious 'modelling' of prison populations. Finland especially has succeeded in steadily reducing its prisoner rates through consistent penal law and sentencing reforms (from 190 per 100000 inhabitants in 1950, to 110 in 1977, 55 in 1995 and 54 in 1998).[250]

The Netherlands on the contrary are an impressive example of expansionist policy: formerly the 'liberal' leader of a moderate and 'reductionist' sentencing and prison policy, often presented as a model in contrast to more repressive policies (compared to England, for example),[251] it has now totally lost this 'leadership' position after implementing a vast prison-building programme and doubling its prison capacity. Until the early 1990s, Germany also maintained a moderate penal philosophy, extending the application of alternatives to imprisonment such as suspended sentences, probation, mediation and diversion, especially in the field of juvenile justice (14- to 21-year-old offenders). However, two reform laws of 1998, increasing the minimum penalties for violent and sexual offences and restrictions on parole for these prisoners, resulted in a sharp increase in prisoners rates from the beginning of 1998. As a result, overcrowding – a problem that did not exist in the 1980s – re-emerged.

Prison overcrowding in western European countries is also a problem in Belgium, France, Greece, Italy, Portugal and Spain (1997 data). In most countries of central and eastern Europe, dramatic overcrowding has become one of the major problems of prison systems, especially in Bulgaria (where the prison population is 158% of capacity), Estonia (163%), Romania (140%), Hungary (125%) and the Czech Republic (114%).[252] However, overcrowding in most countries does not concern all prisons. Major and critical overcrowding is often concentrated in pre-trial detention and in closed (maximum security) prisons.

On the other hand those countries that have been able to stabilise their prison populations, such as Austria and the Scandinavian countries, do not face problems of overcrowding today. They are good examples of the fact that the size of prison populations is not fate but the result of criminal policies. A comparison of prison systems therefore must consider penal philosophies and policies as well as the infrastructure conditions of implementation of certain penal policies that determine the size and structure of prison populations. In general we certainly can learn from 'good practices' such as in Austria or the Scandinavian countries as well as from very problematic developments in the Russian Federation and the states of the former Soviet Union.

Although the republics of the former Soviet Union are trying to find new solutions and to develop new penal philosophies they are, like the Russian Federation, still underdeveloped in many aspects of prison organisation and prison living conditions. Community sanctions have only limited acceptance in society and the criminal-justice agencies and lack of infrastructure (the probation service, and so on) impede the extension of effective community sanctions. Furthermore, the abolition of the death penalty has contributed to an increase in the average length of time spent in prison.

Prison policies

Philosophies of execution of prison sentences

The influence of the European Prison Rules in the development of prison reform laws is now important in central and eastern European countries. The basic principles spelt out in the Rules, of respect for human dignity and individual human rights of prisoners, impartiality, preparation for their social reintegration and the need for independent inspection and control over prisons, are generally accepted as the leading moral standards for detention in Europe. However, the official rhetoric and the actual practice may differ, due to economic shortages and political priorities. In the Russian Federation, the Baltic states and other eastern European countries it is even difficult to provide enough food, medical and hygienic facilities, sanitary installations, clothing or bedding.[253] Tuberculosis has become a major problem in both Russian and Latvian prisons.

The creation of the European Committee for the Prevention of Torture and Inhuman or Degrading Treatment or Punishment (CPT) in 1989 proved to be an important instrument in the monitoring and fostering of European standards on prison conditions and prevention of ill-treatment during detention. It recommended a combination of regular, periodical visits and *ad hoc* visits to places of detention, with an emphasis on co-operation but with independence from governments, and the elaboration of a consistent set of standards and recommendations through the publication of general (and national) reports. These have been influential in prison reforms. Unacceptable living conditions and insufficient legal guarantees for prisoners were found in many European countries, in both east and west, and have stimulated the closure of cells or wings, refurbishment programmes, more independent control over prisons and the strengthening of the legal position of prisoners.

For example, prisoners benefit from independent complaint committees in the Netherlands, an ombudsman in Poland and the United Kingdom, judicial control in Germany and France, a parliamentary human rights commissioner in Hungary, a human rights office in Latvia, and so on. However, the very characteristics of prisons as closed and total institutions result in these mechanisms of inspection and control not being naturally effective. A wide variety of elements must be covered, from the prevention of torture or ill-treatment to the daily aspects of prison life, to decisions about disciplinary sanctions or early release. This requires the presence of several, co-existing systems of control and inspection, covering as many areas as possible and relaying each other over time: permanent and periodic; local, national and international; administrative and judicial.[254]

The philosophy of re-integration gains importance again after a period of emphasis on deterrence and humane containment. New empirical evidence in the United States as well as in Europe[255] shows that the 'nothing works' doctrine, upheld during the 1980s, was wrong. German studies in the field of social therapeutic institutions also give indications of moderate treatment effects.[256] The German constitutional court in its decision on prison labour of 1 July 1998 stated that re-integration as a constitutionally guaranteed principle obliges state authorities to provide effective means for rehabilitation. Adequate remuneration for prison work is only one element of such a rehabilitative approach.[257] On the other hand, it has been said that the treatment and training paradigm was a rhetorical doctrine that never squared with the reality of prison life.[258]

The danger that the treatment philosophy will contribute to longer sentences and to a justification of imprisonment is, however, not a necessary consequence of the rehabilitation model. A combination of what in some countries sails under the flag of re-socialisation, in others under harm reduction, normalisation or humane containment, seems to be a solution. The danger of the humane-containment model could be that the aspirations of prison authorities are orientated rather to low standards of prison services than to improving rehabilitative efforts. On the other hand, for example, the principles named under the heading of humane containment[259] fit very well into the principle of re-socialisation according to the German Prison Act and penal law: minimum use of custody (for the minimum length of time consistent with public safety), minimum use of security (in Germany, for example, priority to open prisons)[260] and normalisation.[261]

The growing attention in the 1980s and 1990s given to drug and sexual offences and their prevention showed the limits of a purely retributive policy and re-introduced the idea of providing treatment programmes, either in prison or upon release, but on a voluntary basis in order to avoid abuse and simulations.

Preparation for re-integration requires that prison conditions differ as little as possible from conditions in society. This principle of normalisation should be understood on two levels: on the individual level, in recognising a prisoner as a person with a variety of social identities and not only as a criminal, and on a collective level, in offering collective services which are as similar as possible to those in the outside community. These two forms of normalisation should form the basis of staff contacts with prisoners and daily prison regimes, which should allow prisoners to take up individual and social responsibilities and thus reduce the debilitating and harmful effects of detention. Involvement of community agencies in prisons strengthens this normalisation and facilitates the preparation of prisoners for release.

However, prison reform in both western and central/eastern European countries is under pressure of budget restrictions. Privatisation seems to be one option, but apparently only in some countries (such as the United Kingdom and France). In Germany, reform proposals to introduce economic systems of control and of global budgets are discussed under the general reform of public administration. Privatisation is accepted only for building, not for running, prisons (except certain services providing food or medical treatment, cleaning clothes, and so on). The issue of privatisation must be seen in the broader context of state power and social control. The philosophical debate on whether the entire management of prisons can be handed over to the private sector, including the use of organised force, disciplinary decisions, and so on, is linked to discussions on the (changing) role of the state, and divergences in political and legal cultures between common-law countries, where the state is considered as a mediator, and civil-law countries, where the state fulfils a supreme role.

Major problems and 'good practices'

Penal inflation and prison overcrowding

The penal inflation mentioned above (see under Mechanisms of change) has often led to serious prison overcrowding. The effects of crowding have been described in the literature as affecting individual health, increasing inter-personal violence and leading to more stressful situations and feelings of insecurity for both prisoners and staff.

According to the CPT, overcrowding may sometimes in itself result in inhuman and degrading treatment or punishment. The Council of Europe in Recommendation No. R (99) 22 of September 1999 reflects this situation and recommends measures to counteract overcrowding. However; the combination of overcrowding, lack of sanitation and lack of activities found in many prisons across Europe, western and eastern, was systematically considered to amount to inhuman and degrading treatment. An extreme example is the situation in the Russian Federation: in some prisons twice as many prisoners are housed as beds are available. Prisoners must share beds by sleeping in shifts. The high number of inmates dying of tuberculosis each year (more than 10 000) is also related to such overcrowding.

Solutions have been sought in three major ways: the expansion of prison capacity (for example in the Netherlands), collective pardons, amnesties and early releases ('back-door strategy' in Belgium, France), and reduction of the application and length of detentions ('front-door strategy' in Finland). The expansion of prison capacity, probably the most frequently applied option, may temporarily relieve overcrowding but fails to stem penal inflation and thus inevitably results in more and more prison building and overcrowding. Early release and parole may be important instruments for a successful social re-integration of prisoners, but fail as a means to reduce prison populations when judges compensate for what they feel to be 'abusive' measures through ever longer prison sentences.[262] As shown by the impressive example of Finland, only a combination of 'back-door' and 'front-door' strategy effectively succeeds in regulating prison populations in the long run, but demands a thorough and consistent reductionist policy from legislation to prosecution, sentencing and release, including decriminalisation, lowering of penal scales, non-custodial sanctions and parole.[263]

Prison regimes

The risks of imprisonment are manifold: the risk of escape or riot, the risk of violence or victimisation, the risk of deterioration of the health of prisoners, and the risk of arbitrary or oppressive treatment by staff. The harmful effects of detention affect the prisoner's behaviour not only in prison but also later upon release. It is therefore also in society's interests that prison management should focus primarily on the prevention of such risks, by pursuing an equal priority and balance between four duties: custody (to prevent escapes), order (to ensure order and safety inside the prisons for prisoners and staff), care (to foster the physical and mental well-being of the prisoners) and justice (fair treatment, consistent outcomes, effective grievance procedures, motivation and explanation of decisions by staff).[264]

Attaining this balance is not easy, especially when public or political pressure tends to prioritise custody and order over care and justice, without realising the importance of the latter in attaining the former. This is linked to the exclusive reliance on the passive security of walls, bars and electronic devices, while experience shows that in the 'post-authoritarian' prison, such 'passive security' cannot succeed without the dynamic security of high-quality staff-inmate contacts, relationships and communication. Moreover, custody and order have proven to have often-competing aims, thus presenting prison administrations with permanent dilemmas. For example, the prioritisation of the occasional but high-consequence risk of riot or escape through stringent security measures may reduce the quality of life for prisoners in such a way as to stimulate frustration and opposition and hence bring about exactly the behaviour that prison management sought to suppress.[265]

It is precisely the combination of the four duties in a daily prison regime that contributes to dynamic security: the legitimacy of security measures and their acceptance by prisoners will be reinforced if they are part of a broader and active regime, while contacts between prisoners and staff during activities facilitate better mutual understanding. In such an active regime, prison labour, education and contacts with the outside world are of paramount importance.

Prison labour has a rather ambivalent status in today's prisons. Compulsory for sentenced prisoners but not for remand prisoners, it is apparently part of the punishment of imprisonment. However, it is a generally accepted international standard that deprivation of liberty is the only and sufficient penalty of imprisonment, and should not be made more severe by adding other punishment. Some scholars have thus questioned the compulsory nature of prison labour.[266] On the other hand, shortages of labour in many prisons have turned it more into a privilege than a punishment and it is often the only means of income for prisoners.

In central and eastern European countries, where prison labour was part of the former state economy, the recent economic and political changes have sharply reduced the availability of work for prisoners. In some countries prison labour is seen as a specific application of every citizen's constitutional right to work: prisons should hence provide inmates with useful work and adequate remuneration, thus developing their work experience and assisting their re-integration into society.[267] Some prisons (in Sweden and Germany; in the latter case especially where prisoners are admitted to work release programmes) offer normal wages to prisoners, thus allowing them to take personal responsibility for their families and victims.

Most prison systems do not provide substantial remuneration for prison work. An exception might be the new Austrian legislation of 1993, which provides in principle the same wages that nationally have been bargained between employers and employees. However, 75% of the wages are deducted for accommodation and food, and prisoners keep only 25% of the wages for their personal use. This is still five times more than a German prisoner receives. However, the German Federal Constitutional Court in a recent decision[268] declared the existing practice unconstitutional and ordered the state to introduce a more equitable system of rewards for working prisoners before the end of the year 2000.

The judgment of the German Court is an important precedent, not only for Germany but also for other countries in which it is accepted that the state has a (constitutional) duty to provide sentenced prisoners with the means of leading a crime-free and socially responsible life upon release.[269] According to the German Court, compulsory prison labour is a justifiable exception to a general prohibition on forced labour only when it is used for this purpose. Moreover, the Court is clear that only appropriately rewarded labour can serve to re-socialise, for the prison labourer must experience, like any worker in a free society, the nexus between work and reward.

Some countries make a great effort to adjust prison work to the management methods of modern business administration (for example, Germany, Britain, Austria, Switzerland). In attempting to create prison industries, prison management must deal with serious problems and structural disadvantages. Prison industries are located in isolated places and tend not to attract capital investment. In many instances there are restrictions on their ability to market their products. In addition, the prisoners who make up the workforce often have a poor work record, are poorly educated and are addicted to drugs or alcohol and generally unmotivated to work.[270]

Education and vocational training are also important aspects of prison regimes, taking into account the often low socio-economic status of prisoners, their limited education and lack of (or irregular) professional experience. European Union programmes such as Budgetline for the re-integration of offenders (1993-96) and the European Union Initiative for Employment (1998-99) fostered co-operation between prison administrations and community labour organisations in developing training courses in prison, combined with employment schemes after release, thus improving prisoners' chances of finding work after release.

Opening the prisons through contacts with the outside world has been a major reform aspect since the 1980s in most western European countries and the same tendencies can be found in eastern Europe. It reduces the totalitarian character of the institutions and hence the risks of imprisonment, enhances the possibilities for social re-integration of the offender, and can be performed without undue financial efforts: for example, unsupervised long-term visits by family (spouse, parents, children), unlimited correspondence, access to media and involvement of local communities and agencies.

Indeed, most prisoners eventually return into society. Therefore it is also in the interest of society that this release be actively prepared. A balance must hence be struck between the risks of release and the risks of continued detention. Systematic prison furloughs (parole) are used in many countries both as a form of harm reduction and as preparation for (early) release (for example, Belgium, Germany, the Scandinavian countries, Hungary), and have very low failure rates.[271] Semi-detention is also sometimes used as an intermediate stage between detention and early release, allowing a prisoner to work in the outside community during the daytime.

Early release systems differ widely between countries: from a quasi-automatic release without conditions, unless individual contra-indications prevent its application (for example, after serving two-thirds of the sentence in the Netherlands) to individually granted parole with supervision over several years, based on good behaviour and/or social re-integration, after serving part of the sentence, the range of which differs again between countries and between offenders or prisoners. There is a theoretical minimum of one-third for non-recidivists in Belgium, two-thirds for recidivists; from two-thirds for low-security prisoners to four-fifths for high security prisoners in Hungary;

from two-thirds for sentences of less than two years to half for sentences of more than two years in Sweden; after serving three-quarters in Spain, a third or a half in the Czech Republic, half for first-time offenders serving sentences of up to two years and two-thirds for all other prisoners in Germany. The significance of these variations can however only be evaluated through the application of parole in practice and its relation to the length of sentences pronounced by the judges.

Severe prison overcrowding has pressured some countries into the application of collective forms of early release, such as collective pardons, amnesties or provisional releases without possibilities of after-care (for example, France and Belgium). Although they may temporarily relieve pressure in prisons, they often have negative side-effects such as inequality between and uncertainty for prisoners, loss of legitimacy of the release system with penal practitioners and the public, and more severe sentencing. The lack of preparation for such releases among prisoners and after-care services has also proven to be counter-productive.

Specific categories of prisoners

Juvenile prisoners

All European countries avoid imprisonment of juvenile offenders. Crime policy in this field has been strongly influenced by international recommendations and standard minimum rules (such as the United Nations' so-called Beijing rules or the standard minimum rules for juveniles deprived of their liberty).[272] Recommendation No. R (87) 20 (1987) of the Council of Europe on 'Social reactions to juvenile delinquency' emphasises the use of imprisonment only as a last resort and for the shortest time possible.

In the 1980s and 1990s many countries strengthened their efforts to avoid incarceration of juveniles by extending the scope of community sanctions (mediation, intermediate sanctions, community service and so on, as in Austria, England/Wales, Germany and the Netherlands). This evolution actually can be observed also in central and eastern European countries (Slovenia, Croatia, Czech Republic).[273] On the other hand, from the beginning of the 1990s there was a reverse trend of institutionalisation. The English Criminal Justice Act of 1994 introduced the secure training order for 12- to 14-year-old children. The Crime and Public Order Act of 1998 also expanded the possibilities for more severe reactions ("no more excuses"). Other European countries re-opened previously-closed facilities under the regime of the welfare authorities. In general, however, the juvenile justice systems have kept the policy of imprisonment and institutionalisation as a last resort.

Comparing the number of juveniles in young offender institutions is difficult as countries define the age group of juveniles differently. In most countries this means persons under the age of 18. However, in Austria the age limit is 19, while in Germany all those sentenced for crimes committed before the age of 21 are held in 'juvenile' prisons. Thus in Germany more than 90% of all juvenile prisoners are between the ages of 18 and 25. The minimum age of criminal responsibility varies from 7 years to 16 or 18; however, most countries do not allow imprisonment for juveniles younger than 14 or 15. Those children or juveniles held in residential care institutions of the juvenile welfare authorities are not counted as juvenile prisoners, although the restrictions on liberty and living conditions in the institutions are similar.

According to the prison statistics of the Council of Europe in 1997, the proportion of juveniles in prison in western European countries was only up to 1.5% (with the exception of Greece, Turkey and the United Kingdom), whereas in central and eastern European countries the proportion was between 1% (Hungary) and 5.6% (Romania). The proportion seems to have declined since 1994.[274]

Juvenile prison regimes and living conditions are more moderate and better than those in prisons for adults. Most juvenile prisons emphasise specific school education programmes and vocational training. Many newer prisons provide social therapeutic communities providing treatment or social training courses and include new methods of organising leisure-time activities.[275] The ratio of staff to prisoner is better than in prisons for adults; and social workers, teachers, vocational training staff and psychologists are involved. More repressive regimes such as in the American 'boot camps'[276] are not seen as an adequate method of education. Nowhere in Europe have boot camps been considered (in some countries such as Germany constitutional grounds would not permit the introduction of such programmes).

Although in many respects juvenile prisons seem to be less negative than prisons for adults (one important reason is that they generally have a smaller capacity), in many countries they also share the problems of prison subculture, violence and drugs. In eastern Europe, often old facilities are still used and prison conditions do not meet the minimum standards of humane containment.

Some countries allow the transfer of juvenile prisoners to prisons for adults in exceptional cases. In other cases the strict separation of juveniles from adults cannot always be guaranteed. Both practices deserve criticism as they do not correspond to rehabilitative goals.

Female prisoners

Female prisoners represent only 4% to 6% of the prison population in most European countries. Exceptions are Portugal and Spain where in 1997 9% to 10% of all prisoners were females.[277] This generally small proportion leads to specific problems. Some countries have only one prison for female prisoners, with differences in internal security (Hungary, Czech Republic, Latvia). This may allow for more adequate employment and care services, but often results in the women being detained at great distance from their social relations, thus hampering visits and preparation for their social re-integration.

In other countries, sometimes in addition to the first option, female prisoners are detained in special wings within male prisons, for example, local remand prisons (Belgium, Germany, Switzerland, Sweden, Spain, Austria, Denmark). This places them closer to their social background, but results in more secure circumstances than would otherwise be necessary, with female prisoners often lacking an adequate regime and activities. The best practice seems to be a combination of local prisons with an adequate regime, activities and care.

Mothers with small children are a special problem. The dilemma of whether to raise small children away from their mother or in a prison environment is well known. Many countries have special prison units for mothers with babies or small children, usually up to 2 or 3 years of age. An interesting solution to the dilemma in some countries (Belgium, Denmark) is to bring the children to normal day-care centres in the community during the day, allowing for normal surroundings and contacts outside the prison, while the mother takes care of the child in the evening. This supposes, of course, that the prison location is sufficiently near the community.

A growing awareness that both the absence of, and the normal prison visits to, an imprisoned parent (either mother or father) are traumatic for children and parents alike, has led to the fostering of more, longer and unrestricted or unsupervised visits, which allow the prisoner to take up his/her parent role in a more adequate manner. In some countries, community volunteers or organisations accompany the children to the prison and offer support and guidance to the children and parents who so wish (for example, Relais Parents-Enfants in France, Belgium; children's agencies). In others, a mother can interrupt the execution of her sentence in order to visit her children for up to thirty days a year (Czech Republic).

Foreign prisoners and ethnic minorities

Foreign prisoners constitute an important proportion of prison populations throughout western Europe (58% in Switzerland, 41% in Belgium, 25% to 29% in Germany, France, Sweden and Austria; in a few countries such as Norway or Spain with 14%-15%, and generally in central and eastern European countries, they do not play a specific important role).[278] The concept of foreigner includes, however, very different categories: non-residents detained for trans-border or international crimes, ethnic minorities or second- or third-generation 'immigrants', illegal aliens or asylum seekers detained for administrative reasons. Each category raises specific questions.

Non-residents detained for international crimes such as drug smuggling often come from African or South American countries and are imprisoned in European prisons without having any local ties or relations. They serve relatively long sentences, without possibility of family visits or prison furloughs, and language barriers may cause important communication problems and result in factual isolation. Moreover, their eventual expulsion is sometimes seen as making any efforts at social re-integration superfluous. However, an active regime, with work and education, is equally important in reducing the harmful effects of imprisonment, and should therefore not be withheld from non-resident prisoners, especially when serving longer sentences. In some countries, language courses teaching basics of the national language(s) are offered to foreign prisoners, thus reducing communication problems and social isolation. Facilitating contacts with their diplomatic or consular authorities and fostering visits by volunteers may also help in this respect.

The Convention on the transfer of sentenced persons, which came into force in the Council of Europe in 1985 and has been ratified by most member states, aims to provide opportunities for foreign prisoners to serve their sentences in their home country if they so wish, for the sake of social rehabilitation and humanitarian considerations. Efforts are currently undertaken to broaden the application of this convention, sometimes hampered by differences in legal incriminations or release provisions and lengthy procedures.

Ethnic minorities are often overrepresented in European prisons, especially juveniles and young male adults: Turks in Germany, Moroccans in France, Belgium and the Netherlands, Roma in Hungary, the Czech Republic and Bulgaria, Russians in the Baltic states, blacks in England and Wales, and so on.

In Germany the so-called *Aussiedler* from the Russian Federation and other eastern countries (who legally receive German passports if their ancestors are of German origin) raise serious problems as they sometimes do not succeed in integrating into German society (partly owing to language problems). They are usually legal residents and may even be national citizens, and prison systems often provide opportunities for compliance with religious and dietary obligations (for example, Islam). They still face many problems, often related to broader attitudes towards them in outside society: from conflicts between prisoners or with prison staff arising from religious and cultural differences or social and political antagonisms, to outright racism and discrimination. Training of prison staff in multiculturalism and the presence of prison staff belonging to the same ethnic minority group may help to defuse the escalation of conflicts.

Family visits and language do not often raise problems for ethnic minorities, as these prisoners were usually born or raised in the country. However, many countries allow for expulsion of foreigners to their country of origin after serving their sentence, even of third-generation 'immigrants' who no longer have ties there. In such a case, they will usually also be denied normal prison furloughs for fear of absconding. In these cases the public administration authorities that decide on expulsion overrule the prison authorities which – under the uncertainty of whether the offender will be expelled – put him or her under conditions of a maximum security regime although the prisoner would not otherwise be a security problem. Such expulsions very often result in subsequent illegal entries and new detentions. If all important family and social ties are present in the country of immigration, it seems preferable and more humane to allow for re-integration into their normal social background.

Illegal aliens and asylum seekers may be held in prisons or in prison-like closed 'detention centres' for administrative reasons. Increased mobility throughout Europe, armed conflicts and economic hardships have sharply increased the number of such detainees in most European countries, while at the same time reducing public and political tolerance towards this population. In many countries, the CPT found their situation of detention to be very alarming, by the combination of poor living conditions, lack of activities and contacts, language and communication problems, the indeterminate but often lengthy detentions and the uncertain outcome of asylum or appeal procedures.

The CPT recommends that special attention be paid to providing legal and medical aid, the selection and training of staff, the right to communication through an interpreter when necessary, and providing guarantees against expulsions holding a risk of ill-treatment in the country of origin.[279] The tragic death of illegal aliens during forced expulsion (for example, in Belgium in 1998, in Austria in 1999) confirmed the CPT's concern over the use of violence during such expulsions. In 1998 the CPT was also concerned over Germany's practice of detention of immigration detainees at Frankfurt am Main airport as well as the procedures for enforcement of removal orders.[280]

Remand prisoners

The (disproportionate) use of pre-trial detention is widely criticised in many European countries. Although the European Convention on Human Rights clearly guarantees the presumption of innocence (cf. Article 6 II, which in many countries is a constitutional principle) the living conditions in remand prisons generally are worse than those for sentenced prisoners.[281] The grounds for pre-trial detention vary in the different legislations and practices. For example, in Belgium more than 90% of remand orders are based on the fear that the defendant might commit further offences whereas in Germany 95% are based on the risk that the defendant might not appear at the trial. In some countries pre-trial detention is imposed regularly if a very serious crime has been committed; in Belgium and France disturbing public order may be a ground for pre-trial detention.

As the legal prerequisites are so vague, it often happens that the real grounds for pre-trial detention are not based on the law (grounds such as 'crisis intervention', giving a 'taste of prison', 'short sharp shock', especially to young offenders, or to use pre-trial detention as short-term imprisonment, eventually preparing a probation term). The length of pre-trial remand often determines the later sentencing decision. The risk of being sent to pre-trial detention is especially high for foreigners and ethic minorities. Pre-trial detention under certain circumstances tends to be abused for purposes of immigration or criminal policy.[282] In general the same vulnerable groups can be identified as suffering from extensive use of pre-trial detention as suffer from ordinary detention (foreigners, ethnic minorities, juveniles, drug users, 'difficult' and 'dangerous' detainees, and so on).[283]

Pre-trial detention faces special regime problems: remand prisoners are not obliged to work but prison authorities should offer work if the detainees wish to do so. In reality this is rarely possible because of shortages of working facilities even for sentenced prisoners. Visits and correspondence are under the supervision of the judicial authorities and therefore sometimes more restricted. In some countries it is rather the exception than the rule that remand prisoners receive a relaxation of their regime. Leisure-time activities are also limited, and often pre-trial detainees are kept in their cells for 23 hours a day. Separation from sentenced prisoners cannot always be guaranteed. The situation in central and eastern European countries does not meet the minimum standards relevant to the Council of Europe's basic instruments. Russian remand prisons, for example, are extremely overcrowded and inmates suffer from inhumane conditions for very long periods.

The proportion of pre-trial detainees within the total prison population in western Europe varies from 9% in Finland or 17% in Sweden to 26% in England and Wales, 28% in Spain, up to 36% in Portugal, 41% in France or even 48% in Italy. Similar differences can be found in central and eastern Europe (1994: 19% in Bulgaria and Slovenia in comparison to 39% in Estonia and 47% in the Czech Republic).[284] These figures demonstrate the different patterns and use of pre-trial detention in the context of criminal law and the importance of criminal political attitudes and strategies determining the practice.

Long-term prisoners

Many European countries face increasing prison populations owing to the increasing length of prison sentences, the abolition of the death penalty or restrictions on early release. According to a questionnaire of the Council of Europe this is especially true for Bulgaria, France, Ireland, Portugal, Romania and the United Kingdom.[285] This results in a rising proportion of long-term prisoners in prisons. Long-term prisoners, usually sentenced for serious offences, are not necessarily dangerous inside the prison either for prison staff or fellow prisoners. On the contrary, they are often known to contribute to the stability of a prison, as they are more interested in organising their prison life in as peaceful a way as possible. However, as the above-mentioned deprivations, detrimental effects and coping mechanisms in prison increase with the duration of detention, long-term prisoners should receive special attention from prison management.

Long-term prisoners go through three phases of detention: 'doing your time' or forgetting your past and making prison your whole life, 'making the change' or giving up the psychological mechanisms that protect you in prison in order to prepare for release, and 'hitting the street' or starting a new life in a new world outside. Each phase is distinct and requires difficult adaptation. Prisoners must choose whether or not they will adjust to each phase, and while most prisoners do adjust, some may adapt to one phase and make little effort to move on to the next.[286]

The dilemma facing both prisoners and prison administrations is that measures that may improve 'doing your time' (institutional adjustment) may be counterproductive for 'hitting the street' (adjustment to a changed society). For example, visits by family and friends are often considered by prisoners as their greatest source of support, but also their greatest source of pain. Their powerlessness towards outside events can make such visits stressful and remind them of what they are missing. Some prisoners will end these relationships abruptly and concentrate on relations inside the prison, thus maybe facilitating institutional adjustment but hampering their prospects for release. In fact, several studies found that forms of inmate adaptation that seemed desirable from the point of view of 'control' or institutional adjustment were counter-productive in terms of post-release success:[287]

well-adjusted prisoners and inmates with the highest-status prison jobs (clerk, bookkeeper) had the highest failure rates on leaving the prison, while inmates with a moderate number of disciplinary reports (5-10) were more likely to succeed after release than those with either less than 5 or more than 10 reports.

To reduce the detrimental effects of long-term incarcerations, both during detention and after release, prison regimes should focus on the fulfilment of certain basic needs:[288]

- comfort: access to basic comforts such as food, shelter, medical services and protection from physical harm; access to sensory and cognitive stimulation; response to the need for recognition (status), independence, protection, acceptance by other people;
- control: the fundamental need of human beings to believe that they exercise some form of control over their fate and environment; this can be answered by offering prisoners a number of choices (for example, between activities, possibilities of association) and by encouraging prisoner participation in the organisation of prison life;
- meaning: every human being's existence must have some meaning, which encompasses religious, philosophical or experiential concerns; education and training courses can thus offer long-term goals and motivations which help prisoners retain a sense of worth and self-esteem.

It is argued that if the means to satisfy these basic needs are not provided by the legitimate structure of the institution, then they will be sought elsewhere (such as the prisoner subculture).[289]

Such 'good practices' have also been advocated by the Council of Europe Recommendation No. R (76) 2 on the treatment of long-term prisoners and can be found in certain prisons in Europe, where long-term prisoners are held in closed institutions ensuring a secure perimeter, but offering the inmates an active and liberal regime inside: an open-door regime inside the units (Belgium, Czech Republic), a variety of high-standard prison labour, education and vocational training offered by outside agencies and leading to official degrees (Belgium), forms of prisoners' participation through elected representatives ('prisoners' committees' in some prisons in the Netherlands) or consultation between prisoners and staff within the living-unit (Denmark). Experience in western European prisons shows that there is no need for segregation of life-sentence prisoners from other long-term prisoners, their regime and security requirements being similar (cf. Recommendation No. R (76) 2).

Long prison sentences are imposed for serious crimes and express the censure and retribution of society for past deeds. The execution of prison sentences must however look forward to the future and prepare for the eventual re-integration of the prisoner into society. Taking into account the detrimental effects of such detentions on the inmate, the execution can become counterproductive for both the prisoner and society. Early release and parole are hence important tools in adapting the execution of a prison sentence to changed circumstances, especially for long-term prisoners, and guiding the inmate towards a gradual re-adaptation to freedom (cf. Recommendation No. R (76) 2).

In most countries, life-sentence prisoners are also eligible for parole, with minimum terms to be served, varying from 10 or 14 years in Belgium, 15 years in Germany to 25 years in the Russian Federation and Latvia, where life sentences were only recently introduced. While some lifers will never leave prison, a majority are released after serving an average of 12 years in Sweden, 13 years in Belgium, 14 years in England and Wales. The increasing restrictions on remission or parole for certain categories of offenders, especially violent and sexual offenders, or for long-term or life-sentence prisoners in general, lead to ever longer periods of imprisonment (France, United Kingdom, Austria). This complicates both the social re-integration and the management of long-term prisoners, the possibility of early release being a major reward for good behaviour inside prisons.

Apart from parole, the adjustment from prison life to society upon release is also fostered by providing prisoners with opportunities to connect with the outside world during their incarceration, by way of contacts (visits, correspondence, telephone) with persons and services that are not connected with the correctional services (family and friends, community agencies, volunteer visitors). The building of prisons for long-term prisoners in remote locations, sometimes considered preferable for security reasons, is thus counter-productive in the long run. Some countries also provide possibilities of progression to open prisons or to semi-detention, allowing prisoners to leave the institution by day to work in the outside community (eg Germany, the Netherlands, Portugal, Sweden; Denmark, Belgium), or have developed intermediate resources such as half-way houses or foster homes (Sweden, Czech Republic).

'Dangerous' prisoners

Although much used in penal and prison practice, and even in some legislation, 'dangerousness' is a highly controversial concept, being defined differently in different countries and periods, settings and ideologies. For example, at the end of the nineteenth century the concept of 'dangerous offenders' referred to special categories of delinquents, such as juveniles, vagrants, the mentally ill and habitual property offenders, while at the end of the twentieth century, it is applied mainly to violent and sexual offenders in western countries, while others use it to designate political opponents, economic or environmental delinquents.

The social construction of 'dangerousness' by each different setting, according to criteria relating to its own functioning, is also obvious within the criminal-justice system. Offenders considered 'dangerous' by society and by the courts, because they have committed a serious violent offence, will be sentenced to a long prison term, maybe a life sentence. They will, however, not necessarily be considered 'dangerous' by the prison system, because they do not threaten essential functions of the prison as an institution: to prevent escapes, to guarantee order and discipline, to appear rational, legitimate, effective and efficient to the public. Many scientists therefore refrain from using concepts such as 'dangerous personality', which they consider to be unscientific, and prefer to point to 'dangerous' situations or interactions.[290]

With regard to prisoners, a distinction is – and should – hence be made between a 'dangerous' offender (who has committed a serious crime), an escape-risk prisoner (who presents a security problem) and a difficult prisoner (who presents a control-problem).[291]

'Dangerous' offenders will usually be long-term prisoners. A systematic security 'over-classification' of such prisoners on the basis of their offence may lead to serious problems inside prison (see Major problems and 'good practices' above: 'custody' versus 'order').

The risk of escape by a prisoner is not necessarily linked to the length of sentence, but public outcry is much stronger when a 'serious' offender escapes. Such prisoners are often the object of special and stringent security measures. Different models can be distinguished: concentration in special security units, either with very strict individual isolation or with a more open and liberal regime, individual dispersal with or without systematic transfers (*'carrousel system'*) or segregation from other prisoners. CPT has expressed concern about the application of lengthy individual isolation and frequent transfers in a carrousel system[292] and found some regimes of extreme segregation to have lasting psychological consequences on the inmates and to amount to inhuman and degrading treatment. Special security measures should hence be compensated by an active regime, intensive staff-inmate relations and professional contacts and supervision.

The concept of 'difficult' prisoner again refers to a variety of problems: aggressive behaviour towards staff and/or fellow inmates (for example, towards vulnerable prisoners), recalcitrant prisoners, prisoners with many disciplinary breaches. Research and prison experience, however, show the interaction between such behaviour with the environment. Prisoners who are known to present intractable control problems in one establishment may present little or no problem in another. Concentration of such prisoners in special units has a turbulent history in many countries: units with an open and liberal regime usually got fairly good results but appeared as a premium for bad behaviour, while units with a very strict segregation regime concentrated and enhanced resentment against the system and could result in inhumane treatment.

As only a small number of prisoners present permanent problems, thought to be linked to mental disturbance, an adequate regime and handling by staff at the normal location, a consistent and fair complaint and disciplinary procedure and an occasional transfer when conflicts are escalating can defuse problems with most 'troublesome' prisoners. Vulnerable prisoners, such as sexual offenders, can often remain at the normal location when staff make it quite clear that bullying or aggression will not be accepted, and when prisoners have much to lose by such behaviour. Such problems may however be more difficult to control in large dormitory-systems (such as in central and eastern Europe prisons).

Some mental disturbances can indeed lead to aggressive and unpredictable behaviour, which should be handled with professional treatment. Prisons are often faced with a lack of sufficient psychiatric personnel, so some countries have established special units for aggressive mentally-ill offenders and psychiatric patients in community hospitals.

Drug users

The repressive drug policy in most western European countries has resulted in increased figures of drug addicts and persons sentenced according to drug laws. In western Europe users and addicts of illegal drugs prevail (for example, in France in 1998 about 20% of all inmates), in central and eastern European countries alcohol addicts are the main problem. The (western) policy concerning illegal drugs had a major impact on prison regimes and great emphasis was given to control and security aspects.

However, it seems to be impossible to create drug-free prisons. On the other hand, special units have been established where addicts are undergoing drug therapy of their own volition in so-called drug-free prisons or departments. Prisons certainly are not the best places for drug therapy and therefore much legislation provides alternatives to imprisonment if the inmate is ready to follow special treatment programmes outside prison (Denmark, Germany). However, those prisons offering drug treatment do not seem to have worse results than other extra-mural programmes. Their efficiency is difficult to measure and therefore the results of different programmes are often not comparable. In some countries methadone or other substitute programmes are also running in prisons (sometimes with the aim of systematically reducing the dose such as in the Netherlands),[292] whereas others strongly refuse to do so. In Switzerland and Germany in some prisons the exchange of needles has been allowed by the prison authorities in order to prevent HIV-infection.

The incarceration of drug users, especially of those using only soft drugs, generally cannot be accepted. It has been a major error of drug and crime policy to render criminal such drugs as cannabis. Their impact on prisons is detrimental and a change in dealing with drug users (of both soft and hard drugs) should be favoured. Although it is officially forbidden, the use of cannabis products in some Swiss prisons is more or less tolerated by not imposing disciplinary sanctions (similar tendencies can be observed in Belgium).

The option of concentrating drug users in special units does not seem to be a solution as this cultivates the drug subculture. Dispersing drug users would be a better solution although this would influence the regime, creating many security and control problems for other prisoners.

Prison staff

In many European countries there is a growing emphasis on the importance of prison staff. The quality of staff determines prison climate and relations inside prisons, which have been described above under the heading of dynamic security. Different staff groups have difficult roles because of conflicting expectations and responsibilities. Thus a sufficient number of well-trained and supported (for stress) staff is required.

The Scandinavian countries traditionally have the best staff to prisoner ratio (about 1:1) whereas in other western European countries such as Germany the ratio is about 1:2 up to 1:2,5. The central and eastern European countries, but also France, Greece or Spain, have even worse conditions.[294] Some eastern European countries such as the Czech Republic (1:4,0), Hungary (1:4,6), Lithuania (1:6,4), Bulgaria (1:6,7) or the Ukraine (1:14) suffer from specific staff and equipment shortages[2954] that make any meaningful treatment approach almost impossible. However, the figures are not always easy to compare because staff, especially doctors and teachers, often are not employed full-time but come from the outside on an irregular basis.

There are problems of low social prestige and remuneration in many countries. The former totalitarian states face special problems of adaptation of prison staff to new organisation and philosophies. This has also been the case in East Germany after reunification in 1990.[296] The roles of prison wardens have changed in many countries and they are more involved in rehabilitative tasks. Education and staff training has been improved (for example, France). A key role in rehabilitative efforts, however, is that of social workers. The structure of services has also been changed in some countries in order to provide a through-care service from pre-trial detention to prison and after-care (France, some federal states in Germany). In some countries co-operation with outside services has been improved (Belgium).

Conclusion

The major challenges of the prison system seem to be threefold. Firstly, to establish an effective system of prisoners' rights, secondly to improve their daily living conditions (especially in central and eastern Europe) and thirdly to reduce prison overcrowding.

Prisons must be supervised and effectively controlled. Prisoners' rights and humane living conditions can be developed by a variety of control systems: individual complaints procedures, national and international (CPT) inspection systems, ombudsmen, boards of visitors, and so on.[297]

Organisational reforms have been stimulated by budget restrictions (Germany) and do not necessarily lead to reduced services for prisoners. Quality control and the evaluation of prisons by economic standards (cost-benefit analyses) should be seen as a chance to improve the conditions for prisoners and staff. The equipment of prisons with staff involved in rehabilitative programmes should not be reduced, whereas some functions of external security can be replaced by video supervision, and similar monitoring. The decentralisation of power to prison wardens and social workers is ambivalent as the power to decide on relaxation of the regime (including leaves of absence, other privileges) can endanger the relationship of confidence necessary for rehabilitative work.

Improvement of prison conditions is related to economic developments in society. As Rusche and Kirchheimer already stated in the 1930s, the living standard outside prison will limit the living conditions inside. In times of high unemployment it is difficult to provide prisoners with meaningful prison work.[298] When the Prison Act of 1976 was passed in the German Parliament the question of allowing television sets for prisoners in their cells was debated. The legislator refused a more liberal regulation arguing that outside prison it was not self-evident that everybody had access to a television. Subsequently the 1998 amendment of the Prison Act generally allowed the possession of a television set under the general aim of 'normalisation' by emphasising the fact that virtually everybody outside prison has television.

The principle of 'normalisation' in general will be applied to prisoners; however, it depends largely on the orientation of the general political system being more or less based on the idea of the welfare state. Neo-liberal thinking and the reduction of social services can negatively influence the living standards in prison, too. Only in welfare states, where ordinary 'free' society enjoys a wide range of social services, does the principle of normalisation operate progressively. In those countries, such as England and the United States, where social services for marginal groups are, if anything, being reduced, the normalisation principle has problematic consequences.[299]

One of the key issues for developing or guaranteeing humane prison conditions is the reduction of prison overcrowding. The solution is not the extension of prison capacities and following a criminal policy such as in the United States. The good examples of the Scandinavian countries (especially Finland) or of Austria and Slovenia show that even under difficult situations and the increasing phenomena of anomie in society, prison populations can be kept on a rather low level. Whereas in some countries the elimination of short-term imprisonment seems to be promising (Switzerland, Scandinavian countries), in other countries the shortening of the periods prisoners have to serve would be an option (Germany). In Germany, prison sentences have been made an exceptional sanction (*ultima ratio*), but those who serve prison sentences stay in prison for rather long periods. Restricting the conditions for parole is counter-productive to a 'reductionist' approach. It cannot be justified by security arguments as empirical studies show that parole has been a successful strategy. Extending, not reducing, the scope of early release should be required.

Another increasing problem in Germany and other countries is that of fine defaulters. The increasing economic problems of offenders limit the scope for imposing fines (at the moment representing 83% of all convicted offenders in Germany). Therefore the introduction of community service as an independent sanction seems to be an option for destitute offenders.

The Council of Europe in Recommendation No. R (99) 22 emphasises on the one hand that custodial sanctions should be reconsidered with a view to reducing long sentences and to limiting the use of short custodial sentences. On the other hand, the Council recommends the extension of the scope for community sanctions and measures such as suspended sentences, probation, community service, treatment orders (contract treatment for specific categories of offenders), curfew orders, electronic monitoring, victim-offender mediation, victim compensation, and so on.

The introduction or extension of community sanctions has to be implemented with the aim of replacing custodial sanctions, and not of replacing other community sanctions. Therefore in some countries electronic monitoring seems to be inappropriate (such as in Germany) as short-term imprisonment for offenders with relatively good prognosis is not a quantitative problem: these offenders are regularly and efficiently dealt with by the probation services. In Sweden the situation is different as traditionally, for example, traffic offenders are sentenced to short-term prison sentences, which can be replaced by curfew orders and electronic monitoring.

So the strategies of combating prison overcrowding must be seen in the national context of the existing sanction system and the system of early release. The field of innovative criminal policies shows a wide range of possible alternatives to the deprivation of liberty. Therefore, expanding prison capacities is the worst and most expensive way of handling the problem.[300] In general we may conclude that prisons are not the solution for solving social problems. They are expensive and a waste of human and societal resources unless limited to being a last resort of crime policy.

Conclusion – where do we go from here?

Christopher Nuttall

Within the field of crime policy, I believe that the European institution that will have the most influence in the next twenty years will be the European Court of Human Rights. The next most important development will be minimum rules for prisons and community sentences. Several of the authors who have contributed to this volume have emphasised the populist push for tougher sanctions and for reversing some of the civilising trends of the second half of the twentieth century. They have made it clear that political leaders must take a lead and demonstrate that harshness and severity will not guarantee safety and security. Because this seems difficult for some to accept, the European Court of Human Rights will be obliged to ensure that the rights of all the people in the criminal-justice system – victims, workers, accused and offenders – are upheld. Democracy cannot be defended by authoritarian means.

People everywhere want to feel safe and secure. They do not want their societies threatened by disorder, civil war or criminals. They want civil peace – a state in which there is confidence that the government and those who exercise formal social control will not behave in an arbitrary manner, where those who work in the justice system work efficiently, fairly, effectively and in an uncorrupted fashion and where crime and fear of crime are minimised. There must be a state of trust between citizens and those elected to carry out the tasks of government on their behalf. Criminal-justice policy exists to produce civil peace.

Thus, fairness and justice must be at the centre of justice systems – but so must effectiveness, efficiency and knowledge. And they must respond to society's constant changes.

The period from 1950 to 2000 saw many changes in priorities for criminal-justice policy. In 1950 many societies used the justice system to defend vested interests – whether of the state or of the rich and powerful. Now they must consider the wishes of all. If they do not do so already, they will certainly have to do so in the near future.

In the twentieth century, the second world war demonstrated the full horrors of racism and genocide. Since then Europeans have put great effort into minimising the destructive effects of discrimination and tribalism. But we have not won the battle yet. Racism on an individual and a community level will be with us for many years. Laws are needed to demonstrate that such attitudes and actions cannot be tolerated by civilised societies. But as long as people feel frightened by their neighbours simply because they have a different culture and customs, we will not make real progress.

Today, violence against women is at least recognised as a real crime – even if it still exists. Fifty years ago it was largely ignored by both the police and the justice system. Now it makes up 20% to 25% of recorded crimes of violence in some countries, not because it has become any more prevalent (the evidence is that it is actually falling), but because it is now recognised. This will continue to be a major problem, which must be approached with determination and care.

Crime prevention has been a major development since the 1980s but it must be seen to be at the centre of crime policy. The traditional ways of preventing crime (cops, courts and corrections) have basically failed or are useful only for extreme cases. It costs about thirty times as much to prevent a burglary by sending someone to prison as it does to prevent it through good crime prevention techniques. When the politicians and criminal-justice practitioners succeed in getting people to understand this, then we will be able to make real progress. This is work for the next thirty years.

In some parts of Europe corruption and organised crime are fundamental threats and the chapter by Kauko Aromaa has shown how prevalent they are in some parts of Europe. Of course, official records miss the vast majority of such crimes, so the situation is even worse than official records suggest. Corruption and organised crime undermine the very foundations of societies and if they are not dealt with those societies will not even begin to achieve civil peace. These areas will need enormous effort in the future. International agreements and co-operation are vital and it is an area in which the Council of Europe has a major role to play. However, such societies (and they know which ones they are) must want to change.

Another problem for the future must continue to be drug use, its sale and distribution. Studies of several European countries stated that drug dependency lies behind up to one-third of all property crime. Serious drug use is a symptom of social exclusion. It is the refuge of the unemployed, the depressed and the desperate. If it continues to be seen as wilful and delinquent then we will not make real progress. We must recognise that cutting demand is the only real way to make any progress (cutting supply only pushes up the price and increases crime). We must carefully examine all the arguments – medical, ethical, social and economic – if we are to reduce this source of misery and crime. My guess is that in thirty years the prohibition of drugs will look as ineffective and criminogenic as the prohibition of alcohol in the United States in the early part of the last century seems to us now.

Nevertheless, there is some hope for improvement. Many countries of Europe have seen the connection between social exclusion, poor education, lack of economic development, bad housing and crime, and are trying to tackle all these issues.

Crime has been falling in the United States for 20 years now and for several years in many European countries, which shows something can be done. The sorts of actions that can prevent or reduce crime are:

- efficient policing – particularly that which is intelligence-led and targeted on 'hot spots';
- effective crime prevention methods, where crimes are made harder to commit and opportunities are reduced;
- drug-treatment programmes;
- penal treatments based on information as to what is effective in reducing re-offending ("what works" principles);
- information and evidence about the effectiveness of programmes and actions;
- much better pre-school education for disadvantaged children (see the success of Head Start in the USA);
- help and support for parents in need;
- information for the general public which allows people to understand the complexity of crime and its cures;
- the will to end corruption.

However, if the confidence of the people is lost then we cannot win. So offenders must not be seen to get away with crime. Victims must not be doubly victimised and the response of the courts must be proportionate to the seriousness of the crime.

One more warning – and then a final note of optimism

We have to break the cycles of despondency and fashion.

One of the barriers to communication within Europe (or anywhere else for that matter) is that various countries are on different cycles in dealing with crime. We need to get on to the same cycle. (Ideally, of course, we would avoid cyclical thinking completely – but that is very difficult.)

Dealing with crime is very difficult. The major problem is people's perception that it is easy to solve.

The United Kingdom went through two complete cycles in the twentieth century. In the first quarter (or so) criminal-justice policy used harshly-administered imprisonment to deal with crime. But crime rose and many saw the degradation of prison as adding to the likelihood that an offender would re-offend. There followed a reaction to the widespread use of prison. The movement to minimise prison use started in the late 1930s, was interrupted by the war, was developed by the government after the war and reached its peak in the 1970s when the use of imprisonment was at its lowest.

But crime continued to rise. This brought a reaction to the use of community penalties and early release in the 1980s. The increased use of prison did not stop the rise in crime and so there was a quick reaction to it, culminating in the Criminal Justice Act of 1991, which tried to limit the use of imprisonment by the courts. But crime still rose! There was another reaction. The use of prison increased again. This is where the United Kingdom is at the moment.

Now crime is going up again in Britain so we can expect another reaction to the use of imprisonment and a return to the cheaper non-custodial penalties.

Other countries in Europe and North America have done exactly the same – but not all at the same time. For example some countries, which introduced community penalties later than the United Kingdom, are just going into an imprisonment mode and those which increased imprisonment later are going into a community mode!

The real problem is that up to now whether people were sent to prison or dealt with in the community was irrelevant as far as re-offending is concerned! Both methods are equally ineffective and criminal-justice policy switches from one to the other as each policy fails to reduce crime.

To break this cycle we must recognise that no one method will reduce crime. There should be more evaluative research and development, better communication and an exchange of good practice as well as a will to work together to reduce crime and the effects of victimisation.

Let me paint a final optimistic view of what the future may hold. Crime has been going down in the United States for twenty years and more recently in many European countries. One of the reasons that has been suggested is that the great disruptions which followed the second world war are now past and society is beginning to settle down. A recent discovery is that the most effective way of controlling crime is through informal social control, which communities can exert on the behaviour of residents and non-residents (modern examples are Ireland and Japan). Communities which have been destabilised and where people do not know each other and do not feel responsible for the behaviour of their neighbours cannot exert such informal social control. Disruption has been the major characteristic of post-war societies in western Europe and post-communist societies in eastern and central Europe, but there is hope that order and continuity are reasserting themselves. If this is happening we could well see much lower crime rates.

American research has clearly shown that the communities that exert informal social control can have crime rates up to 50% lower than those in which there is no social cohesion and informal social control. If social cohesion and community stability are returning naturally then we can expect the beneficial effects to be felt over the next decades. If not, then we are beginning to build up knowledge that will enable us to work with communities to help the process develop.

Informal social control is often seen as relating only to a golden age long gone. This does not have to be. And a plan might look like this:

- obtain local political co-operation;
- identify neighbourhoods for the development work, using as indicators:
  - high crime,
  - low employment,
  - high poverty,
  - relatively low population density,

  - near area of much higher social capital,
  - high proportion socially excluded;
- development team and resources identified;
- identify current neighbourhood or residents' associations;
- identify current and potential neighbourhood leaders;
- widespread publicity about the projects – including potential benefits;
- involve local radio;
- if necessary start a neighbourhood newsletter to be distributed to everyone;
- invite all interested to an initial neighbourhood meeting;
- have series of neighbourhood meetings given publicity by door-to-door canvassing by local residents;
- leadership development programmes launched;
- residents trained in conflict resolution, community organising and leadership skills;
- neighbourhood clean-up;
- neighbourhood celebration;
- neighbourhood needs assessment;
- formulation of multi-institutional, multi-purpose steering groups for project (?);
- mutual-support groups formed (teen parents, grandparents, elderly, etc.);
- sub-neighbourhood social and civic activities;
- new vision of neighbourhood developed, articulated and agreed upon by residents' meeting;
- establish safe places for children to go if they feel threatened;
- establish mentoring, big brother/sister activities;
- encourage neighbourhood sports teams;
- enhance self-reliance by education and encouragement;
- involve local schools in the project.

The relatively long-term outcomes that would indicate we were well on the road to success would be:

- high level of 'intergenerational closure';
- residents believe this is a good place to bring up children;
- residential stability even when incomes going up;
- inter-group relations good;
- residents believe they can be successful in achieving goals;
- neighbourhood projects are being used as a model in other neighbourhoods;
- neighbourhood institutions have strong resource base;
- neighbourhood is seen as a good place for investment;

- residents feel comfortable acting when neighbour or neighbour's child does something wrong;
- residents get access to political leadership;
- volunteerism is strong;
- residents running most of the significant cultural, social, economic and political institutions in the community;
- vulnerable population well-cared for.

The result would be improved increased income and improved education, crime, health and physical infrastructures on a neighbourhood level.

Producing the social cohesion that will encourage informal social control will not be easy but the benefits could be enormous – not just in reducing crime but in the overall increase in the quality of life.

Notes

1 Van Dijk , Jan J. M. "More than a Matter of Security: Trends in Crime Prevention in Europe' in F. Heidensohn and M. Farrell (eds), *Crime In Europe,* Routledge (London: 1990).

2 Cf. Barberet, Rosemary. 'Indicators of Crime and of the Performance of the Criminal Justice System' in Matti Joutsen (ed.), *Five Issues in European Criminal Justice: Corruption, Women in the Criminal Justice System, Criminal Policy Indicators, Community Crime Prevention and Computer Crime,* European Institute for Crime Prevention and Control, affiliated with the United Nations (HEUNI), Publication Series No. 34, pp. 156-168 (1999).

3 Van Dijk, Jan J. M., Killias, Martin, and Mayhew, Pat. *Experiences of Crime across the World: Key Findings from the 1989 International Crime Survey,* Kluwer Law and Taxation Publishers (Dewenter-Boston: 1990).

4 Van Dijk describes the starting point to the present situation assessment for five western European countries. This description is very general, taking a look at all police-recorded crime in five western European countries, Sweden, the Federal Republic of Germany, England and Wales, the Netherlands, and Denmark.

5 Van Dijk 1998.

6 Van Dijk 1998, pp. 51-53.

7 Van Dijk 1998, pp. 51-53.

8 Basically, this is the same division as was used by the Council of Europe Expert Committee on Organised Crime in 1996.

i. Scandinavia (Denmark, Finland, Iceland, Norway, Sweden)

ii. Western Europe (Belgium, Ireland, Luxembourg, the Netherlands, United Kingdom)

iii. West central Europe (Austria, Germany, Liechtenstein, Switzerland)

iv. South-western Europe (Andorra, France, Italy, Malta, Portugal, San Marino, Spain)

v. The Balkans (Albania, Bosnia, Bulgaria, Croatia, "the former Yugoslav Republic of Macedonia", Romania, Slovenia, Federal Republic of Yugoslavia)

vi. East central Europe (Czech Republic, Hungary, Poland, Slovakia)

vii. South-eastern Europe (Cyprus, Greece, Turkey)

viii. The Baltic states (Estonia, Latvia, Lithuania)

ix. Eastern Europe (Belarus, Moldova, Russian Federation, Ukraine).

9 Aromaa, Kauko, and Lehti, Martti. *Foreign Companies and Crime in Eastern Europe. The Security Environment in St. Petersburg and Estonia in 1995,* National Research Institute of Legal Policy, Publication No. 135 (Helsinki: 1996).

10 Cf. Junninen, Mika, and Aromaa, Kauko. *Crime across the Border. Finnish Professional Criminals and Estonian Crime Opportunities,* National Institute of Legal Policy, Research Communication 45 (Helsinki: 1999).

11 Verstraeten, R. 'De burgerlijke partij in het gerechtelijk onderzoek. Het slachtoffer in het strafproces', Maklu Publishers (Antwerp-Apeldoorn: 1990).

12 Van Dijk, J. J. M. 'Strafrechtshervormingen ten behoeve van het slachtoffer in internationaal perspectief' in *Justitiële Verkenningen* (1988).

13 García-Pablos de Molina, A. 'La Víctima del Delito', 22 pp., 1991, unpublished note.

14 Ash, M. 'On Witnesses: A Radical Critique of Criminal Court Procedures' in *Notre Dame Lawyer,* 48 (1972), pp. 493-502.

15 Knudten, R. D., Meade, A., and Doerner, W. 'The victim in the administration of criminal justice: problems and perceptions' in McDonald, W. (ed), *Criminal Justice and the Victim,* Sage (London: 1976).

16 Fattah, E. 'The United Nations Declaration of Basic Principles of Justice for Victims of Crime and Abuse of Power' in Fattah, E. (ed.), *Towards a Critical Victimology,* Macmillan (London: 1992).

17 Galaway, B., and Hudson, (eds), *Perspectives on Crime Victims,* C.V. Mosby (St. Louis: 1981).

18 Fattah, E., op. cit. (1992).

19 Zauberman, R., and Robert, P., *Du côté des victimes. Un autre regard sur la délinquence,* L'Harmattan (Paris: 1995).

20 Castan, N. and Y. 'Beroep op, behoefte aan en gevoel voor recht tegenover de officiële rechtspleging gedurende de 18e eeuw in Frankrijk' in *Tijdschrift voor Criminologie* (1978).

21 Griffiths, C. and Belleau, C. 'Restoration, Reconciliation and Healing: the Revitalization of Culture and Tradition in Addressing Crime and Victimization in Canadian Aboriginal Communities' in Fattah, E., and Peters, T. *Support of Crime Victims in a Comparative Perspective,* Leuven University Press (Leuven: 1998), and Roberts, S. *Order and Dispute. An Introduction to Legal Anthropology,* Penguin (Middlesex: 1979).

22 Van Kerckvoorde, J. *Een maat voor het kwaad?,* Leuven University Press (Leuven: 1995).

23 Geis, G. *Crime Victims: practices and prospects* in Lurigio et al. (eds), (:1990), and Mawby, R. I. and Walklate, S. *Critical Victimology,* Sage (London: 1994).

24 Mawby and Walklate, op. cit., 1994; Roberts, S. op. cit. (1990).

25 Van Kerckvoorde, op. cit. (1986, 1995); Zedner, L. 'Victims' in *The Oxford Handbook of Criminology,* 2nd edn (Oxford: 1997).

26 García-Pablos de Molina, A. *Manual de Criminologia,* Espasa Calpe (Madrid: 1988) and op. cit. (1991).

27 Clark, L., and Lewis, D. 'Rape: the Price of Coercive Sexuality' in *Toronto Women's Press* (1977).

28 Van Dijk, J. J. M. 'L'évaluation de l'impact des régimes d'indemnisation et des programmes d'assistance aux victimes d'infraction' in *Annales de Droit de Liège* (1984).

29 Martin, D. 'Le Mouvement d'aide aux Victimes en Belgique Francophone: Tendances, Problèmes Actuels et Perspectives' in *Revue de Droit Pénal et de Criminologie* (1989).

30 Weiss, K. and Borges, S. 'Victimology and Rape: the case of the legitimate victim' in *Issues in Criminology* (1973).

31 Rock, P. Helping *Victims of Crime. The Home Office and the Rise of Victim Support in England and Wales,* Clarendon Press (Oxford: 1990).

32 Viano, E. 'Victimology: A new focus of research and practice' in *Victims' rights and legal reforms, Oñati Proceedings* (Oñati: 1991).

33 Zedner refers to the research of Maxfield, M. G. *Fear of Crime in England and Wales,* HORS 78, MHSO (London: 1984), Garofalo, J. 'Victimization and the Fear of Crime' in *Journal of Research in Crime and Delinquency* (1979), and Skogan, W. G. 'The Impact of Victimization on Fear' in *Crime and Delinquency* (1986).

34 Gottfredson, 1989; Lurigio, A. J. 'Healing the psychological wounds of criminal victimization: predicting postcrime distress and recovery' in Lurigio, A. J., Skogan, W. G., and Davis, R. C. (eds.). *Victims of Crime: Problems, Policies and Programs,* Sage (Newbury Park, CA: 1990) and Resick, P.A.

35 Research carried out by Maguire, M. 'The Impact of Burglary upon Victims' in British Journal of Criminology (1980), and Maguire, M., and Corbett, C. *The Effects of Crime and the Work of Victim Support Schemes,* Gower (Aldershot: 1987).

36 For the impact of burglary, see also Burt and Katz (1985).

37 Mawby, R. I., and Gill, M. L. *Crime Victims: Needs, Services and the Voluntary Sector,* Tavistock (London: 1987) and Mawby (1992).

38 Fattah, E., *Understanding Criminal Victimisation* (1991).

39 Figures of the International Crime Survey, 1992.

40 Dignan, J., and Cavadino, M. 'Towards a Framework for Conceptualising and Evaluating Models of Criminal Justice from a Victim's Perspective' in *International Review of Victimology* (1996); Peters, T., and Goethals, J. (eds). *De achterkant van de criminaliteit. Over victimologie, slachtofferhulp en strafrechtsbedeling,* Kluwer Law Publishers, Belgium (Antwerp: 1993); Reeves, H. 'The victim support perspective' in Wright, M., and Galaway, B. (eds). *Mediation and criminal justice: victims, offenders and community,* Sage (London: 1989); and Young, M. *Restorative Community Justice: a call for action,* National Organization for Victim Assistance (Washington: 1996).

41 Aertsen, I., and Peters, T. 'Mediation for Reparation: The Victim's Perspective' in *European Journal of Crime, Criminal Law and Criminal Justice,* vol. 6/2 (1998).

42 Commentary on the preamble to the recommendation, Council of Europe Recommendation No. R (99) 19.

43 Aertsen, I. 'Mediation bei schweren Straftaten – auf dem Weg zu einer neuen Rechtskultur?' in *Mediationsverfahren: Horizonte, Grenzen, Innensichten (Jahrbuch für Rechts- und Kriminalsoziologie),* Pelikan, C. (ed.) Nomos (Baden-Baden: 1999).

44 Weitekamp, E. 'The paradigm of restorative justice: potentials, possibilities and pitfalls'. Keynote lecture for the 9th International Symposium on Victimology (unpublished) Amsterdam, 1997.

45 See, for example, Dünkel, F. 'Täter-Opfer Ausgleich. German experiences with mediation in a European perspective' in *European Journal on Criminal Policy and Research,* no. 4.4 (1996).

46 Bazemore, G., and Walgrave, L. 'Restorative Juvenile Justice: In Search of Fundamentals and an Outline for Systemic Reform' in Bazemore, G., and Walgrave, L. (eds) *Restorative Juvenile Justice: Repairing the Harm of Youth Crime,* Criminal Justice Press (Monsey: 1999); McCold, P. 'Restorative Justice – Variations on a Theme' in Walgrave. L. (ed.) *Restorative Justice for Juveniles. Potentialities, Risks and Problems,* Leuven University Press (Leuven: 1998); and Wright, M. *Justice for victims and offenders. A restorative response to crime* (2nd edn), Waterside Press (Winchester: 1996).

47 Zehr, H. *Changing Lenses: A new focus for criminal justice,* Herald Press (Scottsdale: 1990).

48 Peters, T. 'Probleemoplossing en herstel als functies van de straf' in *Panoptikon* (1996); and Walgrave, L. 'Restorative justice for juveniles: just a technique or a fully-fledged alternative?' in *The Howard Journal of Criminal Justice* (1995).

49 Van Ness, D. 'Legal Issues of Restorative Justice' in Bazemore, G., and Walgrave, L. (eds) op. cit. (1999).

50 See variety of definitions of crime prevention in de Waard, J. 'A many-sided battle: definitions of crime prevention' in *Balance and partnership. Towards a role of law enforcement in drug prevention,* Seminar on Best Practices in Drug Prevention by the Law Enforcement Authorities, Helsinki 12-13 July 1999. Police Department Publication 14/ 1999, Helsinki.

51 For example, the classic study on capital punishment from 1959, by Thorsten Sellin.

52 For example the Swedish 1966 study on recidivism after different kinds of penalties, by Börjeson, Bengt. *Om påföljders verkningar. En undersökning av prognosen för unga lagöverträdare efter olika slag av behandling,* Uppsala (1966).

53 A study by W. C. Bailey from 1966 summarised one hundred earlier treatment studies and laid down the fundamental work for the later slogan "nothing works". See Bailey, W. C. 'Correctional Outcome: an evaluation of 100 reports' in *The Journal of Criminal Law, Criminology and Police Science,* 57 (1966), pp. 153-160.

54 See a current overview on European crime prevention agencies in Bünmegelözés európában (Crime Prevention in Europe), Országos Bünmegelözési Tanács (Budapest: 1998).

55 Tonry, M., and Farrington, D. 'Strategic Approaches to Crime Prevention' in Tonry, M., and Farrington, D. (eds), *Building a Safer Society. Strategic Approaches to Crime Prevention. Crime and Justice,* vol. 19, University of Chicago Press (Chicago: 1995).

56 Bailleau, F., and Garioud, G. 'Social strategies aimed at avoiding the production of criminalisable behaviour' in *New social strategies and the criminal justice system.* Proceedings of the 19th Criminological Research Conference 1990. *Criminological Research,* vol. XXIX (Council of Europe: 1994).

57 Garland, D. "The Limits of the Sovereign State" in *The British Journal of Criminology,* vol. 36, no. 4 (Autumn 1996).

58 The following passage describes three European models of crime prevention. The description is a typology. The three models described have a lot of common; similarities will not be pointed out in the typology.

59 See for example Graham, J., and Bennett, T. *Crime Prevention Strategies in Europe and North America,* HEUNI Publications Series No. 28 (Helsinki: 1995).

60 Sherman, Lawrence, Gottfredson, Denise, MacKenzie, Doris, Eck, John, Reuter, Peter and Bushway, Shawn *Preventing crime; what works, what's promising, what doesn't.* A report to the United States Congress, Department of Criminology and Criminal Justice, University of Maryland, Internet, 1997.

61 Ekblom, P., Law, H., and Sutton, M. *Safer cities and domestic burglaries,* Home Office Research Studies 164, Home Office (London: 1996).

62 Reply by the United Kingdom to the Select Committee's questionnaire 1984. Select Committee of Experts on the organisation of Crime Prevention. Council of Europe. – As early as 1961 C. R. Hewitt, one of early advocates for situational crime prevention, wrote in his book *Common sense about crime & punishment:* "... 'crime prevention' in the narrow sense dealt with here is positive and dynamic only in the fact that it seeks to remove or minimise opportunity."

63 See for example the programme of the EU seminar arranged in London 1998 by the Home Office.

64 Waller, I., Welsh, C., and Sansfacon, D. *Crime Prevention Digest 1997. Successes, Benefits and Directions from Seven Countries.* International Centre for the Prevention of Crime (Montreal: 1997).

65 Van Dijk J. J. M., 'Towards a research-based crime reduction policy; Crime prevention as a cost-effective policy option', paper presented at the European Union Conference "Crime Prevention: towards a European level' Nordwijk, 1997.

66 See the booklet Crime Prevention in the Nordic Context – The Nordic Model.

67 For example, the Danish criminologist Berl Kutchinsky 1990.

68 See a collection of success stories in Belgium in van Limbergen, K., Walgrave, S., and Dekegel, I. 1996. *Promising Practices. Crime prevention in Belgium. 10 Examples* (V.S.P.P.: 1966).

69 Mayhew, P., and Van Dijk, J. J. M. *Criminal victimisation in eleven industrialised countries: key findings from the 1996 International Crime Victims Survey,* Ministry of Justice, Research and Documentation Centre (The Hague: 1997).

70 Even European collections of best practices in crime prevention used to refer mainly to projects that originated in the USA, see for example Graham and Bennett, op. cit. (1995).

71 Strandskog, Tog. 'Vold. En erfaringsrapport om det voldsforebyggende arbeide gjennomført ved Senja politikammer' Harstad 1991-1994 med etterord skrevet i januar 1997, Senja Politikammer (Harstad: 1997).

72 Andenæs, M. in Rispo, M. (translation by). *Il codice penale norvegese,* Cedam (Padua: 1998), p. 1 ff.

73 Gallas, W. 'Der dogmatische Teil des Alternativ-Entwurf' in *ZStW* (1968), p. 98 ff and Leferenz, 'Der Entwurf des allgemeinen Teil des StGBs in Kriminologischer Sicht' in *ZStW* (1958), p. 25 ff.

74 Dolcini, E., and Paliero, C. E. "L'illecito amministrativo (Ordnungswidrigkeit) nell'ordinamento della Repubblica Federale di Germania: disciplina, sfera di applicazione, linee di political legislativa" in *Riv. It. Dir. Proc. Pen.,* Giuffré (Milan: 1980), p. 1134 ff.

75 Torre, G. (translation by). *Il codice penale portoghese,* Cedam (Padua: 1997) and de Figueredo Dias, J. 'Il codice penale portoghese del 1982 e la sua riforma' in *Riv. It. Dir. Proc. Pen,* Giuffré (Milan: 1995), p. 25 ff.

76 Pradel, J. *Droit pénal général,* 9th edn (Paris: 1994); AA.VV., 1985; pp. 43-56, 121-135, 251-278, 279-282. The *Code-Pénal-Réform (Lois no. 92-683 a 686 du juillet 1992)* (Paris: 1992).

77 Articles 131-39 of the *code pénal réform* envisage as "criminal sanctions" for the legal entity, dissolution, temporary interdiction from carrying out the activity, legal surveillance, the permanent or temporary closure of one or more plants, temporary exclusion from public markets, temporary or permanent interdiction from making public saving appeals, the interdiction for five years or more from issuing cheques, the confiscation of the goods related to the offence or used to commit it, the publication of the sentence. Finally, Articles 131-40 and 131-41 envisage 'sanctions for infringements' such as a fine, the interdiction from issuing a cheque for a year or more, and confiscation.

78 Naronte, *Il codice penale spagnolo,* Cedam (Padua: 1998); AA. VV., 1995, pp. 85-108, 171-194.

79 Casabona, C. M. R. 'I reati relativi alle manipolazioni genetiche nel codice penale spagnolo del 1995' in *Riv. It. Proc. Pen.*, Giuffré (Milan: 1998), p. 204 ff.

80 Rispo, op. cit. (1998).

81 *Documenti Giustizia,* 1992, p. 311 ff; Ind. Pen., 1992, p. 579 ff. This project, like the Pagliaro project, aims at protecting the constitutional legal entities. It also attempts to overcome the offence-infringement dichotomy by limiting the penal sphere to offences only and using pecuniary sanctions for infringements.

82 Law 205 of 25 June 1999.

83 See *Kazenski zakonik Republike Slovenije, Udradni list,* No. 63 of 13 October 1994.

84 Ljubo Bavcon, in Fišer, Z., Folla, N., and Ukmar, M.. (translation by). *Il codice penale sloveno,* Cedam (Padua: 1998), p. 1 ff.

85 Insolera, G. 'Qualche osservazione in margine alla nuova legge penale Croata' in Ind. Pen. Cedam (Padua: 1999), p. 437 ff; and Pavi_ic, B. 'Modelli di riforma del sistema delle incriminazioni nei paesi in transizione: Repubblica di Croazia' in *Ind. Pen.,* Cedam (Padua: 1998), p. 645 ff.

86 Schröeder, H. Bedinarz (translation by). *Strafgesetzbuch der Russischen Föderaction* (Freiburg im Breisgau: 1998).

87 See the laws dealing with organised crime; L. 19/03/1990, No, 55; D.L. 13/05/1991, No. 152; L. 356/1992.

88 Chiavario, M. *Procedura penale: un codice tra "storia" e crònaca,* 2nd edn Utet (Turin: 1996), p. 34 ff, 108 ff, 144 ff, 178 ff.

89 Möhrenschlager, M. 'Revision des Umweltstrafrecht. Das zewite Gesetz zur Bekämpfung der Umweltkriminalität' (I and II) in *NStZ* (1994), p. 513 ff, and 566 ff.

90 Rodrigo Arias. *Derecho penal y protección del medio ambiente,* (Madrid: 1992), p. 245 ff; and Alonso (1998), p. 393 ff.

91 Heine, G. (ed.) *Umweltstrafrecht in mittel und südeuropäischen Ländern* (Freiburg im Bresgau: 1991), p. 370 ff.

92 Huenerfeld, Portugal in Heine, G. (ed.) *Umweltstrafrecht in mittel und südeuropäischen Ländern* (Freiburg im Bresgau: 1997), p. 359 ff.

93 Spaniol-Hilgers, in Heine, op. cit. (1997), p. 421.

94 In addition to the less recent set of laws, fragmentally spread all over single texts dealing with security and health, as well as in addition to some types of offences set out in the Penal Code, environmental protection in Italy is currently dealt with by the law on the peaceful use of nuclear energy (Law No. 1860 of 31 December 1962), by the law on environmental pollution (the so-called "antismog" Law No. 650 of 13 July 1966), by the law on water pollution (the so-called Merli Law – No. 319 of 10 May 1976 modified by Law 650 of 24 December 1979), and, finally, by the law decree on waste matter (the so-called Ronchey Decree – No. 22 of 5 February 1997). On this issue, see, among others, *Italien,* in Heine (1997), p. 267 ff.

95 In particular, the aim of this project was to include Title VI-*bis,* regarding environmental offences, in addition to common dispositions, containing four offences: environmental pollution, destruction of the natural heritage, illicit waste traffic and environmental fraud. Manna (1998), No. 4.

96 Some authors refer to it as a presumed threat. See Parodi-Giusini *I reati di pericolo tra dogmatica e politica criminale,* Milan, Giuffré (1990), p. 217 ff.

97 We are referring to those offences that represent an abstract threat because the judgment must not consider all the elements available; they are concrete because

the judge must, for each single case, take action to establish whether they pose a threat. Parodi-Giusini, 1990, p. 245 ff; Schroeder, F. C., 1982, pp. 11-14.

98 In Italy, unlike crimes, infringements are punished by merely establishing the guilt: as a result, the judge will only have to prove intent only to establish the penalty (see Donini (1996), p. 70 ff).

99 This is because, since the infringement is of an administrative origin, it adapts well to its connotation in terms of *Verwaltungstrafrecht*. Furthermore, infringements are less serious acts and can therefore easily be detracted from the need to guarantee the principle of offensiveness. On this point, see Donini (1996), p. 158.

100 It should be made clear, however, that this project envisaged two infringements in addition to the crime model. These are environmental pollution and the unauthorised conduct of research activities.

101 Leigh, L. H. *The criminal liability of corporations in English law* (London: 1969).

102 Tiedemann, K. '§264 StGB Subventionsbetrug' in *LK*, 2nd edn (Berlin-New York: 1988), p. 1169 ff.

103 Weber, M. *Economía y Sociedad, Fondo de Cultural Económica* (Mexico City: 1987).

104 Benjamin, W. 'Para una crítica de la violencia' in *Para una crítica de la violencia y otros ensayos*, vol. IV of Iluminaciones, Taurus (Madrid: 1991).

105 Mitchell Waldrop, M. *Complexity*, Penguin Books, Viking Press (London: 1993), p. 11.

106 Recasens, A. 'Les policies a Catalunya. La policia integral I la sea connexió amb les altres policies'. Pending publication in a collective volume (1999).

107 Recommendation 1247/1994 by the Parliamentary Assembly concerning extending the Council of Europe.

108 Taibo, C. *Crisis y cambio en la Europa del Este*. Alianza (Madrid: 1995) and Cao Huy Thuan, et al. *Regards sur le changement en Union Sovietique*, PUF (Paris: 1990).

109 Weber, M. op. cit. (1987), pp. 1056-1057.

110 Recasens, A. *L'espai policial europeu: del desarmament del Leviathan a la construcció del seu futur*, Rapport Fundació Bofill (1995).

111 Xiberras, M. *Les théories de l'exclusion*, Armand Colin (Paris: 1998); Wieviorka, M. *El espacio del racismo*, Paidos (Barcelona: 1992); Wieviorka, M. *Violence en France*, Senil (Paris: 1999) and *Revista Catalana de Seguretat Pública*, 2/99 (1999).

112 Faget, J. *La médiation, essai de politique pénale*, Eres (Toulouse: 1997) and Morineau, J. *L'esprit de la médiation*, Eres (Toulouse: 1998).

113 Body-Gendrot, S. *Les villes face à l'insecurité*, Bayard (Paris: 1998) and Dieu, F. *Politiques publiques de la securité*, L'Harmattan (Paris: 1999).

114 Paniagua, J. L. and Gutiérrez F. (1983); Ballbé, M. (1983); Martín Villa, R. (1984); Barcelona Llop, J. (1997).

115 Palau, A. (1996).

116 Pagon, M. *Policing in central and eastern Europe*, College of Police and Security Studies (Ljubljana: 1998) and Recasens, A. (1996).

117 Blanc, H. *Le dossier noir des mafias russes*, Balzac-le-Grist (Paris: 1998).

118 Anderson, M. *Policing the World, Interpol and the Politics of International Police Co-operation*, Clarendon Press (Oxford: 1989); Benyon, J. *Police Co-operation in Europe: An Investigation*, University of Leicester, Centre for the Study of Public Order (Leicester: 1994); Bigo, D. *L'Europe des polices et de la sécurité intérieure*,

Complèxe (Paris: 1992) and Recasens, A. 'El espacio policial europeo: un futuro en construcción' in *Cuadernos de la Guardia Civil,* no. 14 (1995).

119 See Zaitch, Damián. 'Viejos conocidos, nuevos enemigos. Discursos y políticas sobre el delito organizado en la Nueva Europa'. Congreso Internacional sobre la problemática de las drogas: mitos y realidades. Colombia, 27-31 October, 1997.

120 European Parliament. 'Deuxième Rapport de la Commission des libertés publiques et des affaires intérieures: Sur l'entrée en vigueur des conventions de Schengen'. Rapporteur M. Lode van Outrive. PE 202.540, 5 November 1992. European Parliament. 'Report of the Committee on Civil Liberties and Internal Affairs: On Co-operation in the field of justice and internal affairs under the Treaty on European Union (Title VI and other provisions)'. Rapporteur Mr. Carlos Robles Piquer. PE 204.587, 1 July 1993. European Parliament. 'Report of the Committee on Civil Liberties and Internal Affairs: On participation by the European Parliament in international agreements by the member states and the Union on co-operation in the fields of justice and home affairs'. Rapporteur Mr. Georg Jarzembowski, PE 206.245, 21 December 1993.

121 Roberts, C. 'Unidad antidrogas de Europol' in *Focus,* no. 4 (August 1994), quoted in *Ciencia Policial,* No. 28 (January-February 1995), p. 118.

122 Guillaute, M. *Mémoire sur la Reformation de la Police en France,* Hermann (Paris: 1974).

123 Emsley, C. *Policing and its context 1750-1870,* Macmillan (London: 1983), p. 66 ff.

124 Soliciteur Général du Canada. *Une vision de l'avenir de la police au Canada: police-défi 2000 – Document de réfléxion,* Ministry of Supply and Services (Ottawa: 1990).

125 Normandeau, A. 'Balance y perspectivas de la policia comunitaria' in *Prevenció,* No. 10 (January 1998), pp. 17-18 and IHESI. 'Les partages de la sécurité' in *Les Cahiers de la Sécurité intérieure,* No. 33, third trimestre, (Paris: 1998).

126 Jankowski, B. 'La police de proximité: regard de la recherche sur un nouveau style de police' in IHESI, *Les Cahiers de la Sécurité intérieure,* No. 13 (May-July 1998), pp. 209 to 230, and Ferret, J. and Ocqueteau, F. *Evaluer la police de proximité,* La Documentation française (Paris: 1998).

127 Normandeau, A. (1994).

128 Wilson, J. G., and Kelling, G. L. 'Broken Windows' in *The Atlantic Monthly,* Vol. 249, No. 3 (March, 1982), pp. 29-38.

129 Brodeur, J. P. 'L'évaluation des programmes d'intervention sécuritaire. Quelques remarques sur les expériences canadienne et américaine' in Ferret, J. and Ocqueteau, F. op. cit. (1998), p. 18.

130 Other authors, such as Macallair, D. and Taqi-Eddin, K. *Shattering 'Broken Windows': An Analysis of San Francisco's Alternative Crime Policies,* The Justice Policy Institute (San Francisco: 1999), and Stauffer, E. 'La zéro tolérance et la baisse de la criminalité dans la ville de New York' in *Revue Internationale de Criminologie et de Police Technique et Scientifique,* No. 2 (April-June, 1999), pp. 151-162, also express their doubts, and contrast the drop in the crime rate in New York with that of other American cities.

131 Hayes B. (1997).

132 Among others, *Revue internationale de droit penal* 56 (1985), 1-2, 57 (1986), 3-4, 63 (1992), 1-2, 66 (1995), 3-4; multilateral meetings organised by the Council of Europe within the THEMIS programme: *The Transformation of the Prokuratura into a Body compatible with the democratic principles of Law,* CE Publishing (Strasbourg: 1996), *The Prokuratura in a State governed by the Rule of Law,* CE

Publishing (Strasbourg: 1997), *The role of the public prosecution office in a democratic Society,* CE Publishing (Strasbourg: 1997). The European Committee on Crime Problems of the Council of Europe has initiated a project 'The Role of the Public Prosecution in the Criminal Justice Field'. The preparatory materials for this project have been made available to the author who wishes to express her sincere thanks emphasising, however, that the views in the articles are her sole responsibility.

133 For example Pradel, Jean. *Droit Pénal Comparé,* Dalloz (Paris: 1995).

134 *Delays in the criminal justice systems,* Council of Europe (Strasbourg: 1992).

135 Pradel, op. cit. (1995), p. 322 ff.

136 Whenever illustration of individual countries is given, the data refer to the document PC-PR(97) 1.Rev.3 of the Council of Europe containing national replies to a CoE questionnaire on the public prosecution office.

137 Pradel, op. cit. (1995), pp. 322-323.

138 Doc. PC-PR(97) 1 Rev.3, p. 3-11. According to the replies, half of the CoE member-states dispose of such units in one or another way.

139 Pradel, op. cit. (1995), p. 325.

140 Skuratov, Y. 'Conceptual questions relating to the development of the Prokuratura' in *The Prokuratura in a State governed by the Rule of Law,* Council of Europe (Strasbourg: 1997), pp. 11-22, esp. 14-15 see also Toczilovski, V. N. 'O kocepcii prokuroskoj vlasti', *Sov. gos. i pravo* (Moskow: 1990), pp. 9, 39-46. The problem of the general control of legality will be dealt with later.

141 PC-PR (97) 1 Rev.3, 27–32.

142 Pradel, op. cit. (1995), p. 327.

143 Esp. Cariti, G. 'Dependence or Independence of the Public Prosecution Office' in *The role of the public prosecution office in a democratic society,* pp. 13–22, esp. 17 18.

144 Document PC-PR (99)-3.

145 Among others, Pradel (1995), pp. 322-323; Toman, J. 'The Development of the constitutional and legal status of Public Prosecution Offices' in publ. cited in ft. 9, 30.

146 Toman, J. 'The Role of the Public Prosecution Office in the criminal field', in *The role of the Public Prosecution Office in a democratic society,* 127–133.

147 Skuratov, Y., op. cit. (1998), 11–13.

148 *Les Systèmes comparés de justice pénale: de la diversité au rapprochement,* AIDP, 17/1998.

149 Dc.PC-PR(97) 1 rev. 3, 103.

150 Dc. PC-PR(97) 1 rev. 3, 74 and following. Denmark reports that prosecution office and police are integrated at a local level. The local head of police is also the local prosecution office head. But this practice seems to be rather an exception.

151 Buisson, J. 'The Role of Public Prosecution Office in the Criminal Field' in CE, op. cit. in ft. 12, 58-59.

152 Roxin, C. *Strafverfahrensrecht,* C. H. Beck (1995), 63 64.

153 Hessmer, H., and Otto, H.-U. (eds). *Restorative Justice on Trial,* Eds. Kluwer Academic Publishers (1992), and Jung, Heike. 'Plea Bargaining and its Repercussions on the Theory of Criminal Procedure' in *European Journal of Crime, Criminal Law and Criminal Justice,* 5 (1997), 2, 112-122.

154 Recommendation No. R (87) of the Council of Europe on simplification procedures is one of the documents aimed at alleviating these problems.

155 Among others, vast literature in *Restorative Justice on Trial,* ft. 22.

156 Op. cit. in ft. 22, Part V: Toward a restoration of Justice, 525-583. At the Council of Europe a recommendation on mediation is being prepared at present.

157 Jung, H. 'Plea Bargaining and its repercussions on the theory of criminal procedure' in *European Journal of Crime, Criminology and Criminal Justice,* 5 (1997), p. 112.

158 Jung, H. op. cit. (1997), p. 115.

159 *Corpus iuris,* introducing penal provisions for the purpose of the financial interests of the European Union, under the direction of M. Delmas-Marty, *Economica* (1997).

160 There are five sections in this chapter: (1) trends in sentencing policy in the 1990s; (2) new initiatives in sentencing guidance; (3) changes in the law relating to the aims and principles of sentencing; (4) developments in judicial training and research; and (5) influences on the development of sentencing practice.

161 See further Traskman, P.-O. 'The Dragon's Egg: Drugs-Related Crime Control' in Snare, A. (ed.) 'Beware of Punishment', *Scandinavian Studies in Criminology,* Vol. 14, Pax (Oslo: 1995), and Pieth, M. 'The Prevention of Money Laundering: a Comparative Analysis' in *European Journal of Crime, Criminal Law and Criminal Justice,* 2 (1998).

162 See Wasik, M. and Von Hirsch, A. 'Civil Disqualification...' in *Cambridge Law Journal* (1998).

163 See generally Council of Europe Recommendation No. R (87) 18 on the simplification of criminal justice.

164 Tak, P. J. P. 'Changes in Sentencing in the Netherlands, 1970-1995' in Frase, R., and Tonry, M. (eds) *Punishment and Penal Systems in Western Countries,* Oxford University Press (New York: 2000) – forthcoming.

165 Ashworth, A. 'The Decline of English Sentencing and Other Stories' in Frase and Tonry, op. cit. (2000).

166 Albrecht, H.-J. 'Sentencing and Punishment in Germany' in Tonry, M., and Hatlestad, K. (eds) *Sentencing in Overcrowded Times: a Comparative Perspective,* Oxford University Press (New York: 1997).

167 Lappi-Seppala, T. 'The Decline of the Repressive Ideal: Criminal Policy and Penal Practices in Finland' in Frase and Tonry, op. cit. (2000).

168 Snacken, S. 'Surpopulation des Prisons et Sanctions Alternatives' in Mary, P. (ed.) *Travail d'intérêt Général et Mediation Pénale: Socialisation du Pénal ou Pénalisation du Social?* Bruylant (Brussels: 1997).

169 Hulsman, "Penal reform in the Netherlands" in *Howard Journal,* XX, 1981, p.150.

170 Braithwaite, J., *Crime, Shame and Reintegration,* Cambridge University Press, 1989.

171 Bard, K. 'Some General Traits of the Criminal Justice Systems of the Socialist Countries with special reference to Hungary' in *Papers in Crime Policy,* HEUNI (Helsinki: 1986), pp. 6-7, and Krapac, D. 'The Position of the Victim in Criminal Justice: a Restrained Central and Eastern European perspective on Victim-Offender mediation' in *European Journal of Crime, Criminal Law and Criminal Justice,* 3 (1995).

172 The European Court of Human Rights held in *T v. U.K., V v. U.K.* (judgments of 16 December 1999).

173 Šelih, A. 'Juvenile Criminal Law and Change: Trends in some East- and Central-European Countries' in *European Journal of Crime, Criminal Law and Criminal Justice,* 2 (1996).

174 Eser, A. and Huber, B. (eds) *Strafsentwicklung in Europa, 5.1 and 5.2,* Max Planck Institut für auslandisches und internationales Strafrecht (Freiburg: 1994), pp. 1099, 1204.

175 Tubex, H., and Snacken, S. 'L'Evolution des Longues Peines: Aperçu International et Analyse des Causes' in *Deviances et Société,* 19, 2 (1995).

176 Kensey, A., and Tournier, P. 'French Prison Numbers Stable Since 1988, but Populations Changing' in *Overcrowded Times,* 9, 4 (1998).

177 Tornudd, P. 'Sentencing and Punishment in Finland' in Tonry and Hatlestad, op. cit. (1997).

178 Killias, M., Kuhn, A., and Ronez, S. 'Sentencing in Switzerland' in Tonry and Hatlestad, op. cit. (1997).

179 Hebenton, B., and Spencer, J. 'Law Enforcement in Societies in Transition' in *European Journal of Crime, Criminal Law and Criminal Justice,* 1, 29 (1998).

180 Kyvsgaard, B. 'Penal Sanctions and the Use of Imprisonment in Denmark' in *Overcrowded Times, 9*, No. 6 (1998), p. 9.

181 See Traskman, op. cit. (1995).

182 Tak, P. J. P. 'Changes in Sentencing in the Netherlands' in Tonry and Hatlestad, op.cit. (2000).

183 Tubex and Snacken, op cit. (1995).

184 De Pauw, W. 'Sentencing of Drug Offences: Focus on Ethnic Minorities' (unpublished paper for American Society of Criminology conference: author at wdepauw@vub.ac.be (1998).

185 Kensey and Tournier, op. cit. (1998).

186 Weigend, op. cit. (1997).

187 Killias, Kuhn and Ronez, op. cit. (1997).

188 Hebenton and Spencer, op. cit. (1998).

189 Eser and Huber, op. cit. (1997), p. 577.

190 Tak, op. cit. (2000).

191 Kensey and Tournier, op. cit. (1998), p. 13.

192 Eser and Huber, op. cit. (1997), p. 621.

193 Eser and Huber, op. cit. (1997), p. 484.

194 Killias, Kuhn and Ronez, op. cit. (1997), p. 207.

195 Tak, op. cit. (2000).

196 De la Cuesta, J. L., and Varona, G. 'An Approach to the New Spanish Penal Code of 1995' in *European Journal of Crime, Criminal Law and Criminal Justice,* Vol. 3 (1996), p. 230.

197 Eser and Huber, op. cit. (1997), pp. 672, 683.

198 Albrecht, op. cit. (1997), p. 187.

199 Kensey and Tournier, op. cit. (1998), p. 15.

200 De Pauw, op. cit. (1998).

201 Hood, R. *Race and Sentencing,* Oxford University Press (Oxford: 1992), pp. 124-130.

202 Hebenton and Spencer, op. cit (1998), p. 38.

203 See, for example Eser and Huber, op. cit. (1994), p. 1016, on Austria.

204 Recent movements towards abolition of the death penalty in central and eastern European states are discussed by Hood (1996, pp. 16-23). An increased use of the sentence of imprisonment for life has been noted in several countries. In England and Wales, where life imprisonment is the mandatory sentence for murder and a discretionary sentence for many serious crimes, there are now more than 4,000 people serving life imprisonment. The use of life imprisonment has increased to a lesser extent in several other countries, including France. But, in contrast to this, life imprisonment has been abolished as a sentence in Norway, Portugal and Slovenia; and the German Constitutional Court has held that the sentence of life imprisonment must be reserved for a small number of well-defined types of case, and that the sentence must always preserve the possibility of release back into the community.

205 Larsson, P. 'Norway Prison Use up Slightly' in *Overcrowded Times,* 10, No. 1 (1999), p. 11.

206 See, for example, Eser and Huber, op. cit. (1994), p. 1099 on Poland and p. 1204 on Russia.

207 For discussion, see Victor, D. 'Politics and the Penal System – a Drama in Progress' in Snare, op. cit. (1995), and Morgan, R. 'Imprisonment in England and Wales: Flood Tide, but on the Turn?' in *Overcrowded Times, 9*, no. 6 (1998).

208 Hamai, K. 'Prison Population in Japan Stable for 30 Years' in *Overcrowded Times,* 10, no. 1 (1999).

209 Jareborg, N. 'The Swedish Sentencing Reform' in Clarkson, C., and Morgan, R. (eds). *The Politics of Sentencing Reform,* Oxford University Press (Oxford: 1995).

210 Ashworth, A. *Sentencing and Criminal Justice,* 3rd edn, Butterworths (London: 2000), ch. 3.

211 Tornudd, op.cit. (1997), p. 190, and Lappi-Seppala, op. cit. (2000).

212 Duff, P., and Hutton, N. (eds). *Criminal Justice in Scotland,* Ashgate-Dartmouth (Aldershot: 1999), p. 6.

213 Bard, op. cit. (1986).

214 Ashworth, op. cit. (2000), ch. 10.

215 Tak, op. cit. (2000).

216 Lappi-Seppala, op. cit. (2000).

217 Ashworth, A. op. cit. (2000).

218 De Pauw, op. cit. (1998).

219 Flood-Page, C., and Mackie, A. *Sentencing Practice: an examination of decisions in magistrates' courts and the Crown Court in the mid-1990s,* Home Office Research Study 180, Home Office (London: 1998); see also the Scottish research reported by Hutton, N. 'Sentencing in Scotland' in Duff and Hutton, op. cit. (1999), p. 175.

220 Council of Europe (1974), p. 13.

221 Hutton, op. cit. (1999), pp. 177-179.

222 For a general overview of the history and development of alternatives to imprisonment, see A. M. Van Kalmthout and P. J. P. Tak, *Sanctions Systems in the member states of the Council of Europe,* (Deventer/Boston: 1988, Part 1, and 1992, Part 2); J. Junger-Tas, *Alternatives to Prison Sentences: Experiences and Developments,* (Amsterdam-New York: 1994).

223 See eg: Eighth Congress of the United Nations on the Prevention of Crime and the Treatment of Offenders, Havana 1990, a/conf. 144/28/Rev.1; Council of

Europe: 1. Resolution (65) on suspended sentences, probation and other alternatives to imprisonment; 2. Resolution (70) on the practical organisation of measures for the supervision and after-care of conditionally sentenced or conditionally released offenders; 3. Resolution (76) 10 on certain alternative penal measures to imprisonment; Recommendation No. R (82) 16 on the European Rules on Community Sanctions and Measures.

224 UN General Assembly Resolution 45/110: UN Standard Minimum Rules for Non-Custodial Measures (Tokyo Rules), Havana 1990.

225 Recommendation No. R (92) 16 and explanatory memorandum, Strasbourg 1992.

226 Válková, J. 'The legal framework for community sanctions and measures' in *CEP Bulletin,* 11 (1999), pp. 1-3.

227 See Office fédéral de la statistique 1997, *Le travail d'intérêt général en 1997,* (Neuchâtel: 1998), p. 6.

228 UN Centre for International Crime Prevention, Model Law on Juvenile Justice (Vienna: September 1997).

229 See: Faget, J. 'Le TIG, beaucoup d'espoir..., des résultats mitigés' in *Bulletin du CLCJ* (1 February 1997).

230 See Killias, M. 'Community service without net-widening: a question of implementation? Some lessons from the Swiss Experiment' in Albrecht, H.-J. and Van Kalmthout, A. M. *Community Sanctions and Measures in Europe,* Max Planck Institute (Freiburg: 2000), to be published.

231 Worral, A. *Punishment in the Community: the Future of Criminal Justice* (London: 1997).

232 Rule 24 states: "Any instructions of the implementing authority, including in particular those in relation to control requirements, shall be practical, precise and limited to what is necessary for the effective implementation of the sanction or measure."

233 See eg Micro, G. 'Community Service and Custody in Scotland', *Howard Journal,* 29/2 (1990), pp. 101-113.

234 See May, T. 'Probation and Community Sanctions', op. cit., pp. 881-87.

235 Davreux, S. et al., 'Evaluation de l'application de la loi organisant une procedure de médiation pénale en Belgique du 1/1/1996 au 31/12/1996', Bruxelles, Ministère de la Justice (1997). For the net-widening effect in England/Wales and the Netherlands see: Ken Pease, 'Community Service Orders' in Tonry, M. and Morris, N. (eds'), *Crime and Justice. An Annual Review of Research,* 6 (1985), pp. 51-94, and Spaans, E. C. 'Community Service in the Netherlands: its Effects on Recidivism and Net-Widening', *International Criminal Justice Review,* 8 (1998) pp. 1-14.

236 Fanchiotti, V. 'Alternatives to Imprisonment in the Italian Criminal Justice System' in Albrecht, H.-J. and Van Kalmthout, A. M. *Community Sanctions and Measures in Europe,* Max Planck Institute (Freiburg: 2000), to be published.

237 Rule 90 of the European Rules states: "Evaluation of community sanctions and measures should include, but not be limited to, objective assessment of the extent to which their use:
– conforms to the expectations of law makers, judicial authorities, deciding authorities, implementing authorities and the community concerning the goals of community sanctions and measures;
– contributes to a reduction in the rates of imprisonment;
– enables the offence-related needs of offenders to be met;

- is cost-effective;
- contributes to the reduction of crime in the community.

238 See eg Andersen, J. G. *Borgerne og lovene (The Citizens and the Laws)* (Aarhus University Press: 1998), and NIPO, *Groot* maatschappelijk *draagvlak voor Taakstraffen (Great Societal Support for Task Penalties),* NIPO (Den Haag: 1998).

239 Kyvskaard, B. 'Community sanctions and measures in Denmark', in: Albrecht and Van Kalmthout, *Community Sanctions and Measures in Europe,* op. cit. (to be published in 2000).

240 See Kuhn, A., Tournier, P., and Walmsley, R. *Draft report on prison overcrowding and prison population inflation,* in: Restricted PC-CP (Council of Europe: 1999), p. 20 and Figures 2 and 3.

241 Zimring, F. E. and Hawkins, G. *The scale of imprisonment,* University of Chicago Press (Chicago and London: 1991), and HEUNI, *Prison population in Europe and in North America. Problems and solutions* (Helsinki: 1997); and Kuhn, A. 'Sanctions and their severity' in *Crime and criminal justice in Europe and North America* (Helsinki: 1998).

242 See Snacken, Beyens and Tubex, op. cit. (1995); Beyens, in HEUNI, op. cit. (1997), pp. 161-186.

243 Blumstein, A., Sentencing and the prison crowding problem' in Gottfredson, S. D., and McConville, S. (eds) *America's correctional crisis,* Greenwood Press (Connecticut: 1987)

244 Zimring and Hawkins, op. cit. (1991).

245 Box, S. *Recession, crime and punishment,* Macmillan Education (Hong Kong, London: 1987).

246 Vanneste, Ch. 'L'évolution de la population pénitentiaire belge de 1830 á nos jours: comment et pourquoi? Des logiques socio-économiques á leur traduction pénale' in *Revue de Droit Pénale et de Criminologie* (1999). Godefroy, T., and Lafargue, B. *Changements économiques et répression pénale. Plus de chômage, plus d'emprisonnement?* CESDIP (Paris: 1991), and Melossi, D. 'An introduction: fifty years later, punishment and social structure in comparataive analysis' in *Contemporary Crisis* (1989).

247 Chiricos, T. G., and Bales, W. D. 'Unemployment and punishment: an empirical assessment' in *Criminology* (1991), and De Pauw, W. *Sentencing of drug offences: focus on ethnic minorities,* paper presented at the American Society of Criminology 50th Annual Meeting, November 11-14, 1998 (Washington, D.C.: 1999).

248 Walker, N. and Hough, M. (eds). *Public attitudes to sentencing.* Surveys from five countries, Cambridge Studies in Cirminology, Gower (Aldershot: 1988).

249 Weiss, R. and South, N. *Comparing prison systems,* Gordon and Breach (Amsterdam: 1998), p. 12; eg, the Labour Party in UK or the Social Democrats in Germany.

250 See Lappi-Seppälä, T. *Regulating the prison population.* Experiences from a long-term policy in Finland, National Research Institute of Legal Policy, Research Communication 38 (Helsinki: 1998).

251 Downes, D. *Contrasts in tolerance. Post-war penal policy in the Netherlands and England and Wales,* Clarendon Press (Oxford: 1988).

252 See Tournier, op. cit.

253 Walmsley, R. *Prison systems in Central and Eastern Europe,* HEUNI (Helsinki: 1996).

254 Penal Reform International, Monitoring prison conditions in Europe (Paris: 1997), and Koeppel, K. *Kontrolle des Strafvollzugs – individueller Rechtsschutz und generale Aufsicht – Ein Rechtsvergleich,* (Mönchengladbach: 1999).

255 Sherman, L. W. et al. *Preventing crime, What works, what doesn't, what's promising?* US Department of Justice, Office of Justice programs, National Institute of Justice, 1998 (full report under http://www.preventingcrime.org) and Lipton, D. S. *The effectiveness of correctional treatment revisited thirty years later: Preliminary meta-analytic findings from the CDATE study.* Paper presented at the 12th International Congress on Criminology, Seoul, 1998 (doug.lipton@ndri.org), and Goldblatt, P. and Lewis, C. (eds), *Reducing offending: an assessment of research evidence on ways of dealing with offending behaviour,* Home Office Research Study 187 (London: 1998).

256 Lösel, F. 'Sprechen Evaluationsergebnisse von Meta-Analysen für einen frischen Wind in der Straftäterbehandlung?' in Egg, R. (ed.) *Sozialtherapie in den 90er Jahren* (Wiesbaden: 1993), and Dünkel, F. *Empirische Forschung im Strafvollzug – Bestandsaufnahme und Perspektiven,* Forum (Berlin: 1996).

257 See BVerfG NStZ (1998), 478.

258 See Morgan, R. 'Imprisonment: Current concerns and a brief history since 1945' in Maguire, M., Morgan, R., and Reiner, R. *The Oxford Handbook of Criminology,* 2nd edn, Clarendon Press (Oxford: 1997), p. 1146.

259 Morgan, op. cit.

260 See sect. 10 of the Prison Act.

261 See King, R. D. and Morgan, R. *The future of the prison system,* Gower (Aldershot: 1980) and Morgan, op. cit. (1997), p. 1146.

262 Snacken, S. et al. 'Changing prison populations in Western countries: fate or policy?' in *European Journal of Crime, Criminal Law and Criminal Justice* (1995).

263 Törnudd, in HEUNI, op. cit. (1997) and Lappi-Seppälä, op. cit. (1998).

264 See Morgan, R. 'Following Woolf: the prospects for prison policy' in *Journal of Law and Society* (1992), and Sparks, R. et al. *Prisons and the problem of order,* Clarendon Studies in Criminology, Clarendon Press (Oxford: 1996).

265 Sparks et al., op. cit (1996), p. 91.

266 De Jonge, G. 'Still "slaves of the state" – Prison labour and international law' in Van Zyl Smit, D. and Dünkel, F. *Prison labour – Salvation or Slavery?,* Dartmouth (Ashgate: 1999).

267 For example, the Hungarian Prison Act, 1979.

268 From 1 July 1998, see BVerfG *NStZ* 1998, p. 478.

269 Rotman, E. 'Do criminal offenders have a constitutional right to rehabilitation?' in *Journal of Criminal Law and Criminology* (1986).

270 See van Zyl Smit and Dünkel, op. cit (1999).

271 See Dünkel, F., op. cit. (1996).

272 See United Nations (1991).

273 See Dünkel, F., Van Kalmthout, A., and Schüler-Springorum, H. (eds). *Entwichlungstendenzen und Reformstrategien im Jugendstrafrecht im europäischen Vergleich,* (Mönchengladbach: 1997).

274 See Kuhn, Tournier and Walmsley, op. cit. (1999), p. 29.

275 Also outside prison, see Dünkel, F., op. cit. (1999).

276 See Gescher, N. *Boot Camp-Programme in den USA – Ein Fallbeispiel zum Formenwandel in der amerikanischen Kriminalpolitik,* (Mönchengladbach: 1998).

277 See Kuhn, Tournier and Walmsley, op. cit. (1999), p. 24.

278 See Kuhn, Tournier and Walmsley, op. cit. (1999), pp. 26, 30.

279 See 7th General Report, CPT/Inf (97), p. 10.

280 For allegations of the use of excessive force, see 9th General Report on the CPT's activities, CPT/Inf (99), vol. 12, p. 8.

281 See Dünkel, F., and Vagg, J. (eds). *Waiting for trial – International perspectives on the user of pre-trial detention and the rights and living conditions of prisoners waiting for trial,* Max-Planck-Instit ut für ausländisches und internationales Strafrecht (Freiburg im Breisgau: 1994).

282 See Dünkel, op. cit. (1994).

283 See Dünkel and Vagg, op. cit. (1994), p. 938.

284 See Kuhn, op. cit. (1998).

285 See Kuhn, Tournier and Walmsley, op. cit. (1999), p. 22.

286 Cobden, J. and Stewart, G. 'Breaking out: a perspective on long-term imprisonment and the process of release' in *Canadian Journal of Criminology* (1984).

287 Ditchfield, J. *Control in prisons: a review of the literature,* Home Office Research Study 118 (London: 1990).

288 McKay, H. B. et al. *The effects of long-term incarceration. And a proposed strategy for future research,* Solicitor General of Canada, Research Division (Ottawa: 1979).

289 McKay et al., op. cit. (1979), p. 55.

290 Floud, J. 'Dangerousness and criminal justice' in *British Journal of Criminology* (1982), and Nash, M. "Dangerousness revisited" in *International Journal of the Sociology of Law* (1992).

291 See also the Explanatory Memorandum to Recommendation No. R (82) 17 of the Council of Europe.

292 Second General Report, CPT/Inf (92) 3.

293 See Van Zyl Smit, D., and Dünkel, F. (eds). *Imprisonment today and tomorrow – International perspectives on prisoners' rights and prison conditions,* 2nd edn, Kluwer (Deventer and Boston: 2000).

294 See Van Zyl Smit and Dünkel, op. cit. (2000).

295 See Council of Europe, SPACE 1997, p. 19.

296 See Dünkel, F. 'Imprisonment in transition – The situation in the new states of the Federal Republic of Germany' in *British Journal of Criminology* (1995).

297 See Koeppel, op. cit. (1999).

298 Rusche, G., and Kirchheimer, O. *Punishment and social structure,* Russel & Russel (New York: 1968) and Weiss, in Weiss and South, op. cit. (1998), p. 466.

299 See Van Zyl Smit and Dünkel, op. cit. (2000).

300 See Kuhn, Tournier and Walmsley, op. cit. (1999), pp. 39 ff., 47 ff.

Sales agents for publications of the Council of Europe
Agents de vente des publications du Conseil de l'Europe

AUSTRALIA/AUSTRALIE
Hunter Publications, 58A, Gipps Street
AUS-3066 COLLINGWOOD, Victoria
Tel.: (61) 3 9417 5361
Fax: (61) 3 9419 7154
E-mail: Sales@hunter-pubs.com.au
http://www.hunter-pubs.com.au

AUSTRIA/AUTRICHE
Gerold und Co., Graben 31
A-1011 WIEN 1
Tel.: (43) 1 533 5014
Fax: (43) 1 533 5014 18
E-mail: buch@gerold.telecom.at
http://www.gerold.at

BELGIUM/BELGIQUE
La Librairie européenne SA
50, avenue A. Jonnart
B-1200 BRUXELLES 20
Tel.: (32) 2 734 0281
Fax: (32) 2 735 0860
E-mail: info@libeurop.be
http://www.libeurop.be

Jean de Lannoy
202, avenue du Roi
B-1190 BRUXELLES
Tel.: (32) 2 538 4308
Fax: (32) 2 538 0841
E-mail: jean.de.lannoy@euronet.be
http://www.jean-de-lannoy.be

CANADA
Renouf Publishing Company Limited
5369 Chemin Canotek Road
CDN-OTTAWA, Ontario, K1J 9J3
Tel.: (1) 613 745 2665
Fax: (1) 613 745 7660
E-mail: order.dept@renoufbooks.com
http://www.renoufbooks.com

CZECH REPUBLIC/ RÉPUBLIQUE TCHÈQUE
USIS, Publication Service
Havelkova 22
CZ-130 00 PRAHA 3
Tel./Fax: (420) 2 2423 1114

DENMARK/DANEMARK
Munksgaard
35 Norre Sogade, PO Box 173
DK-1005 KØBENHAVN K
Tel.: (45) 7 733 3333
Fax: (45) 7 733 3377
E-mail: direct@munksgaarddirect.dk
http://www.munksgaarddirect.dk

FINLAND/FINLANDE
Akateeminen Kirjakauppa
Keskuskatu 1, PO Box 218
FIN-00381 HELSINKI
Tel.: (358) 9 121 41
Fax: (358) 9 121 4450
E-mail: akatilaus@stockmann.fi
http://www.akatilaus.akateeminen.com

GERMANY/ALLEMAGNE
UNO Verlag
Proppelsdorfer Allee 55
D-53115 BONN
Tel.: (49) 2 28 94 90 231
Fax: (49) 2 28 21 74 92
E-mail: unoverlag@aol.com
http://www.uno-verlag.de

GREECE/GRÈCE
Librairie Kauffmann
Mavrokordatou 9
GR-ATHINAI 106 78
Tel.: (30) 1 38 29 283
Fax: (30) 1 38 33 967

HUNGARY/HONGRIE
Euro Info Service
Hungexpo Europa Kozpont ter 1
H-1101 BUDAPEST
Tel.: (361) 264 8270
Fax: (361) 264 8271
E-mail: euroinfo@euroinfo.hu
http://www.euroinfo.hu

ITALY/ITALIE
Libreria Commissionaria Sansoni
Via Duca di Calabria 1/1, CP 552
I-50125 FIRENZE
Tel.: (39) 556 4831
Fax: (39) 556 41257
E-mail: licosa@licosa.com
http://www.licosa.com

NETHERLANDS/PAYS-BAS
De Lindeboom Internationale Publikaties
PO Box 202, MA de Ruyterstraat 20 A
NL-7480 AE HAAKSBERGEN
Tel.: (31) 53 574 0004
Fax: (31) 53 572 9296
E-mail: lindeboo@worldonline.nl
http://home-1-worldonline.nl/~lindeboo/

NORWAY/NORVÈGE
Akademika, A/S Universitetsbokhandel
PO Box 84, Blindern
N-0314 OSLO
Tel.: (47) 22 85 30 30
Fax: (47) 23 12 24 20

POLAND/POLOGNE
Głowna Księgarnia Naukowa
im. B. Prusa
Krakowskie Przedmiescie 7
PL-00-068 WARSZAWA
Tel.: (48) 29 22 66
Fax: (48) 22 26 64 49
E-mail: inter@internews.com.pl
http://www.internews.com.pl

PORTUGAL
Livraria Portugal
Rua do Carmo, 70
P-1200 LISBOA
Tel.: (351) 13 47 49 82
Fax: (351) 13 47 02 64
E-mail: liv.portugal@mail.telepac.pt

SPAIN/ESPAGNE
Mundi-Prensa Libros SA
Castelló 37
E-28001 MADRID
Tel.: (34) 914 36 37 00
Fax: (34) 915 75 39 98
E-mail: libreria@mundiprensa.es
http://www.mundiprensa.com

SWITZERLAND/SUISSE
BERSY
Route d'Uvrier 15
CH-1958 LIVRIER/SION
Tel.: (41) 27 203 73 30
Fax: (41) 27 203 73 32
E-mail: bersy@freesurf.ch

UNITED KINGDOM/ROYAUME-UNI
TSO (formerly HMSO)
51 Nine Elms Lane
GB-LONDON SW8 5DR
Tel.: (44) 171 873 8372
Fax: (44) 171 873 8200
E-mail: customer.services@theso.co.uk
http://www.the-stationery-office.co.uk
http://www.itsofficial.net

UNITED STATES and CANADA/ ÉTATS-UNIS et CANADA
Manhattan Publishing Company
468 Albany Post Road, PO Box 850
CROTON-ON-HUDSON,
NY 10520, USA
Tel.: (1) 914 271 5194
Fax: (1) 914 271 5856
E-mail: Info@manhattanpublishing.com
http://www.manhattanpublishing.com

STRASBOURG
Librairie Kléber
Palais de l'Europe
F-67075 STRASBOURG Cedex
Fax: (33) 03 88 52 91 21

Council of Europe Publishing/Editions du Conseil de l'Europe
F-67075 Strasbourg Cedex
Tel.: (33) 03 88 41 25 81 – Fax: (33) 03 88 41 39 10
E-mail: publishing@coe.int – Web site: http://book.coe.fr

